D0099701

STALKING GOD

Stalking God

MY UNORTHODOX SEARCH FOR SOMETHING TO BELIEVE IN

ANJALI KUMAR

SEAL PRESS

Seal Press
Hachette Book Group
1700 Fourth Street
Berkeley, California
sealpress.com

Printed in the United States of America

Published by Seal Press, an imprint of Perseus Books, LLC,
a subsidiary of Hachette Book Group, Inc.
The Seal Press name and logo is a trademark of the Hachette Book Group.

The publisher is not responsible for websites (or their content)
that are not owned by the publisher.

Cover design by Jennifer Carrow
Print book interior design by Sagecraft Book Design

Library of Congress Cataloging-in-Publication Data
Names: Kumar, Anjali, 1973– author.
Title: Stalking God : my unorthodox search for something to believe in / by
Anjali Kumar.
Description: Berkeley, California : Seal Press, 2018. | Includes
bibliographical references and index.
Identifiers: LCCN 2017029619 (print) | LCCN 2017030918 (ebook) | ISBN
9781580056625 (ebook) | ISBN 9781580056618 (hardcover : alkaline paper)
Subjects: LCSH: Kumar, Anjali, 1973—Religion. | Kumar, Anjali,
1973—Philosophy. | Kumar, Anjali, 1973—Travel. | Spiritual
biography–United States. | Pilgrims and pilgrimages. | Religious life. |
Spiritual life. | Spirituality. | Women lawyers—United States—Biography.
| BISAC: BIOGRAPHY & AUTOBIOGRAPHY / Personal Memoirs.
Classification: LCC BL73.K84 (ebook) | LCC BL73.K84 A3 2018 (print) | DDC
204.092 [B] —dc23
LC record available at https://lccn.loc.gov/2017029619
LSC-C

10   9   8   7   6   5   4   3   2   1

To my parents and my sister Avanti

for building me a nest

To Atul for showing me my wings

And to Zia for reminding me I could fly . . .

if I just had a little faith

Contents

As for me, all I know is that I know nothing.

—SOCRATES

Cuz I've gotta have faith. I gotta have faith.
Cuz I've gotta have faith faith faith.
I've gotta have faith faith faith.

—GEORGE MICHAEL

Are you there God? It's me, Anjali.

—ANJALI KUMAR

Author's Note

The events and people in this book are all real, but in some cases I have changed names, artfully disguised details, and altered the timeline to protect the identities of the private individuals who shared this journey with me. I did this out of respect and in a manner that kept the integrity of my experience intact. I know that if I had experienced a forty-five-minute orgasm in front of a group of complete strangers or was a practicing witch who hadn't come completely "out of the broom closet" to my boss, I would want my name and any identifying markers altered just a bit too. As for my sister, Avanti, I realize that you didn't want anyone to know that you went with me to have "invisible" surgery and get your eyeballs scraped by a faith healer in Brazil, so I completely left you out of that chapter and pretended that I went alone (you're welcome). As for everyone else—all my family, friends, and colleagues whose names and specifics I didn't disguise (sorry, Mom)—I pretty much threw you under the bus. Just roll with it.

—Anjali

Introduction

In 2010, when my daughter Zia was born, I decided that I needed to find God. I told myself that she would eventually ask me questions that I couldn't answer—and that completely unraveled me. I was senior counsel at Google at the time, and, as a lawyer, when people asked me a question, I was used to giving them an answer backed with certitude. And precedent. Or if all else failed, at least I could Google a satisfactory answer.

I also found that having a child—actually creating a life—had changed me. It didn't help that I had struggled to get pregnant, enduring multiple, heartbreaking miscarriages, or that right after Zia was born, my doula commented, "She is from another time," after pointing out that Zia was holding the fingers of her left hand in gyan mudra—a prayer position used in yoga and meditation. Then a few days into Zia's life, when my father asked me when I would be taking her to our temple, my spiritual skepticism, complacency, and lassitude abruptly ended. I felt what could only be described as a newfound sense of spiritual curiosity.

Curiosity sparked by a new and completely unanticipated sense of spiritual urgency. And perhaps a touch of panic.

Now that I had a child, I wanted—needed—to believe in something bigger than myself. Not just to believe in the possibility that there is more but to know with a degree of "legal" certainty that there is something deeper and bigger than just *this*. So as the months following Zia's birth unfolded, I made a firm commitment to myself—and to her—that I would make a valiant effort to find us a comfortable spiritual home. It became patently clear that my somewhat eclectic multicultural upbringing had given me deep spiritual footings but not the structure they were intended to support.

I had the foundation but not the house.

AT THE ONSET of this mission—which I didn't embark on in a serious manner until Zia was one year old—I knew that I wouldn't be looking for God in the usual places or in the traditional sense. Growing up, I had been exposed, first- and secondhand, to a broad sampling of both Western and Eastern religions. I was born to Indian parents and raised in America, where my family was culturally Hindu and practiced a strict and relatively unknown (at least in the West) Indian religion called Jainism. Incongruently, I was educated by Catholic nuns—well, at least until I came home from school one day in fifth grade and announced with confidence that Jesus would save us all, after which my parents promptly enrolled me in the local public school.

As a child I spoke both English and Hindi; by the time my daughter was born, I was reasonably fluent in French and Italian as well. I was well educated, well traveled, and worldly. To add to the religious and spiritual mix, my husband, Atul, an interventional cardiologist, is Hindu. As a man of science, he finds comfort in research and data and doesn't share my spiritual thirst or my anxiety about the unknown. But for me, science wasn't enough. And religiously and spiritually speaking, nothing I had experienced thus far was a perfect fit. I was walking barefoot, so to speak. Not because I wanted to but because I had a closet full of uncomfortable shoes.

SINCE I HADN'T been able to find God—or a satiating spiritual connection—in any of the obvious places, I decided to widen my net. This wasn't an out-and-out rejection of the traditional religion that I grew up with; rather it was a deep, spiritual curiosity that left me yearning to find out if there's *more*. So when I headed out to find God—him or her or it—I was looking elsewhere and everywhere. And I went all-in. I wanted to experience each of these belief systems and practices in the flesh. Nothing was off-limits or too unorthodox.

WHAT I FOUND was unexpected, to say the least.

Early on, what I encountered was somewhat encouraging, at times even bordering on the spiritual. That inspired me to keep looking.

But more often what I experienced was perplexing. Or hilarious.

Other times, what I unearthed could only be described as shocking, intellectually discordant, or downright baffling. Or just plain-old disappointing. What I observed ranged from the very profound to the stunningly dumbfounding.

And it was crowded. I had to wait in a lot of lines. It seems everyone is looking for God—or at least one of his spiritual bedfellows.

WHEN I FIRST mentioned my quest to friends and colleagues, I didn't know how they would react. So I was initially cautious. I whispered tentatively in a few, select ears.

To my relief, no one pulled back or judged me. Instead they lit up, became animated, whispered back.

A few even shouted from the mountaintops.

After all, finding a comfortable spiritual home affects us in so many fundamental ways. It provides clear direction and adds meaning and purpose to everything we do—not just for our families and on a personal level but in our work too. And having meaningful work grounded in a higher purpose beyond the material and the here and now is profoundly life altering.

THERE IS COMPELLING evidence that religious beliefs are not solely a result of indoctrination, that humans are born with a natural instinct to believe in divine power, which helps explain why so many of us are seeking. Broaching this topic with family, friends, and colleagues—many of them lawyers, doctors, and engineers—opened up an unexpected dialogue. Quite a few of them scribbled down names of people they thought I should meet, people they referred to as goddesses, gurus, and saints. Many of them told me, with detail and fervor, about their spiritual journeys, some successful, others disastrous and disappointing.

Then they invited me to places. Lots of places.

Apparently, while I had been negotiating contracts at Google, the rest of the world had been on a quest to find enlightenment, spiritual clarity, and salvation.

I was late to the party.

WHEN A COWORKER named Gopi heard about my quest, he suggested that I meet a healer from India known as Hugging Amma. In addition to being on the marketing team, Gopi taught yoga at Google and occasionally sent me spiritual missives—sweet, inspirational sayings conveyed via e-mail. He thought I might benefit from meeting Amma, and I was intrigued. Besides, in a few weeks Amma was going to be in New York City hugging her followers at a convention center just a quick cab ride from my apartment.

Amma has a global reputation as a healing saint and a guru. She travels around the world and frequently embarks on multicity tours across the United States, delivering her message of kindness and love with the simple warmth and connection of an embrace. Over the last three decades she has dispensed more than 34 million hugs.

Amma supports a network of charities under the umbrella organization Embracing the World, which reportedly takes in over $20 million a year. Hugging is apparently big business.

And there's no question that she helps people. After the tsunami hit in 2004, Amma had over 6,000 homes built in southern India. She has properties in Asia, Europe, and the United States—including an ashram in the Indian state of Kerala, where she built a state-of-the-art university and a medical school. But she also bought a mansion in Maryland said to be worth almost $8 million, so she's definitely helping Amma too, as she sells her Amma-themed merchandise: Amma-branded jewelry, clothing, dolls, and even watches, which I was told keep "Amma Time"—whatever that is.

Amma's "children," as she calls her followers, swear that she's a spiritual healer. Her critics suggest she's a guru of self-promotion. Either way, her following is undeniably enormous. I contemplated Gopi's suggestion by asking myself if I believed that spiritual salvation and enlightenment lay in something as simple and pure, as innocent and fundamental, as a hug.

Or an aggregate 34 million hugs.

I was skeptical, but then I reminded myself that millions around the world believe that Amma is a healing saint. Besides, I reasoned, Gopi is an enviably spiritual and happy man, so I should at least give Hugging Amma a shot.

Then I reminded myself that there was some soft science behind this too. Hugs release oxytocin, the "feel-good" hormone, and touch is recognized as an important element in psychological and physical healing and well-being. Maybe that alone explains it? Or maybe this was just the lawyer in me trying to find a concrete explanation for the inexplicable.

As for her critics, I rationalized that money and spirituality are always an awkward, unsavory mix. Doesn't the Catholic Church have the highest net worth of any institution on earth? Don't Mormons pay 10 percent of their income to the church? And don't some people who practice Judaism "pay to pray," with temples charging for seats or memberships? Don't many religious organizations and a lot of spiritual leaders own real estate and sell related paraphernalia?

THE DAY I went to see Amma, I changed my clothes three times. I had absolutely no idea what to wear to meet a saint. (Add to that the fact that July in New York can be brutally hot, and I didn't want to be sweaty for my hug.) Work clothes felt oddly formal, a loose-fitting, colorful Indian salwaar kameez seemed too costumey, jeans would be sweltering, and everything else in my closet was better suited for a night out on the town. Yoga pants, on the other hand, seemed directionally correct; I worried that they were too casual and informal—even bordering on cliché—but settled on them with a loose-fitting button-down shirt anyway.

When I finally arrived at the convention center to meet Amma, thousands of people were milling about in the front of the hall. And they were shopping. I had walked into what appeared to be an Amma-themed tchotchke sale. All the merchandise I had read about—the dolls and perfume and jewelry—was for sale. The hug might be free, but a watch with Amma's face on it will set you back $25.

I got in line for the ticket to hug Amma, thinking how this didn't feel any more spiritual than hanging out at a flea market. I spent the next four hours standing and waiting with thousands of other people. Some, just like me, were looking for something they were pre-wired to want but probably would never find; many others were fervent believers, sure they had already found it.

At noon, there was a sudden flurry of activity when some of Amma's children (identifiable by what looked like beauty pageant sashes) rolled out a red carpet. Amma entered to palpable excitement. I was standing close enough that I unintentionally ended up in a makeshift receiving line, which made it possible to reach out and touch her hand. I was wearing my new Amma watch on my wrist and had a few other Amma incidentals tucked away in my purse.

She was wearing a white cotton sari. She is all of four feet tall. For some reason, I thought she would be bigger. Maybe like Michael Jordan.

When my number was finally called and I was next in the crowd to receive a hug, the movement around me accelerated. Amma's front man asked me what language I spoke. I stumbled, then said, "Hindi." Oddly, he leaned over and told her that I spoke English, apparently deciding I wasn't Indian enough.

When I approached Amma, one of Amma's children pushed me down on my knees, and Amma pulled me in to a long bear hug. I wasn't sure how this worked—what I was supposed to do or how I should feel. As a New Yorker, hugging strangers didn't come naturally to me. When I started to wonder who should instigate the release, I awkwardly tried to pull away. But she held on to me with the firmness and conviction of an uncomfortably overfamiliar distant relative while chanting something in my ear, whispering in a language I did not recognize. I surrendered to the moment.

Her words felt comforting, even though I didn't understand them. I tried my best to hold on to them but I couldn't.

I can report that Amma smelled of sandalwood and rose and hugged with such conviction and passion that for a brief moment, mid-hug, after I had allowed the energy and emotion to engulf me, I thought she might just be selling what I was shopping for. I was hoping she would tell me something profound or answer those questions that plagued me . . . the questions that Zia would be asking me.

Why are we here?
What is the meaning of life?
What happens when we die?
Is there a God?

When she released me from the embrace, Amma held me at arm's length, then looked and smiled at me with such honesty and purity that I felt she, above anyone else, understood who I was. And then—just like that—it was over.

Before sending me on my way, she gave me a packet of sandalwood powder and a kiss.

A kiss made of milk chocolate, wrapped in silver, and manufactured by Hershey.

I WAS SIMULTANEOUSLY over- and underwhelmed. The hug, the sandalwood, the rose, the warmth, the energy, the conviction, the whispered words, her smile—all were, on many levels, compelling, even spiritual. In the depth of her embrace I had thought, at least fleetingly, that I felt something approaching otherworldly and enlightening.

I was trying really hard. I wanted to get it.

But in the end, the kiss unglued me. She told me to eat it.

Like Holy Communion? The Eucharist from Hershey?

Before I left the building, I was already obsessing about the kiss. *Should I eat it now like she told me to? And if I don't, what if it melts? What happens if I lose it? Can I save some for my husband and Zia? How do you share one little kiss?*

With these thoughts racing around in my head, the questions I'd set out to answer seemed even more elusive. I had been undone by a piece of candy.

I stepped out onto 34th Street to assaulting midday heat. Looking back over my shoulder, I acknowledged that it felt better in there hugging Amma than it did out here in the heat and noise of the city streets. But I knew it wasn't anywhere near enough. I was looking for more than a fleeting sense of comfort. I was looking for more than a sweaty hug at a convention center.

* * *

IN THE NEXT few months, I would wait in more lines. I would follow detailed instructions. Instructions about energy fields and karma, cleansing rituals and seminar logistics. Instructions written by spiritual leaders who took Visa and PayPal and had websites with disclaimers, downloadable liability release forms, and links to Google Maps.

I had to remind myself that the pope uses Twitter, that the liability issues were pro forma, and that I worked for Google. It shouldn't bother me that I was looking for God using the Internet and a credit card while signing disclaimers.

Should it?

I OPENED MY doors to let evil spirits out after I walked around my apartment burning a mixture of Epsom salts and rubbing alcohol. I downloaded a meditation timer app to my phone and snuck into the Mothers' Room at Google to meditate every afternoon. I had my natal chart read by a man dressed like the captain on *The Love*

Boat, joined a laughing yoga group in South Africa via Skype, and stood half naked on a beach in Mexico covered in Mayan clay and honey, trying to visualize a beautiful garden and all my dreams coming true.

I started working with an energy healer in Australia for "distance healing" via Google Hangout. She clears my energy fields quarterly, right before our scheduled video chat. Then she reminds me to envision a white protective light surrounding me while I shower and comments about the negative energy field running under the building I live in. She keeps suggesting that I sell my apartment and move. (Apparently energy healers in Australia have no idea how hard great apartments are to come by in New York.) But it's easy to get hooked and become dependent. When I called her for advice about an issue with a family member and she didn't get back to me for a week, I felt enormous trepidation. I had to remind myself that energy healers take vacations just like the rest of us.

To say that I was pushing my boundaries would be a grand understatement. The law is palpable and definitive, and the corporate legal work that fed and housed me anchored me in the concrete. But in my spare time, on weekends and days off, on my way to and from work, I found myself untethered and yearning for the comfort of another realm.

A realm that eluded me.

AFTER ONE FRIEND told me about a ten-day silent meditation retreat, another confessed that she had had a near-death experience as a child and now speaks to angels. Another gave me the name and address of her facialist in Los Angeles, a celibate Buddhist who keeps a second apartment in downtown New York, goes by the name "Goddess," and channels angels.

I have her on speed dial.

I traveled to Brazil to meet John of God and was introduced to tantric sound healing and transcendental meditation as I SoulCycled and hip-hop yoga-d away my lingering baby weight. I got detailed and reliable first-person accounts of the spiritual exploits of others, along with speculative half-truths, hearsay, and misrepresentations. I heard the plausible and the promising tucked in between reports of routes to salvation that sounded more like spiritual black holes or marketing scams than paths to enlightenment. Each account was richer, stranger, and more implausible than the last.

I lapped them up.

A forty-five-minute orgasm as a route to spiritual healing and enlightenment? Invisible surgery to cure cancer or depression? Count me in.

Yoni worship? Cooch yodeling? A forgiveness coach? Exploring the divine feminine? I signed up for all of it.

Spiritual salvation, inner peace, and the keys to happiness were conveniently offered in weekend packages, midweek seminars, and all-inclusive retreats. Millions subscribe to these wildly popular programs. My inbox was overflowing with brochures and web links forwarded to me by friends and friends of friends, accompanied by notes written in a tenor that ranged from unflinching conviction and awe to cynical curiosity.

There were more than a few giggles. Not everyone believed. But everyone, it seemed, was looking.

So I showed up. In Abadiânia, Brazil, and Ojai, California; in Kyoto, Japan, and Rhinebeck, New York. I traveled in all directions all around the globe. I became a spiritual tourist.

Not one of my friends pointed me toward traditional philosophies or religions. Though this journey I had embarked on might eventually lead me to a spiritual place, it clearly would not be a route to a temple or synagogue or church.

Along the way, I learned to chant, to meditate, and to marvel. I wrestled with my own identity, from my ethnic and cultural roots in India, to my femininity, to my role as a woman, daughter, mother, and wife. I questioned my relationships, my core beliefs, and the possibility of otherness. Mine was a global expedition and a noble quest. I fancied myself an explorer, no different really than Magellan or Columbus. I was looking for a new world.

Because now that I had a daughter, I didn't want to believe that the spiritual world was flat. I couldn't just sit back and accept the possibility that if I set sail to circumnavigate this earth in search of God, I would reach the end and just fall into a void of nothing.

I intended to return home with a spiritual map and the epic stories of self-discovery to go with it. I wanted to be able to tell my daughter, with certitude and conviction, that there is more. And it is glorious.

DON'T GET ME wrong: I was a skeptic extraordinaire. Some of what I had been told was truly unbelievable—often irrational or just plain crazy.

Angels? Witches? Faith healers? Saints? Eyeball scraping and nasal probes? Tree whispering and bioenergy healing? Sweat lodges?

At times what I heard conjured up words like "charlatan" and "ridiculous." I will admit that, at the beginning of this journey, I had a propensity to giggle, even to snicker.

But I self-corrected. I promised myself that, above all, I would show respect and keep an open mind. I knew that if I didn't do that, I would never learn something more expansive than what I already know.

I kept reminding myself that I was doing all of this so I would have answers for Zia when she was old enough to ask those questions. The questions that had unglued me when she was born. The questions that everyone wants answered.

> Why are we here?
> What is the meaning of life?
> What happens when we die?
> Is there a God?

So I shored myself up and dedicated myself to this mission. I had undertaken difficult challenges before: I'd studied biomedical ethics at Brown University, then law at Boston University. I was certain I could do this. I gave myself a year.

I gave myself one year to find God for Zia. The journey ended up taking much longer than that. And what I found was completely unexpected.

This book tells that story.

Chapter 1

JOHN OF GOD
Abadiânia, Brazil

As I opened up to conversations about spirituality, it quickly became clear that I knew many perfectly normal, intelligent, and rational people who held beliefs and engaged in practices that I found highly questionable. Okay, in some cases, absolutely preposterous and full-on nuts. And yet, I envied each of them. I desperately wanted the deep level of conviction and meaning that they had in their lives.

And then, as I stood at the gate at JFK waiting to board a plane to Brazil to visit one of the more questionable of highly questionable spiritual leaders on my long "hit list," rather than open-mindedly embracing the opportunity before me—as I had promised myself I would—I began to backpedal. Mainly because I started thinking about the Catholic Church's warnings about the dangers of yoga.

The church advises Catholics to not practice yoga at all. And if they do stray from the flock to take a cleansing breath or two, they are cautioned to not mistake any spiritual feelings they may experience while in downward dog or warrior pose as in any way relating to God.

The reason this particular fact unnerved me was not completely random. I may not be Catholic, but I spent some of my early, formative years with nuns—and there I was, headed to visit a faith healer. A faith healer who performs miracles and convenes with the dead. A faith healer not sanctioned by the church.

I was pretty sure that was worse than yoga.

IN THAT MOMENT it dawned on me that one tough part of shopping for a new God is the completely irrational fear that the old God you already have ties to, however loose, just might get pissed off and drop you altogether. By boarding this plane, I was straying from the flock—quite a few flocks, in fact. I was an apostate and religious turncoat, a spiritual Benedict Arnold.

And yet I boarded that plane anyway.

* * *

JOÃO TEIXEIRA DE FARIA, John of God (JOG), claims to be a full-trance medium—a pipeline between people here on earth and the spirit world. Granted, that may sound stranger to some of us in the United States than it does to people in Brazil and in many other parts of the world where there are strong cultural beliefs in the existence of mediums who act as vessels of contact with those on the other side—but still.

JOG and his devotees believe that he enters a trancelike state that enables him to channel more than thirty entities—from kings and saints to doctors, scientists, and psychiatrists. This, he professes, gives him the power to heal the sick. JOG believes that he is a conduit—literally, the healing hand of God—and that God ministers to the ill by directing his actions. Even though this sounded completely ludicrous to me, he's treated over 15 million people (some via distance healing), and so far over 8 million have traveled from around the world to see him in person, many at his compound, Casa de Dom Inácio de Loyola or "The Casa," in Abadiânia, Brazil.

There are numerous reports that JOG has cured cancer, eliminated tumors, and restored sight. While individual anecdotal stories of miraculous cures or partial recoveries are widespread, actual documented scientific evidence is hard to come by—and, believe me, I looked. He does, however, offer proof himself in the form of an "evidence room" at The Casa full of crutches and walkers left behind by the "cured."

JOG is popular and controversial enough to have attracted widespread media attention, including from *60 Minutes*, CNN, the *New Yorker*, the *New York Times*, and the big-name media gurus. Dr. Oz was consulted by ABC's *Primetime* with respect to some of JOG's apparent results, including a patient who appeared to have shown remarkable improvement from an inoperable, stage IV glioblastoma multiform with a reported 2 percent rate of remission. While Dr. Oz said that he wouldn't send his own patients to JOG, he thought that "JOG could . . . be on to something," be it the atmosphere in the clinic or the actual hands-on manipulation performed. Oprah reports of her near collapse and overwhelming physical response when she witnessed JOG performing what he calls a "visible" surgery. Yes, the kind that involves a knife and blood. And no, JOG is not a doctor. He has no formal education. In fact, he can neither read nor write.

But according to JOG and his followers, that's okay because God himself, or one of the other entities—not JOG—is cutting you with an unsterilized kitchen knife or probing your nostrils with forceps. Even still, before you get your eyeballs scraped or let him cut an incision in your chest, you might want to remind yourself that you signed a liability release form. (Sorry, but as a lawyer I had to say that.)

OF COURSE, SKEPTICS (like me) are a given. And by and large, the mainstream news reporters appeared less woozy and weak-in-the-knees than Oprah did and far less open-minded than Dr. Oz. But millions of followers have looked to JOG to heal something or to find answers beyond what traditional medicine and conventional religious thinking have to offer. There is no question that, just like Hugging Amma, JOG gives hope to millions. I was struggling to determine whether this is false hope marketed to the desperate by a charlatan or if what he does really works on some level science can't yet explain.

WHEN I SET off for Brazil I recognized that my willingness to travel so far to see JOG meant that I was at least open to the possibility that he is for real. Otherwise I would have stayed home.

So, on top of my concerns about losing whatever weak ties I had to the God and religions I knew as a child, I started to worry about a justification paradigm.

The greater the effort expended to join a group—think of undergoing a rigorous fraternity initiation, or military boot camp, or childbirth—the more positive our perception of the group as a whole will be, regardless of the objective truth behind the actual group experience. This is because we all seek to reconcile any cognitive dissonance we encounter—we want equilibrium between our beliefs, the energy expended to get something, and the objective truth. When there is a discrepancy between two "facts," we adjust one of them so we feel better. In other words, we hoodwink ourselves.

Since I was expending resources to find enlightenment—money, psychological currency, and time away from my job and family—I had to be careful not to convince myself I'd found it just so I could justify the investment. So, at the onset at least, I defected to hard science.

* * *

IN MATHEMATICS, A proof is a set of logical, definitive, and irrefutable steps that take you from a question to its answer. A mathematical proof always begins with a set of pre-established truths called "givens."

All sorts of things—from the Bible and religion to geometry and football—have givens.

- You can eat locusts and beetles but not rabbit, pigs, and shellfish. (Bible)

- You can't have twelve men in a huddle. (football)

- You can't wear any fabric that is woven of wool and linen together. (Bible)

- You can't step out of bounds, then step back in and catch a pass. (football)

- You can't clip below the waist. (Bible and football)

So here are the John of God givens. I received them in a pretrip information e-mail. And just like any lawyer would do, I sifted through them and pulled out the most pertinent and eyebrow-raising facts. Be forewarned that, like so much else in life, they require a considerable leap of faith.

- John of God is referred to as "The entity."

- He prescribes herbs and teas and conducts surgeries. (Yes, the real kind, with an incision and blood but no anesthesia or sterilization.)

- JOG has no formal education. (This includes no medical degree.)

- JOG has been prosecuted for performing medical procedures without a license.

- He drives a Ford 250 pickup truck. (This and the previous were not in the packet. They are just interesting.)

- The Casa is open only on Wednesday, Thursday, and Friday.

- JOG channels more than thirty spirit entities (dead people), many of whom were medical doctors in other times.

- He channels only one entity at a time.

- Unchanneled entities can still participate in your healing.

- You can receive treatment even when you are alone in your hotel room, or en route to Abadiânia, or even prior to getting on the airplane to visit The Casa.

- The cure can occur instantaneously, or it can happen slowly, sometimes three to four months after you leave.

- You must wear all white clothing during your visit as it allows JOG to see the energy around you better.

- Much of the day is spent in one of three "current rooms."

- Current rooms are for silent prayer or meditation.

- No ticket is needed for the current rooms.

- In the current rooms you must sit with your legs uncrossed and your eyes closed.

- The entities cannot work with you if your eyes are open.

- Energy cannot flow through crimped limbs.

- The third current room is where the invisible surgeries take place.

- You can bring pictures of people who want to be healed and present them to JOG as long as you have the person's permission.

- Obviously if the entity prescribes surgery by looking at the picture of your family member or friend, the family member or friend will have to come to Brazil for the procedure.

- But if the sick person is too ill to travel, a family member can have the surgery for him or her. This is called surrogate surgery. JOG can just look at the picture and then operate on you for your friend. (I am not making this up.)

- There is no charge to see JOG.

- You just pay for travel expenses and for prescription treatments, like herbs and crystals.

- JOG enters the room in a trance.

- If you don't speak Portuguese, you will need to have a translator by your side.

- Translators wear blue shirts.

- If you are a first-time visitor, you wait in one line.

- Repeat visitors queue up in a separate line.

- Do not get in the spiritual intervention line unless instructed to do so.

- People returning for surgery wait in the surgery line.

- There are "invisible" and "visible" surgeries.

- A visible surgery means he cuts you. (Unbelievably, people claim it does not hurt.)

- An invisible surgery means JOG operates on a whole group of people without cutting into any of them but just by thinking about doing so, or channeling surgical energy.

- Even after an invisible surgery, you need to recuperate, just as if you had a "real" operation.

- You cannot have a visible surgery if you are under eighteen or over fifty-three or have certain medical conditions. (If you will turn fifty-four in a week, it is still okay.)

- No sex for forty days after the first operation—even if the operation is invisible.

- No sex for eight days after subsequent operations.

- Do not pass by the entity or the current room after surgery, as your auric field remains open.

- Your bed sheets should be white or a pale color when you visit The Casa.

- There is no anesthesia. (I mentioned this already, but I feel like it warrants repeating.)

- After surgery you should put a glass of water next to your bed and ask the entities to remove your sutures. You will sleep for a very long time.

- JOG prescribes herbs after he meets with you—or sees your picture.

- Prescribed herbs can take the form of capsules or tea.

- The capsules cost $20 for a bottle of forty, which will last thirteen days.

- You will be prescribed between one and six different bottles.

- Even though the herbs all look alike, no two regimens are the same, so don't mix up the bottles.

- If you have a chronic condition, you should buy enough for two years.

- You should bring enough Brazilian currency, *reals*, for more herbs than you think you might need—the equivalent of at least US$240 but up to US$1,120.

- You need to drink large quantities of blessed water for forty days after treatment.

- Blessed water is for sale in the bookstore.

- There are ATM machines in town.

- Do not drink alcohol or eat peppery food, gassed bananas, pig meat, or fertilized eggs after you go home.

- Gassed bananas are bananas sprayed with ripening hormones.

- Ungassed bananas are okay to eat.

- Avoid black coffee, cola, smoking, junk food, and sugar after surgery. (And sex. This also warrants repeated mention.)

- The entity may prescribe crystal bed therapy. It costs twenty Brazilian *reals*.

- You sign up for crystal bed therapy in the bookstore.

- The seven crystals above the bed are aligned with the seven chakras of the body.

- The crystals cleanse and energize the body.

- You should have an odd number of sessions (one or three sessions instead of two or four).

- If you want more than that, you have to get permission from JOG.

- If JOG told you to come back again, you don't need a ticket.

- Ask someone in a blue shirt which line you should get in.

- JOG doesn't cure anyone; God does. Well, actually, God is responsible for 25 percent of your cure and the entities for another 25 percent; you are responsible for the remaining 50 percent. (Yes, they are that specific.)

All this information was in the welcome packet, and 8 million people have shown up. Including Oprah and me.

IN DESCRIBING HER experience meeting JOG in Brazil, Oprah said of her initial reaction, "Just being in the presence of so much hope was humbling." Then, when she stood by JOG's side as he performed surgery, she had an overwhelming and inexplicable physical reaction: she heated up and nearly fainted. Someone had to escort her back to her chair. She reported that what she felt was otherworldly. JOG told Oprah that all that heat was the entities entering her body—and it looks like she bought it. Apparently, Oprah Winfrey, the goddess of daytime television, became a believer.

And then there's me.

*   *   *

I HAD TO travel over 4,200 miles from New York to Brasilia, Brazil, by air. Then a cab drove me for two hours through dusty back roads to the JOG compound located in the remote village of Abadiânia. The whole town exists to support JOG's business—he is a tourist attraction, like Lourdes or the Grand Canyon. And all the hotel owners are prepared to deal with the JOG "givens."

The program for most people lasts three days, although many stay longer. Much longer. Though people who have surgery must stay to recover for eight days, some people never leave—because they have found their way home.

My visit involved an orientation, followed by meditation sessions held in the first current room for several hours, two times each day, plus long waits in line to meet JOG. It was like Hugging Amma, without the hug.

Although instructed to wear white clothes, we weren't all in heavenly white. One guy, with a mullet, waiting in line to see JOG was wearing a *Ghostbusters* T-shirt.

Ghostbusters? Maybe it was the only white shirt he owned?

Even still, it was ironic. Or satirical. Or disrespectful. Possibly snarky. But hardly heavenly.

WHEN YOU VISIT JOG, you get to ask him three questions, called "intentions." It sounded so appealing. As I stood in line, I felt a bit like I imagine Dorothy must have when she was waiting to meet the Wizard of Oz. I wasn't in Kansas anymore either, and the promise for me seemed just as simple and equally profound. John of God would take me home.

There was a problem though. I didn't speak Portuguese. I was confused by the translators in the blue shirts. And I got in the wrong line. Two days in a row. Even though I am a lawyer and I read the information packet.

I had wasted two days standing in the wrong line. Then, on the third day, I finally caught on and got in the correct line, slowly making my way to the front. Just like everyone else, I would get to ask JOG three questions. I was planning on asking the questions Zia would later ask me.

Why are we here?
What is the meaning of life?
What happens when we die?
Is there a God?

Yes, I know that's four questions.

I thought it would be easy to drop one, but I couldn't decide which to let go. So now I had another problem. And I started to second-guess myself. I started to think that maybe all my questions were too philosophical. I started to think that maybe I should just ask him something simple and concrete. But what?

I asked someone to hold my place so I could sneak out to dash to the bathroom. When I rounded the corner, I saw JOG standing between the ladies' room and me. I stopped dead in my tracks. He must have been on a break.

I wasn't sure about protocol and etiquette. Should I walk across his path? (The information packet said not to.) Do I speak to him? Nod? Smile? Bow? Genuflect? I glanced back toward the line, then at the door to the bathroom. Then back at JOG.

He was clipping his nails.

I was frozen like a skeptic caught in spiritual headlights. Then I bolted past him and slipped into the ladies' room. I didn't speak, nod, smile, bow, or genuflect. I looked at my feet instead.

There was yet another line to deal with inside the ladies' room. The woman in front of me said she came all this way to ask JOG if her house in Seattle would sell. And he said he didn't know.

I guess JOG knew he was no match for the global recession.

WHEN I LEFT the ladies' room, JOG was, thankfully, gone, and I got back in the main waiting line. As I continued inching my way toward the front, I felt like I was repeating my experience with Hugging Amma. I'd had a lifetime to prepare and yet had thrust myself into a situation that I was ill-prepared for. One that would be over before I knew it. I decided that when my turn came, I should ask JOG to help me find laughter and passion and to learn how to heal and protect my heart.

If I couldn't get answers for the bigger questions, I felt that this was a solid place to start.

Then when my turn came, at the last minute, I changed my mind again and defaulted to the simplest of simple. I told JOG that I wanted to have fun in every aspect of my life.

It wasn't three questions. It wasn't even one question. It was a single statement of intent. A simple wish, like a child might make if presented with a magic genie—or the Wizard of Oz.

JOG said nothing. I mean, *nothing*. He simply waved me through. I had asked him for basic happiness, and he didn't even reply.

I didn't experience the Oprah effect. I didn't heat up or swoon or vibrate. I didn't feel anything.

Instead, I said to myself, *That's it? I came all this way, with all this hope and anticipation and need and . . . that's it?*

Meanwhile, a helper was directing me to a blessing room where I would receive a powerful energy transmission. Like all the rooms in the compound, it was pretty nondescript: white paint, church pews, and pictures of the various dead entities hanging on the walls.

But even in the blessing room, I felt absolutely nothing. No vibration. No heat. No energy transmission. No otherworldliness.

Next, I was sent to the current room to meditate. Just as instructed, I kept my eyes closed and my legs uncrossed. I was silent and uncrimped. I didn't feel energy vibrations when sitting in the current or crystal rooms or when watching a surgery. Unlike

Oprah, I didn't become drained or collapse; no one had to escort me to my chair.

I wish that some such thing of undeniable magnitude had happened to me, because that would make believing so simple. But it didn't.

THEN IT WAS time for the soup break. As I ate the blessed soup, made with blessed water and vegetables—essentially a spiritual minestrone—I began to wonder if I had missed my opportunity. I started to think that maybe I should have asked JOG the profound questions about laughter, passion, and heart. Maybe I was dismissed because I didn't state a worthy intention or ask the right question.

After lunch, I went back to the meditation room. I was still wearing white. I was still silent and unfolded. But I was no longer optimistic. I felt I had absolutely nothing to show for my trip—until I remembered what Norberto had said.

Each morning, as everyone waited in line, a man named Norberto spoke to us in a combination of Portuguese and German, mixed with a little broken English. It was a sermon of sorts to keep us distracted as we inched our way forward. I don't know what he said in Portuguese or German, but the English I understood perfectly. He said, "Smile more, pray more . . . happy more. Drink more water. Eat breakfast. Real breakfast, at a table, with your family."

At first I found it annoying.

I had come all this way to see JOG, but the only advice I received was from someone named Norberto? But as I sat in the meditation room I focused on "Smile more, pray more . . . happy more. Drink more water. Eat breakfast. Real breakfast, at a table, with your family" because I had nothing else.

And then the unexpected happened.

I BEGAN TO feel something. And it was simple.

Not necessarily remarkable. But possibly miraculous in its simplicity.

Like a weight had been lifted.

"Smile more, pray more . . . happy more. Drink more water. Eat breakfast. Real breakfast, at a table, with your family."

Was this energy healing?

Combine one molecule of oxygen with two of hydrogen and you get water. Is it possible that energy healing is that simple? And just as miraculous? So what if I didn't heat up or vibrate? So what if I couldn't see or understand it? So what if it made no sense to me? I turn on my computer every day and get Wi-Fi. I love my husband and my daughter. I can't see any of that either, but it is undeniably real. I decided that I would tell Zia the story of the first microscope and how it changed science. I would tell her that there are so many things that are real and powerful but that we cannot see.

Like love and germs and Wi-Fi.

I SPENT THE rest of the trip reveling in this new, joyful sense of well-being. I ate warm, ripe tomatoes, fresh fish, and passion fruit. I drank blessed water. Lots of blessed water. And I meditated.

On the flight home I smiled at everyone. Including Pedro, the gate attendant. I was on standby for a flight that would get me to New York a few hours earlier than the one I had booked and was an unlikely number twenty-two on the list. Despite the unfavorable odds, I got bumped to the earlier flight. Then I smiled at the flight crew and got moved to an exit-row seat on the plane. I breezed through immigration in Miami, where I got a customs official to laugh. For some reason he wanted to hear all about my trip.

Was it my smile?

I made it home in time to smile at Zia before she went to sleep. She smiled back. It was a beautiful smile. The kind of smile that makes you feel your life is complete.

I felt lighter. Less burdened. Cured of what ailed me. And it actually felt like it might take. I still didn't have any answers. But I didn't care as much. I didn't give a hoot about justification paradigms, or cognitive dissonance, or whether I had hoodwinked myself. I had faith in things that I could not see.

I felt more comfortable in my own skin, what the French call *bien dans sa peau*. I hadn't felt that in . . . well, forever.

THE NEXT MORNING I woke up in New York to the smell of breakfast being cooked by Atul. I smiled. Until I remembered that I had told him about the "eat breakfast with your family" part but not the "no pig meat" part.

I could smell the bacon frying.

By the time I got out of bed, I had already decided to not abide by JOG's "no pig meat" rule. Just this once.

Then I remembered the "no alcohol" rule. And of course there was the JOG mandate to eliminate spicy food, gassed bananas, sugar, and sex for forty days. I could do without the spicy food and the gassed bananas, but the sugar and alcohol and sex loomed problematic.

I had been home for less than twelve hours and I was already facing equilibrium-busting cognitive dissonance. So I did what all true believers do when certain parts of their belief systems don't work for them: I hand-selected what worked for me and created a justifier for the rest. Just like cult members waiting for the apocalypse and Catholics who use birth control.

I took a shower, got dressed, walked into the kitchen, and ate a piece of bacon while thinking about the bottles of Tuscan red we would be drinking at Atul's birthday party later that week and the even more memorable bottles of pinot noir I would bring home from a trip we had planned to Napa Valley.

I picked up Zia from her highchair, and she insisted on feeding me another piece of bacon.

She was laughing, and I was smiling.

I took a sip of the blessed water I'd carted home with me, kissed my bacon-frying husband on the cheek, and said a quick prayer of thanks. Despite the pig meat, the pending alcohol consumption, and the anticipated sex, I still felt more comfortable in my own skin. I was home.

It was flawed. I was hoodwinked. But it felt glorious.

And it lasted all of three days.

Chapter 2

PARAMJI

Tantric Sound Healing,
Ojai, California

Partway through my hunt for God, I was in the car with my mom coming home from the grocery store when she announced that she was an atheist.

It was as though I was driving carefree along the highway of life, then—smack—I hit a deer. Came at me out of nowhere. And then the massive, shocking, wholly unappealing reality of MY MOM IS AN ATHEIST was staring me in the face.

I mean, seriously? I'm thinking, *WTF???*

"Since when?" I asked, trying to sound casual.

Instead of answering she lobbed a second grenade. "I don't believe in gurus and healers either."

We had just been discussing my recent visits to Hugging Amma and John of God (JOG) and spiritual healers in general—who, she proceeded to tell me, were all "nonsense." "They just take your money and don't really do anything."

Not exactly what I wanted to hear.

I responded, "But even if you're right about the gurus and healers when it comes to their value to you, don't you think at least
some of them might have some value to other people?" I was going
to add, "like me," but stopped myself.

"No," she replied. "We need to do the work ourselves. No one
can do it for us."

There you go—that's my mom. Clean and precise. No wavering.

I, on the other hand, am the Queen of Wavering, so I started to
do just that—*maybe she had a point*—then circled back to her original atheist comment.

"Well, even still, I don't see how not believing in gurus and healers would lead you to conclude that there is no God."

Admittedly, it sounded a bit more defensive than I would have
liked. My mother didn't say anything.

I looked over, and she was just blissfully looking out the car
window. But what I saw was a giant obstruction threatening to
block my path to enlightenment.

Then it got worse. As in me-alone-in-my-head-Mom-isn't-
going-to-talk worse.

As we drove in silence I started thinking about the fact that what
she had said actually made no sense. At least the "no God" part didn't.

Followers of the Jain religion, like my parents and most of my
extended family—as well as 4 million other people around the
world (primarily in India)—believe that rather than one God,
there are an infinite number of Gods—that God manifests as the
perfection of each of us as individuals. We are taught that
throughout our lives we are all striving to remove the bad karmas
that block us from becoming our own perfect selves. Doing so
liberates our souls and delivers us to a state of glorious, limitless
knowledge, heavenly bliss, and godlike power called *moksha*,
where we join all the other self-perfected, self-actualized Gods
who have arrived before us, to add to an ever-growing, infinite
pool of enlightenment and perfection.

So that meant that when my mom said, "I don't believe in
God," she was really saying that she didn't believe in the

perfected version of herself—or anyone else. Which was some-how, at least to me as her daughter and as a spiritual seeker hell-bent on self-improvement, much worse and much harder to understand than if she had announced that she didn't believe in a single, all-powerful supreme being.

As I drove down the highway, I kept glancing over at my mother, continuing to wonder how she could be so calm. Then it crossed my mind that if she could be so calm about the whole no-God thing, what exactly was I so worried about? Which of course led me to question what the hell I was doing looking for something my own mother said didn't exist, and then, as I reflected further on the conversation, to wonder whether I was being completely sincere in saying that I was doing the hunt-for-God stuff for Zia in the first place. At which point I had to face the possibility that all the effort I was putting in was both worthless and nothing more than an ex-cuse to do something for me.

Then I missed my exit.

And I don't mean that metaphorically. I actually drove right by it. Didn't even pause.

The truth was

A. my mom might be right that the whole God/guru thing was a bunch of bunk, and

B. I might, in fact, be doing all of this, to a large degree, for myself.

To be perfectly honest, I enjoyed yoga retreats and esoteric spir-itual adventures. Plus things were emerging from it. Patterns. Things of interest. Granted, just small incremental things—but nonetheless (slightly) profound things.

Besides, even though when all was said and done I might not actually find a concrete, definitive, irrefutable spiritual home, I was pretty sure that in going to these gurus and healers and hand-picking and selectively choosing, I'd at least find foundational ele-ments that would work for me—elements that I could gift to Zia.

So I then concluded (arguing with myself, since the only other person in the car was blissfully looking out the window at the—apparently—God-less world) that while many of these healers just might actually be worthless, it made perfect sense that I would have to find my spiritual home before I could help my daughter find hers. Maybe I *was* building the Temple of Me. The perfected me.

Which, upon reflection, sounded a hell of a lot like Jainism and a goddamned justification paradigm all wrapped up in one.

But before I got to the next exit, I had decided, *So frickin' what?* If I did build a Temple of Me—as in, removed those bad karmas or uncovered spiritual practices that led to a more perfect me—I would be better equipped to help Zia build a Temple of Her, and then maybe I wouldn't find myself sitting next to my daughter thirty years from now as she drove down some highway as I calmly told her that she wouldn't find what she was looking for because it didn't exist. Especially if that "thing" she was looking for happened to be something important . . . like God, deep spiritual connection, and cosmic enlightenment rather than, say, the closest shopping mall.

I was quickly drawing a twofold conclusion. First, maybe my mother was wrong and some of these gurus and healers do work for some people (like me). And second, so what if I focus on myself a little and this whole spiritual quest is for me? Would that be so bad?

But my issue with this whole Mom/God thing didn't really have to do with whom I was actually trying to help in my personal quest for deeper meaning. I was more bothered by how certain my mom seemed to be about her conclusion that gurus and healers were all worthless and the world was in fact God-less.

Especially the God-less world part.

How could she tell me that she was an atheist and not be upset, even a little? She had apparently just dismissed God in any and all forms, right along with the perfection of self—just like that.

So what did I do? Did I swear off gurus and healers because my mother, the woman who raised me and whom I respected highly—a woman who frequently had an aura of bliss and certainty about her of a magnitude that I would like to experience just once in my life—had told me that the quest I was on was all a bunch of hogwash with such precision and conviction that it led me to question my own motivations for seeking enlightenment in the first place?

Of course not. I drove to the next exit, got off the highway, turned the car around, and headed home.

EN ROUTE, I reflected on the advice of two near perfect strangers, people I had no history with and absolutely no reason to believe or respect. The first was my facialist—a person who happens to refer to herself as "Goddess." Not as in "a goddess." Just "Goddess." Signs her e-mails that way too.

Seriously—you've got to love a woman who has that much confidence.

My facialist, the Goddess of Skin, had told me that she was a celibate Buddhist (by choice) and hadn't had sex in six years.

I wasn't even sure what that meant (the celibate Buddhist part).

Of course, I knew what celibacy was. And I knew what Buddhism was. I just wasn't sure how they came together in a meaningful way. While she was cleaning my pores, I had started thinking about the no-sex-for-six-years thing and that brought to mind, in a concerning way, the slight dry patch Atul and I were going through. And thinking about that led me to thinking about that other perfect stranger: a woman who had suggested that I embrace my femininity as a means to achieve greater spiritual unity with my husband and the universe by going to Mama Gena's School of Womanly Arts to "liberate my inner bitch" and "explore my pussy." Mama Gena is the powerhouse motivator who teaches classes like "Training Your Man" and "Trust Your Pussy," which are basically seminars in feminine pleasure. As Mama Gena puts it, ice cream and orgasms can be drivers of genuine happiness and success.

Or, "better yet," this stranger then said, her top recommendation was to take a class called SFactor, which she said was "an empowering stripper/pole-dancing workout class right here in the city."

Honestly, both Mama Gena and SFactor were options that on the surface I found a little too *Sex and the City* or bachelorette party–esque for me. So I told this woman that the journey I was on was a bit more spiritual in nature than Mama Gena or SFactor were likely to satisfy—at which point she told me that Mama Gena was her priestess and SFactor classes were her church, which I thought was a pretty funny comment.

But I was (unfortunately and awkwardly) laughing alone.

In any event, this woman had planted the idea of the Divine Feminine in my head, and since I had been reading a bit about Goddess worship at the time anyway, as I was lying there on the skin Goddess/facialist's table in Chelsea while she extracted and exfoliated, I was (loosely and fearfully) entertaining the possibility of throwing caution to the wind and going, not to Mama Gena's or SFactor, but to someplace a bit more concretely spiritual to get my yoni healed.

Yoni means sacred temple in Sanskrit. And divine opening. And vagina. (*Lingam* is the male counterpart.)

There was something undeniably compelling about the ironic juxtaposition of the highly feminine and confident sex-free Buddhist/Goddess and the highly feminine and confident oversexed pole dancer, and at that moment I found both their similarities and their contradictions mildly (okay, extremely) intriguing. I actually wanted the deep level of feminine confidence that both of these women exuded. Plus, the tradition of Goddess worship and the Divine Feminine goes back thousands of years in India and focuses on connecting to the divine within ourselves as a massive source of untapped cosmic energy—which, I have to be honest, after having a baby, sounded rather appealing.

I was intrigued by the concept of feminine power, not only in the life-giving and sexual aspects but also in terms of matriarchy. From visiting India as a child, I remembered my grandmother had carried around a big ring of keys—the likes of which I had only seen on the janitor at my elementary school—that gave her both an air of importance and supreme control over both family and guests.

She wore the keys on a chain attached to the petticoat that held up her sari, and they opened the multiple padlocks on a set of steel closets where the family stored everything of value. And I mean everything. Not only cash and jewelry and clothes but also things of relatively small value, like pistachios and crayons and chocolate. In my eyes my grandmother had extraordinary, unprecedented power because anyone who needed anything—even his or her own clothing—had to go to her to get it. That meant that she knew just about everything about everyone at all times, a construct that I found both intrusive and enviable, especially since my only point of reference for that kind of power was the description of God himself (and Santa) that the nuns (and kids) in Catholic school had drilled into my head.

So instead of listening to my own mother and accepting her God-less world, I decided that I would go see a guru named Shri Param Eswaran (aka Paramji), whom my friend Karen had recently brought to my attention and my mother would surely declare a wholly indisputable, card-carrying charlatan.

Paramji is a self-proclaimed yoni healer and (according to Karen) "cooch yodeler" (use your imagination) who purports to tap into the vibrations of the universe to provide both a greater spiritual connection and better sex. So maybe this was a step in the right direction.

I did, however, have to admit that my mom had a point. A lot of this stuff did smack of crazy. And yes, I also considered that by making the decision to attend a spiritual/yoni healing retreat, I might have been overreacting to—possibly even rebelling against—the Mom/God bomb just a tiny bit.

*   *   *

IF SANTA CLAUS were from India, he would look exactly like Paramji. White beard, broad face, big smile, crinkles around the eyes—and generally sparkly. Heavy around the midsection too—but in Paramji's case more in a yoga-fit-stocky-old-Indian-guru kind of way than in the flabby-Western-too-much-eggnog-and-too-many-cookies kind of way. Couple that with the promise that they both drop off big bags of gifts, then throw in the fact that when I met him, Paramji was drinking tea out of a Santa mug while smoking a cigar, and you'll see why I made the connection.

In Paramji's case, those gifts would be sourced from ancient Vedic tradition—or Spirituality-R-Us depending on your mind-set—and involve awakening your inner Goddess, yoni healing, and womb empowerment. That, and a deep connection to the energy force of the universe. How's that for a Christmas list?

Translation? Greater self-knowledge, self-esteem, happiness, spiritual enlightenment, Goddess status, and better sex all rolled into a four-day retreat. Cost? 432 bucks. If it works, even in an incremental, infinitesimal way—maybe not priceless but clearly a bargain.

PARAMJI IS NOT, in fact, an Indian manifestation of Santa—despite his appearance and promise of gilded, feminine, and otherworldly large-scale, cosmic-level gifts. He is a guru practicing something called Para-Tan sounding or tantric sound healing. I had to Google "Para-Tan sounding" and "Paramji" because I had never heard of it—or him—until Karen brought them to my attention. Unfortunately, the description I had received from her, while compelling, was somewhat confusing and I felt should be taken with a grain of salt the size of, well, a cathedral. And believe me, I was stalwart in my skepticism. Especially after the Mom/God conversation.

Here's what I learned: You (the soundee) lie on the floor, Paramji (the sounder) covers you with a sheet, and then he lies on top of you and chants (sounds) into your seven chakras (energy centers), one at a time. Meanwhile the healing circle of people around you (yes, this is a group activity) also chant (or sound) mantras into your chakras and selected other body parts—for an hour.

The person in the center of the circle (the soundee) is the one being "sounded." Sounding creates "positive electromagnetic signals" that are sent to all the organs, especially the brain. The idea is that these positive electromagnetic signals will create positive emotions that will replace "negative emotional memories."

I had to read these descriptions several times. And I wasn't sure which part made me more uncomfortable: the old Indian guy who would be lying on top of me chanting into my chakras, the fact that perfect strangers would be both watching the whole thing and chanting into my body along with him, or the unscientific use of "electromagnetic signals."

Then the lawyer in me took over, and I reconfirmed where the seven chakras were—even though I already knew—just to be sure. On the long shot that I was going to let anyone chant into them, I wanted to confirm that

A. I hadn't forgotten about any, and
B. none of them were located anywhere I didn't want perfect strangers' mouths to be.

Especially after the mention of yoni healing and womb empowerment.

Unfortunately, my research confirmed that a couple of the chakras were located in questionable areas:

1. **Root chakra:** base of spine (seems okay, maybe)
2. **Sacral chakra:** lower abdomen (not so sure, as it is in the general vicinity of the yoni—my yoni)
3. **Solar plexus chakra:** upper abdomen (seems okay)
4. **Heart chakra:** close to breasts (slightly unnerving)
5. **Throat chakra:** (weird, but okay)
6. **Third-eye chakra:** between the eyebrows (ditto)
7. **Crown chakra:** top of head (fine)

Then I momentarily considered that it was becoming hard to keep engaging in these spiritual practices while keeping an open mind and not starting to feel like a nutbag—or like I'd been conned. Or like I was conning myself. Especially after the Mom-doesn't-believe-in-gurus conversation.

But whenever I started feeling that nutbag, conned way, I'd invariably stumble upon something bright and shiny that I wanted to hold on to. Something slightly scientific, compellingly moving, or straight-up logical. Something mildly convincing, even to a lawyer—a factoid or two that I could actually discuss with the highly intellectual, Western-educated, science- and data-based people I spent my days with. That is, of course, on the days when I wasn't visiting serial huggers, eyeball scrapers, and cooch yodelers.

PARA-TAN SOUNDING IS done in a group because the concept—stemming from ancient Vedic tradition—is to use chanting and mantras to connect to a "collective consciousness." Paramji's goal is to heal the individual as a means to heal, one by one, all of humanity. Which sounded sweet and noble.

Then I read that channeling vibrations into a specific body part allows "vibrational frequency of each Bija (seed) mantra to release emotional blocks and restore the correct spin of the DNA on a cellular level." Which of course, at first, I thought was a lot of nonsense: the correct spin of DNA? *Does DNA spin?*

Ahhh, but then I read that everything spins. As in everything in the universe.

According to string theory, the entire universe is basically humming—all of it and all of us. Add that to the fact that the chanting of mantras has a long, compelling spiritual history, that cancer researchers are using sound—high-intensity focused ultrasound—to successfully destroy prostate cancer cells, that acoustical energy has been used to treat inoperable brain and breast cancer tumors, and that sound waves are being used to heal leg and foot ulcers, and this whole Paramji thing starts to look like it just might be grounded in a bit of hard science, not woo-woo, crazy, charlatan bunk after all.

In fact, Vedic tradition promotes the use of mantras and chanting to align the individual with the universe so that the person can heal. A mantra is a sound to bridge to the other side, to transport you from contained me to uncontained us, from confined (as in a body) to spiritually free (as in connected to something larger than yourself). In other words, chanting is the process of using sound as a pathway to spiritual connections, and the use of Sanskrit mantras dates back thousands of years to both Hindu and Buddhist sages.

Science has proven that chanting has a calming effect, lowers heart rate and blood pressure, changes brain wave activity, increases melatonin (which regulates hormones and helps you sleep), improves cognitive function, alters cellular structure, and elevates oxygen flow to the brain. As for the softer science, just ask anyone who sings in a chorus, and you will likely hear all about the power of communal harmonics and the spiritual connection singers feel as their voices join in unison and rise toward the heavens.

The larger, harder-to-swallow claim, of course, is that these chants can align us with the vibrations of the divine. Ask a yogi, and he will tell you that chanting can tap into a very powerful source of primal energy—kundalini—believed to be a latent power coiled at the base of the spine. When it rises, traveling up the spinal cord to the Sahasrara chakra at the top of the head, it creates the intense sensation of an electrical current while delivering a deep, meditative state of bliss. In the process it provides a sort of personal big bang, one-with-the-universe kind of thing.

And then I stumbled on this: simply attending religious services more than once a week lowers the death rate for women from any cause—including heart disease and cancer—by a whopping 33 percent. And the more you go to religious services, the better your chances of sticking around. The researchers didn't measure the level of commitment to God or religion or whether attendees actually believed in anything—they just looked at the health benefits for those who showed up.

So that is what I decided to do with Paramji—not necessarily to believe wholeheartedly but to show up.

HAVING SAID ALL that, it was still a bit hard for me to shake the charlatan—and possibly creepy—vibe of some old guy lying on top of me, but for good or bad, I was ultimately swayed by geography. A weekend Para-Tan healing retreat would be held just a short flight away from, and just after, a Google sales conference I'd be attending. Which meant that I could lie under the old Indian guru and get sounded, heal my yoni, vibrate with the universe, find God (maybe), and prove my mom wrong, all without spending more than a few extra days away from my family, increasing the price of my plane ticket, or missing any work. Then, when I heard that Ojai, California was like Tuscany with orange groves and avocado trees, I was sold.

Surprisingly, in the days leading up to the retreat, I found myself getting increasingly hopeful. Excited even. The science and sacred history of Goddess worship and the compelling fact that the universe itself vibrates continued to—pardon the play on words—resonate with me. After all, who doesn't want to be a divinely feminine earth mother cosmically pulsing in poetic unison with the harmonic, vibratory universe? I'm serious. That actually sounded far more compelling to me than my mom's this-is-all-there-is-Godless world. In fact, as a lawyer, I have to say that there is a strong case for it being—in an otherworldly sense and at this particular moment in my life—wildly compelling.

On the flip side, I found the "givens"—or the intellectual constructs that underpin tantric sounding, as presented on Paramji's website—though far more streamlined, just as perplexing as the givens laid out in the Bible, by the NFL, and by JOG:

- The person being sounded is a manifestation of a God or Goddess.

- Sounding is making love vibrations.

- Therefore sounding is making love to a God/Goddess (without sex!!). (Note that the "without sex" part, with the parentheses and two exclamation points, is on the website. So is the "making love" part.)

- It is very weird to have an Indian Santa lying on top of you doing this. (This last fact is not on the website; it was my personal observation when I was being sounded.)

Which means that I actually did go to see the Indian Santa with the bag of gifts sourced from the enlightenment shop. And the experience was out there—as in, really out there.

*   *   *

ON THE PLUS side, the people attending the retreat were a colorful group:

Me (Anjali)—skeptic extraordinaire. A corporate lawyer who took a lot of notes and photos (perhaps collecting material for a potential lawsuit if she was injured during sounding). Very fond of both avocados and napping. Not a likely candidate to embrace Goddess status—or worship—because her upbringing by immigrant parents who did not acknowledge her Goddess status, coupled with a strict Catholic school education, gave her a childhood that prudishly bordered on Amish.

Karen—a screenwriter from Hollywood. Hilarious, funny, blond, California/Jersey girl. Likely already a Goddess and attending only to "brush up" on her feminine divinity.

Neve—gorgeous, incredibly sensual, and confident in her womanhood. A Goddess's Goddess who clearly needed no brushing up. Said she's a lesbian. Might actually have enough divinely feminine power to convert nonlesbians.

Jenn—nicknamed (by Paramji) "Norman the Mormon." A healer from outside Salt Lake City, Utah.

Nina—nicknamed (by me) Hippie Jane Seymour. Just wanted to have fun. Her idea of fun might be a bit more wackadoodle than yours or mine, but she added a good vibe.

Nick—first experience with anything like this (join the club). Had a solid teddy bear/Billy Zane look to him. Friends with Neve. Their relationship was loving and beautiful to watch. (Made me think that maybe Neve was not actually a lesbian.)

Jane and Greg—Jane was an actress. Incredibly smart, definitely on a search. Greg was her boyfriend.

Shivani—a white woman who changed her name (I'm assuming) to an Indian one over the course of her spiritual journey. (Paramji admitted to me when we met that when he saw my name on the list he just assumed I was white and had changed my name to an Indian one because "Indian people don't do these things.")

Molly—an artist living in Ojai who hosted us for the retreat. She is the owner of many avocado trees.

ON THE SURFACE, the retreat was peaceful and restful, with lots of yoga and great vegan food, hikes in the countryside, and long afternoon naps. We were staying at a pretty house with an outdoor meditation building and a pool. Add in some live music and singing—and an abundance of avocados—and it was, as retreats go, not bad. Actually, it was really nice.

And then there were the private meetings with Paramji (weird and disconcerting but in some ways productive), the sounding of the others in the group (out there, as in really, really out there), my sounding (sadly pedestrian), and the weekend capper: Neve and the forty-five-minute orgasm. After witnessing that, I was pretty sure the Yoni Sisters on the Quest for the Golden Lingam had found it: Paramji.

And I mean, holy cow.
But first, the private meetings with Paramji.

* * *

HERE IS SOME of what Paramji told me when I met with him over the weekend (not necessarily in this order):

- I am human by birth. (So far we were in agreement.)

- My animal symbol is the male monkey. (I was okay with this too. I like monkeys; they're cute and smart and limber—and chatty, just like me.)

- I should (must) sleep with my head facing east. (I was not so sure this would work without moving to a new apartment or getting new bedroom furniture [or a new husband], since my apartment [and husband] were configured in such a way that I had slept facing south for our entire marriage.)

- I need to stop wearing a bra. (Interesting, and would consider. But more on this shortly.)

Here's where he lost me. He said that I should *must* change my name to something beginning with Bu, or Bhaa, or Pha, or Dha. (Not happening—as in, really NOT HAPPENING.) I (politely) resisted, but Paramji was insistent.

"How about Bhuvaneshwari?" he asked. I shook my head.

"Why not?"

"Because Anjali is my name."

"You have to change your name. It doesn't empower you."

I tried again by stating the obvious. "But it's my name."

He said, "Some cuckoo named you."

I told him that cuckoo was my mother. He wasn't impressed.

PARAMJI DISMISSED MY mother—along with the whole tradition of parents naming their babies—with a wave of his hand, saying, "That's what happens when Indians get Westernized."

I was about to object but decided (uncharacteristically) to keep my mouth shut. Then Paramji said, "Your mother named you Anjali because she forgot that you were a Goddess."

I have to admit, he got me there. That part was probably true.

NONETHELESS, I COULD not see myself going by something beginning with Bu, or Bhaa, or Pha, or Dha or explaining to my mother or husband or daughter—or boss and colleagues (good lord!)—that I was changing my name to something beginning with Bu, or Bhaa, or Pha, or Dha and that I was doing so

A. because my mother was cuckoo when she named me, and, parenthetically,
B. because when she named me she had "forgotten" I was a Goddess.

I'm pretty sure no one ever thought I was a Goddess. Not my mother, not my husband (okay, maybe once or twice), not my daughter, my friends, or my boss, and not me. Especially not me.

And therein, as Paramji would say, lay all my problems.

*   *   *

PARAMJI BEGAN A sounding by asking, "Are you ready to make love?"

Say, whaaat?? Or so I thought to myself the first time this happened, until I remembered that his website stated he would say exactly that.

Luckily, I didn't have to go first. Shivani volunteered. Paramji covered her with a sheet and then lay on top of her. We were all gathered around her at her different chakra "stations." When he began to chant/sound into her neck, we chanted (sounded) her as well. It was like we were in a temple worshiping her.

And then she had multiple, off-the-charts energy surges—convulsions almost. I couldn't decide if someone should offer her a cigarette or call 911. She was writhing and undulating, her arms were flapping, and she rose up. As in levitated. I was thinking, *I want this; I don't want this. I want to stay; I want to go.*

While watching Shivani, I felt third-eye pressure between my brows—the chakra attributed to spiritual insight, wisdom, and intuition—like a fly on my forehead. I didn't know if I believed this was real or put-on. But the chanting itself, in unison, was harmonic, elevating, and compelling. The mantras and sounds felt undeniably transcendent. As the hour went on, there was a strong feeling of connection in the joined voices and the melodic patterns. There was something beautiful and fully human and intimate and sensual about it.

This strange place I was visiting wholly defied categorization.

In some small ways, I felt like I was getting in touch with my roots in India—but instead of feeling like I was coming home, I felt uncomfortable, even a little afraid. This was undeniably crazy-assed shit.

But there was another good and surprising part—hardly orgasmic bliss, but still, I was happy to take it: it stopped the noise in my head.

THE NEXT DAY, I started out as Miss Yoni for Jane. This sounds like a beauty pageant for vaginas, but it actually means my "station" was sitting at her crown chakra with her head straight up in between my legs, right up against my yoni. Her boyfriend, Greg, was sounding her, meaning he was the one laying on her. (Paramji sounded only the women, and the women of the group sounded the men—if they were comfortable doing so, which I was decidedly not; those who came as a couple could sound each other.)

Greg looked like an eager-to-please puppy and was working so hard to do it right. It was disconcerting to watch. It was clearly an out-of-body experience for Jane too, since her kundalini was definitely rising. She too was undulating and writhing around like she was having multiple orgasms—or dying, I couldn't tell which. When it was over and Jane was asked to describe it, she was completely overcome with emotion and said she had a strong sense of

Christ energy from Greg. She then said that she had the recurring thought *John of God, John of God, John of God.*

I MUST SAY, that totally startled me. I started to worry that the JOG message somehow came from me—as in, it came from me and my yoni—because this was the first time I had felt the vibrations everyone else had experienced so powerfully throughout the weekend. I felt them running up and down my right side (mostly in my right calf, which admittedly could have been nothing more than my leg falling asleep). And I also felt them in the area below my navel, what I would normally call my stomach but now realized was the sacral chakra that included my lady parts. It was a pulsing vibration. Not necessarily an amazing sensation—and certainly not remotely orgasmic—but not bad either. It was just a humming. Like a tremor that was apparently intended not for me at all but to project JOG in Brazil to Jane.

When it was Neve's turn, I knew something extraordinary was going to happen because here was a woman who exuded the most sensual female energy of anyone I have ever met. Ever.

Neve was a cross between Angelina Jolie and Kim Kardashian in a manner that translated to grand-scale feminine intimidation—as if all other women might as well hand in their sex organs and call it a day. In the presence of Neve, no one else was womanly enough.

When Paramji sounded Neve, I was assigned to her left hand. I was 100 percent focused on that hand, as if I had no other responsibility in the world but to lie face down on the floor repeating the Bija sounds into her palm, possibly for the rest of my life: "Om om om, breem breem breem." Her response to her sounding was out there. Levitation, gyration, vibration, and exultation like I have never seen before. Not in a church, not on TV, and certainly not in a bedroom. To put it in Evangelical Christian terms—a full-blown, Pentecostal, born-again, saw-the-light, heathen, sexual splitting of the atom. In Sanskrit and yogic terms—a kundalini or Shakti awakening, an unfolding of the divine serpent fire. Or to put it in simpler, Western pop-cultural terms, it was the Iron Lotus of orgasms. The Iron Lotus is a mythical, impossible-to-execute, figure skating move from the film *Blades of Glory*; it is so complex—mechanically speaking—that it defies the laws of physics and carries the risk of decapitation. By ice skate blade. Which was almost what happened to me toward the end of Neve's throes of passion: she hit me smack in the face with her flailing legs as I was chanting into her left hand.

Recovering from the facial injury, I had a momentary flash of the scene in *When Harry Met Sally* where Meg Ryan, sitting across from Billy Crystal in Katz's Delicatessen, fakes a protracted (and epic) orgasm—after which a lady at the next table says to the server, "I'll have what she's having."

After witnessing Neve's performance—which, quite frankly, just thirty seconds in had put Meg Ryan's to shame—Paramji saw my I'd-like-one-of-those-multiorgasmic-fits-please expression and said, "You could have that with your husband." At which point I replied, "Sign me up."

And Paramji said, "Not so fast, Bhu."

THE PROBLEM WAS that sounding is as much about your openness to receive as it is about what is being done to you. I was far more likely to be restrained and guarded (okay, uptight and skeptical)—and therefore less likely to undulate, let alone levitate.

So on the second-to-last day, when it was finally my turn to be sounded, I wasn't particularly optimistic. I lay down on the floor and pulled the sheet over myself, and Paramji got on top of me—which released a whole firestorm of contradictory feelings. It was, on the one hand, definitely weird and creepy. And yet, in a small but open-minded way, maybe a little soothing.

He started sounding into my throat. Karen was sounding into the top of my head and Neve into one of my hands. Shivani chanted into one of my feet. There was a harmonic humming noise. My eyes were closed. I felt the vibrations—heard the vibrations as if I were holed up in a hive of buzzing bees. It was intimate and sensual but not sexual—despite the man lying on top of me. I flipped back and forth between thinking *This is kind of nice* and *What the hell am I doing here?* As well as *This is* way *too intimate for me.* At times I was afraid. At other times Paramji felt comforting, like a panic blanket. Sometimes I wanted to push him off me; then I wanted him to stay—to see where this would take me.

The chanting was affronting; it was loud, then it was soft. I tried to relax and lose myself in "Om shrim hrim krim hum sauh . . . " Eventually I fell into a deep meditation. In many ways it felt very loving. I was touched that everyone came together for me, which made me feel calm and present. In some ways it felt like a sacred and special dance. Like we were in a secret, ancient temple sharing a lovely and special ritual.

But, alas, no rising of the kundalini. No vibratory surge of energy. No undulation. No levitation. No electrical current. Did I feel conflicted? Yes. Orgasmic or transcendent? Absolutely not.

In the end it was just kind of thought provoking and interesting. And at different points my mind felt quiet—really still—for brief but pleasant blocks of time. Like Santa had brought me noise-canceling headphones.

* * *

THE LAST NIGHT at dinner, we had amazing organic vegetarian food with hot chai and coconut milk ice cream at a nearby restaurant as Jane and Greg's friend played guitar for us.

The dinner conversation was all over the place. Jenn was telling us about growing up Mormon and how, after fifteen years of marriage and going to church and doing everything right, she just got sick of it and thought, *Shit, is this all there is? That can't be.* So she started exploring other things.

Then Paramji told us we shouldn't wear bras. He said they were terrible things, and Goddesses didn't need them. He then demonstrated breast exercises right there in the restaurant. He gave us a boob-lift mantra too: "Uh, rhe, dom, da, ra, guy, num . . . " He told us to chant this after the one-hour daily meditation he'd assigned.

Honestly, I kept getting drawn in, and then Paramji would say something like that and lose me. I can't meditate for an hour every day, I'm not going to change my name, and I'm definitely not going to walk around without a bra. Goddess or not. And I don't remotely believe that chanting "Uh, rhe, dom, da, ra, guy, num" will provide enough support to make a bra unnecessary.

When we were driving back from the restaurant, Karen told us that Paramji gave her an astrological reading and said that her future holds money and great sex. To this Jenn shouted out, "Well heck, I hope my chart says that!"

Then Karen compared religion to beer: "You might like Dos Equis, and I might like a Coors Light, but they are both still beer and will get you buzzed. Like brands of beer, all religions are fundamentally the same, yet, oddly, we all have strong feelings about one over another." Then she said in what appeared to be for her a paramount moment of great clarity and satisfaction, "God is beer."

In that moment I felt gratitude. For them, for this weekend, for their openness and humor. We were all looking for something we were not likely to find, and we knew it.

But that doesn't mean that I left empty-handed.

"MIND YOUR OWN business." That's one of the helpful things Paramji had told me all weekend in our one-on-one meetings. I'd be complaining about various family members and friends and about my husband and my career. Basically carrying the weight of the world on my shoulders and kvetching about it. I was laying blame and harboring latent anger and resentment. Essentially, just whining.

He told me to stop. To "drop it all." To "mind my own business." To focus on me.

"But . . . "

"No 'but.' Mind your own business. Any stuff your husband did, your parents did, and your friends or boss did, that's on them."

I found that concept, unlike my sounding, powerfully liberating. Any stuff Atul went through, that was his business—not mine.

Ditto anything my parents did. I needed to mind my own business. I liked the idea of being responsible for only my own behavior. That I didn't have to carry everyone else's mistakes and transgressions or be angry with them or resentful. That was powerful—stunning even in its simplicity. According to Paramji, I needed to take care of me and love myself. Only then would everyone else be able to love me more fully.

The flip side of that was that everyone else needed to love themselves first too, before they'd be able to love others even more. Paramji said that if we couldn't manage that self-love, then we wouldn't be much good to each other. Which meant that Atul and I had to love ourselves before we could fully love each other—or Zia.

This was, as simple as it sounds, big news and came as a huge relief. It was as if I had been carrying an elephant up the stairs, and while I staggered under its weight, someone (Paramji) calmly pointed to the elevator. Paramji said all that "stuff"—as in everyone else's stuff that I busied myself with—was distracting me from my inner bliss.

No shit.

But was it that easy? Just mind my own business? Let it all go? Take the elevator, so to speak?

Paramji acted like doing so was profoundly simple, no different than changing my name. Just do it. Just like that.

He acted like it was easy too—a wave of the hand, and it's done. The same motion he had used to dismiss my birth name.

He said that holding on to all that stuff was ridiculous. Then I remembered that Dr. Luskin had told me the exact same thing.

A MONTH EARLIER I had taken a stress-management course at Google given by Dr. Fred Luskin, who taught some basic breathing exercises to use in moments of stress at work. The exercises seemed interesting and helpful, but he also mentioned in passing that he had done some work on forgiveness and was in fact the director of the Stanford Forgiveness Project. And that caught my interest even more.

So I drew Dr. Luskin aside and asked, "How do you truly, truly forgive someone?"

He said, "It's simple. You just do it."

Ha! Easy for him to say, I had thought at the time. But now Paramji was saying the same thing.

Dr. Luskin had added, "You make the decision to be the kind of person who forgives and not the person who holds grudges."

Ha! He doesn't know me.

I asked him how long it should take to forgive. "For example, if it's something really bad, are we talking a year or two?"

He laughed. "That seems like enough."

That made me laugh too.

What's the point of holding on to—even hoarding—all the negative stuff? To what end? To prove we are right? To suffer under its weight? To "win"?

Dr. Luskin had said, "If you don't forgive, then you've decided that being right is more important than being happy."

As a lawyer, I was trained to argue my point, to prove I was right. But I started to realize that, in my personal life, I didn't need to be right. I needed—and wanted—to be happy.

And Paramji may have just given me the key to do that. He said that I didn't even need to get to forgiveness. That none of what other people did was even my business in the first place. Paramji had one-upped Luskin.

No one ever explained to me that I wasn't responsible for all the bad things that others around me had done. I collected all that bad stuff and gave it safe harbor. I wore the wounds, picked at the scabs, displayed them as a badge of victimhood—all while anger and resentment festered inside me and I felt sorry for myself.

I never knew how to let go of all this stuff—I never even knew I could. And now I was being told that you just *do it*. You choose happy over unhappy. Just like that. Luskin and Paramji gave me the key to the locker where the good stuff is kept.

AS FOR PARA-TAN sounding? By the time I was at LAX heading home, this is what I concluded:

I didn't get it.

As in, really, really didn't get it.

And it probably wasn't for me.

But, on the flip side? My skin looked amazing. Way better than when I went to the facialist. I think it was all the avocados I ate.

I cancelled my next appointment with Goddess and bought *a lot* of avocados. And began letting things go. Simply off-lifting them from my emotional shelf. Just saying to myself, "That's not on me."

I started to feel a bit lighter, less weighted down. Happier.

And then I began sounding into Zia's feet when she cried. Not because I felt like a Goddess—more out of desperation one day when I couldn't get her to settle down and had already tried everything else. I began repeating, "Om shrim hrim krim hum sauh" into the bottom of her tiny feet, with no expectation whatsoever. And guess what? It worked. As in really, really worked.

Zia settled right down. Fast. She looked peaceful. Her lids got heavy. She fell asleep. I did it whenever she cried, and it always worked. I was the baby whisperer. Sounding became my go-to way to comfort her. Which meant that either this Para-Tan sounding thing really did work and I had tuned Zia into the vibrations of the universe, or I freaked her out so much by chanting into her feet that she stopped crying because she thought I was crazy. Cuckoo. Exactly what Paramji said my mother was.

Either way, calming my baby made me feel divinely feminine. Powerful. Competent. Sated. Like my grandmother in India, for a few brief moments, I was the keeper of the keys.

I didn't heal my yoni in Ojai. But in a small way, I healed my baby. And my heart.

Chapter 3

SOULCYCLE

Tribeca, NYC

By the time my year was almost up, I hadn't found answers. Or God. Or spiritual roots. Or a palatable ideology.

Not even close.

And over the past eleven months I had tried a number of other things, ranging from joining a shaman flash mob in Central Park to rolling hardboiled eggs to celebrate spring to being tickled by a healer to the stars, and none of them had resonated with me. It was evident that, aside from a few small incremental insights and helpful wellness tips—smile more, pray more, eat breakfast with my family, the bad deeds of other people are not on me, and embrace forgiveness—I hadn't made any real progress in the big picture, spiritual sense.

It felt like I had actually lost ground and was even more confounded and adrift now, spiritually speaking, than when I started on this mission. Back when Zia was born, while my religious orientation was far from perfect, it was still *something*. At that point I was—annoyingly and uncomfortably—Jain, and my husband was—enviably and comfortably—Hindu. And if nothing else, we had history there. In the months following, as I blithely sailed out of what were for me two flawed but familiar ports in search of a new and better world—one that would leave me gloriously fulfilled and spiritually sated—I was armed, albeit naively, with fierce confidence that I would find something wholly superior to what I currently had. As with many new endeavors, at the onset there was a whole lot of blue sky and optimism, but at this particular point, with my one-year deadline bearing down and no God in sight, my confidence and enthusiasm were waning.

If I were to be completely objective, I would have to say that I now found myself halfway across the ocean, within arm's reach of neither the shore that I had left behind nor the one I hoped to stake a claim to. Frankly, I was spiritually untethered, an existential anarchist frantically flailing about in the spiritual chop and religious mist with no dry land in sight. I now had both highly dubious GPS coordinates on my current location and absolutely no specific spiritual options to set my sights on—and a looming deadline to boot.

Refusing to accept either the possibility that there is nothing more than a vast spiritual void in a barren spiritual universe or that I had embarked on a failed personal mission, I decided to continue to deny the existence of what could only be characterized as an atheist's abyss of nothing, even though I had, as of yet, no real proof to defend that belief and absolutely no resolution to my spiritual "homelessness" in sight.

Instead, I dug my heels in, licked the wounds inflicted by the realization that I may have, in fact, actually regressed, and resolved to keep looking.

I brazenly told myself, *So what if I have sought but not found?*

I'd just look harder. And in weirder places. And I'd hurry.

Ever the optimist—or absurdly delusional—I then concluded that this was doable. After all, I still had a month left to find my spiritual home.

SINCE I WAS simultaneously both discouraged about my lack of progress and enthused by the options still in front of me, I started thinking about how one of the big product attributes of religion is that it gives us hope. That hope is firmly embedded in the thought that if there is more, then we actually matter.

And then, before I got too caught up in the humbling existential nature of my desire to matter, not just to myself and to my family but in the broadest of senses—to the limitless universe and in the immeasurable expanse of time—I started wondering about how real the hope offered by religion actually is.

That of course led me to dissect the mechanisms driving hope in general, which led me to read far more than I had ever wanted to about brain chemistry. The fact is, hopefulness and heightened expectations raise the dopamine levels in our brains, and elevated dopamine—whatever its source—alters our brains in a way that makes us feel good.

Really good.

Dopamine imparts a feeling of bliss and euphoria, as it increases drive and focus as well as our ability to concentrate. And it doesn't work alone. Dopamine works in concert with a class of neurotransmitters called endorphins and the other happy-addictive-feel-good brain chemicals serotonin and oxytocin.

Researchers have found that Parkinson's patients receiving a placebo in the form of a saline injection—though they were told they were being given a promising experimental drug—showed significant improvement in both measures of physical symptoms and brain imaging. The interesting part of the study wasn't just that a placebo improved their symptoms; rather, it was that the patients who were told that the "fake" experimental drug cost $1,500 per dose improved twice as much as the patients who were led to believe that the same "treatment" only cost $100. Which raises a question: Why would a placebo perceived to cost more improve symptoms at a much greater rate?

The patients who thought they were being given an expensive drug felt greater hope that it just might work. And heightened expectation—high hope—raises the dopamine levels in our brains. In fact, the $1,500-per-shot injections raised dopamine levels just as much as the leading Parkinson's medicine did, and since elevated dopamine relieves the symptoms of Parkinson's, that fake $1,500 injection of saline actually did improve the patient's health.

They were healing themselves by increasing their own dopamine production and effectively "self-medicating" with optimism.

They got better simply because they believed they would.

And this placebo effect doesn't just work with dopamine-depleted Parkinson's patients. There are numerous other examples, including evidence of a placebo effect with "fake" knee surgery.

THERE ARE ALL sorts of other routes to a dopamine spike and a chemical brain state that makes us feel good, including, alcohol, exercise, food, gambling, illicit drugs, meditation, music, and sex. Since we all want to feel good, activities like these can be powerful drivers of behaviors both good and bad—so much so that they are often addictive. And of course, religious and spiritual experiences can provide us with enormous hope—which means they can incite a dopamine spike as well. The fact that hope is a big part of what religion sells and that spiritual experiences raise dopamine levels introduces the unsettling possibility that the feelings of spirituality, immortality, deep conviction, faith—and even belief in miracles— that arise from religious experiences and interactions with faith healers actually indicate a chemically altered brain state rather than anything "godly."

There is no question that religion bottled hope long before medical researchers and big pharma did. Since high hope—whatever its source—can make us feel deep conviction, I began to wonder about the level of feel-good dopamine brain flooding that must go on when one is wholly convinced that there is a loving God and eternal life and that all suffering will cease and we will go on forever in an ethereal heavenly place after our brief stop over here on earth or perhaps will be reincarnated and given another shot at life.

It was also clear that studies about brain chemistry and feel good hormones provide medically plausible explanations for why John of

God's "invisible" surgery—and the efforts of other self-proclaimed "faith healers"—may quite legitimately "cure" some people too. Increased hope raises dopamine. That makes us feel good—even feel less pain—and we cure ourselves by believing.

I had also been reading more about the science behind the collective energy of the crowd, which can be generated by any number of group activities: choirs, religious services, team sports, concerts, raves, and even protest marches and sit-ins. That collective energy takes on a life of its own by creating a feeling of belonging and community—and even euphoria. Sociologist Émile Durkheim explained that when "I" becomes "we," we transcend, and that can give us a powerful feeling of connectedness and immortality. He argued that anything that makes us experience collective emotions as part of a group can be elevated to the level of sacred, and it doesn't seem to matter what that community is based on.

This brought to my mind the following questions:

1. Does elevated dopamine and "I" morphing into "we" create a feeling of hope and collectivism that we label as spirituality but that actually reflects a chemically changed brain state?

2. If so, is a dopamine-soaked brain and heightened community-fueled euphoria enough for me?

I decided to find out.
In the hybrid gym-temple known as SoulCycle.

I CAN GUESS what you are thinking. *Seriously? With one month left to find a spiritual practice you could dedicate your life to, you went to SoulCycle?*

Obviously that sounds ridiculous based on where I was (nowhere) in relation to where I wanted to be (securely seated in the Temple of Me), but when you break it down, SoulCycle delivers the collective energy of the crowd—just without the church. And because SoulCycle also involves exercise and loud music wrapped in spiritual intention-setting, it's primed to raise dopamine levels.

And going to SoulCycle helped clarify a few things for me on a number of levels—enough to mollify and compel the hopefully not-for-long God-less and spiritually homeless me.

Plus, come on. Since one woman had told me that her priestess was Mama Gena—whose teachings involve self-exploration with a feminine bent (think no pants, legs spread, a pink boa, a magic marker, and glitter) with the goal of building positive self-identity, renewed energy, increased confidence, and spiritual health—and her church was the stripper/pole-dancing workout at SFactor, I figured it wouldn't be that weird if SoulCycle became my church.

But believe me, the sardonic irony did not escape me that SoulCycle involved frantically pedaling for forty-five-minutes on a stationary bicycle, with sweat springing from every pore, and ending up exactly where I started.

There is no question that it was the perfect metaphor for my previous year: try hard, get (almost) nowhere.

* * *

SOULCYCLE IS AN intense cardio workout in the form of a spinning class augmented with free weights and a heavy dose of positive thinking set to very loud dance music (with a heavy emphasis on Beyoncé tracks). It has also developed a cult following. The miracle of SoulCycle is in its branding, especially its exclusivity. In big cities like New York, there can be a rush to sign up since there are fewer cycles than would-be cyclists, but what most makes it stand out from regular spinning classes—other than its relatively high cost ($35 to $80 a class)—is the promise that you will tighten your abs, glutes, and quads while frantically spinning to "find your soul." Add to that the feel-good missives on the walls, the dimmed lights, and the candles, all uniquely—and secularly—packaged with a spiritual, music-and-exercise-fueled dopamine kicker.

Plus, the whole thing functions as a turbine for group energy. The bikes are placed very close together, so participants can draft in the slipstream of the collective emotional high of the other cyclers.

It's basically a two-fer. SoulCycle is like going to church while being at the gym.

WHEN I ARRIVED, the class was filled to capacity, the bikes were almost touching, and the front row was already studded with the stars of this congregation. SoulCycle warns attendees not to select front-row bikes unless they're real spinning superstars. (The staff will bump you if you sign up for the front row and you're not up to snuff.) Front row and center is coveted, but the best of the best are those invited to hop on the instructor's bike and, as they put it, "ride the podium." I, on the other hand, intentionally reserved a seat in the far back corner with the other fearful slackers in the hinterlands.

Looking around, I located my preselected bike, squeezed my way through, clipped my shoes into the pedals, and then settled into the saddle. The instructor strode up to her bike positioned on the stage/altar with candles lit around her, turned the microphone on, amped up the music, and started us on our warm-up.

A few minutes in, the gospel voice of Andrew Hozier-Byrne, the obscure Irish singer who rose to stardom after writing the smash hit *Take Me to Church*, literally filled the room with the passion and timbre of a church choir. As this congregation of SoulCyclers pedaled away, the irony of this song choice did not escape me. Hozier wrote *Take Me to Church* as a condemnation of the Catholic Church, and here I was pedaling like a demon looking for a way into any church or temple that I could believe in but going nowhere, as he built me a cathedral out of church-slamming words.

The instructor—think hellfire and brimstone preacher meets Broadway-star hopeful meets hard-core personal trainer—stood on what amounted to a pulpit with her microphone headset on, calling out encouragement like it was the sermon that would save us all. I tried to ignore the self-defeating thinking I was engaged in and convince myself that this SoulCycle thing was nothing less than the gospel truth. Then Hozier reached the chorus in which he damns the church just as I rose from the saddle for a steep climb, desperate for something to believe in.

I tried really hard to believe that this could be my route to salvation—it's hard to resist the promise of health and fitness, taut thighs, a firm butt, and spiritual fulfillment wrapped into one forty-five-minute dopamine-pumping session. But even before the first beads of sweat formed on my forehead, I was already looking toward the door for a way out.

Because that was when the first baby step of progress hit me—right in the back of a faux-spiritual spinning class. I wasn't looking for the right-side, limbic, prefrontal surge of dopamine we get from religion and exercise mixed with rock 'n' roll offered by the nondenominational, spiritual doctrine that is SoulCycle. I was looking for something behemoth and transformative. I was looking for the God Effect—transcendent certainty of oneness with the universe—not a tantalizing and addictive and fleeting euphoria. I wanted something sustainable and omnipotent and spiritually systemic. I wanted to fall off the cliff and believe in the beyond with unabashed certainty and lifelong conviction. I wanted the confirmation of otherness and eternity.

So the first milestone revelation for me, as I furiously pedaled and the flywheel spun at lightning speed, was the realization that I needed to make sure that I didn't mistake momentary surges of dopamine for something godly and otherworldly and eternal. And with that thought firmly planted in my head, I had a second revelation, because it was at that point that the biggest flaw in my find-God-for-Zia plan hit me: I'd been looking for something self-defining and exponential, and there was virtually no chance that I could have found something that big in a single year. It wasn't that I had been looking in the wrong places; the flaw was in setting a deadline in the first place.

I WASN'T SURE why I had thought I could find a spiritual home in a single year. Chalk it up to spending too much time with hard deadlines, legal contracts, and calendars that auto-sync. Or chalk it up to working in a regimented, buttoned-up, time-sensitive profession. Or being a delusional new mother. Or perhaps just being painfully optimistic and naive. Or all of the above.

People have been searching for spiritual answers since the dawn of time, and yet I somehow thought I could get the job done in a single year as I worked full-time and took care of a toddler. So pedaling that bike in the back of a SoulCycle class, I decided to give myself more time. A lot more time.

THEN A THIRD revelation hit me as the familiar beat of Depeche Mode's "Personal Jesus" filled the room. As this congregation of SoulCyclers pedaled at high speed, I was listening to the lyrics thinking that this song was about looking inward and using the godlike power in our hearts to be a Jesus for someone else, and here I was this whole time looking outward, practically begging for a way into any esoteric corner of the spiritual world that I could call home. And I wasn't sure why I believed that the place where I landed spiritually had to be some external belief system.

Because it had just dawned on me that maybe God wasn't "out there." Maybe God was "in here"—inside me.

And then I stopped pedaling altogether because

A. I was desperately out of shape, and this was a really hard class, and
B. it occurred to me that I believed that if God was "out there," he-or-she-or-it would be easier to find than if he-she-it was inside of me.

These three things—dopamine is not God, I needed more time, and God may be internal—while markers of progress, were mildly depressing, as were the physiques of just about everyone in this class, because all those things underscored just how much work I still had to do.

When I walked out of that SoulCycle class that day, I knew that I wouldn't find what I wanted in a spinning class wrapped in a non-denominational quasi-religious service. I knew that I wanted more than a temporary surge in dopamine and more than the collective energy of the group.

But on the upside—and I don't know if it was the dopamine talking—I was certain that I was circling around my stairway to heaven. I was confident that the promise of the divine and eternal life and otherness and more would present itself to me if I just kept looking.

SO, AS ZIA'S birthday approached I gave myself a second year.

Then, as more birthdays came and went, I dropped the deadline altogether. The important thing, I reassured myself, was to not give up.

Along the way, somewhere between the ages of three and four, just as I had feared she would, Zia started asking those questions. The ones I couldn't answer. So I was forced to engage in a bit of spiritual improv. Meaning, like most parents, I made stuff up. Feel-good-don't-worry stuff that I pulled from anywhere I could find it—Jainism, Hinduism, Catholicism, Paganism, *Dora the Explorer*—I used anything that I thought could work.

Then, when I didn't have adequate, reasonable, fathomable answers for her, Zia tried finding them herself. She literally asked Siri on my sister's iPhone, "Is there a God?"

The first time she did it, I was stunned. Why hadn't I thought of that?

THIS IS WHAT Siri said in response: "I'm really not equipped to answer such questions."

I was thinking, *Ha! There you go!*

Frustrated, Zia asked again, this time louder and slower as she enunciated each word, "Siri, Is There a God?"

And this time the voice in the phone said, "My policy is the separation of the spirit and silicon."

Really confused now, Zia tried again. She got the same response: "My policy is the separation of the spirit and silicon."

Then I jumped in, took the phone from her, and promised her the universe.

I said, "Of course there's a God, Zia! And don't worry, Mama will find Him. Or Her."

Chapter 4

WICCA

West Village, NYC

I happened to read an article about how Buddhists in Japan can go online and order a priest for home delivery. Just like a pizza or kombucha or ramen noodles. It's called *obosan-bin*, and you can shop for and order that priest right on Amazon. As in, drop him in the virtual cart next to your shampoo and tampons. The idea is, Why go to a temple when you can have a priest delivered right to your doorstep?

My initial reaction was similar to the one I had when I first saw coffins for sale at Costco. *Wait, Whaaat??*

When I read about *obosan-bin*, I happened to be trying to figure out how to contact a practicing witch, so it occurred to me that witches in America might be a bit like priests in Japan: easier to get a hold of than you might think.

That is, if you shop for them on Amazon. But I learned something.

They're not.

I CAN REPORT that, at least when I looked, there were no witches— or priests, Buddhist or otherwise—available for home delivery on major online retail sites in the United States. But not one to be deterred, I tapped social media and put up a post on Facebook—mainly because I had no idea where else to look for a witch.

That post began just like a lot of my other recent requests had—with an awkward qualifier: "I realize this is an odd question, but . . . "

In this case it was followed by something that sounded completely absurd, even for me: "Does anyone know a witch? Like, a real one?"

I HONESTLY THOUGHT that I had finally shredded—okay, completely destroyed—any modicum of credibility I still had and was going to get responses that ran the gamut from "Ha ha! Very funny, Anjali!" to "You're fired"—likely followed by a string of emojis of black cats and broomsticks along with numerous unfriendings and a few links to websites for mental health professionals.

But that's not what happened. Instead I was bombarded with kind and useful information. And I heard from all sorts of people. I mean, *Seriously?* I was kind of kidding.

But my Facebook friends weren't.

I WAS GIVEN offers of introduction and links to websites and names of neopagan and New Age shops that sold oils, candles, chalices, cloaks, robes, daggers, and crystals. I was sent e-mail addresses of high priestesses and invites to private-message with practicing witches. Unbeknownst to me, I was Facebook friends with someone who knew an expert in West African witchcraft, as well as someone else who used to visit a "major" Santería witch in Harlem who had "chickens in her backyard." The reference to "chickens" seemed oddly random and irrelevant until I Googled "Santería" and learned that followers of this particular form of witchcraft practice animal sacrifice. Yikes.

Another friend sent me a link to an article in *New York Magazine* that discussed the possible witchcraft connection to an unexplained outbreak of severed goat heads littering Prospect Park in Brooklyn. That seemed worse than the chickens.

Then another friend enthusiastically posted that he knew three fairies I could hang with. I was thinking *faeries*, as in, elves, spirits, goblins, and the like . . . but it turned out he was referring to his young daughters and only kidding. But all the other posts were—at least seemingly—legit.

I was apparently, to my shock and awe, well connected in the witch community.

One friend posted, "I know an Irish witch! Want an intro?" Another said, "Our friend Susan is kind of a white witch." And as I contemplated which Susan she was referring to, I realized I had no clue what a "white witch"—let alone an "Irish witch"—even was. The posts kept coming.

"Jamie must know a few!"

Benign, conservative Jamie? Really??

"I heard the most amazing story on a Moth podcast from a woman who studied Wicca. She was incredible. I will find it!"

"*Sabat Magazine* is a new feminist, really good witch publication."

"Check out Enchantments in the East Village."

"And Catland in Brooklyn."

"I know many!"

Really?? I have another conservative, straight-laced friend who knows many witches?

A NUMBER OF posts just expressed enthusiastic support, like "I don't know a witch, but I love this question so much!"

But, hands down, this was my favorite: "Yes."

That was it. Just "Yes."

WHICH WAS INTERESTING, because this openness didn't fit with my impression that witches were usually highly secretive. And then, as I was reading through the posts, contemplating my options, this popped up: "We have a coven. Message me directly," and the hair on the back of my neck stood up.

Minutes later, I got a message from my friend Anna with a link to Reverend Starr Ann RavenHawk and the Wiccan Family Temple website. I clicked on that link, apprehensive that, despite the comforting mention of "family," I'd find references to Satan and Black Magick and the occult—or live chickens and severed goat heads.

But I found the website informative and nonthreatening, even benign and lovely, with no reference to animals, dead or alive. In fact, for a witch website—I mean, come on, people suspected of witchcraft were once burned at the stake—the Wiccan Family Temple website seemed surprisingly pedestrian. So I checked out other "witch" websites, and most of them seemed benign too. Then I went to the Wiccan Family Temple's Facebook page and took note that in a few weeks the group was hosting a potluck supper for something called the Mabon Festival.

First I thought, *Witches have potluck suppers?*

Then I thought, *And they advertise them on Facebook?*

The post said, "Everyone's welcome."

Even still, I wasn't wholly convinced that that meant me.

THEN I GOOGLED "Mabon Festival" and learned that it was a celebration of the autumn equinox, one of eight annual Wicca festivals, called sabbats. And I found a post on the Facebook page by a witch saying she couldn't attend this upcoming event because she had to go to a bachelorette party.

It all seemed so normal.

So I decided to go. Even though at that point I didn't even know what Wicca was.

I made that choice mainly because it seemed way better than option B: messaging the guy with the coven.

* * *

THE FACEBOOK INVITE indicated what supplies were needed for the Eleventh Annual Mabon Ritual & Witches ThanksGiving

Dinner and who would be bringing them. The supplies, just like the website, seemed pretty ordinary: an altar cloth, Mabon incense and anointing oil, hand instruments—drums and rattles—leaves and gourds, and a bell and ringer. I was pleased to note the conspicuous omission of mentions of cauldrons and live chickens and goat heads and daggers and poison potions and "Keep Away Hate Oil" and "Bat's Blood Oil" and other ominous-sounding incidental items that I'd read about or had seen for sale at butcher shops and *botánicas*—local neighborhood bodegas around NYC that "serve all your spiritual needs"—apparently including those associated with death rituals, evil spells, and animal sacrifices.

The attendees of the Mabon Festival were asked to bring food: meat, vegetables, and bread. It also suggested that guests come wearing "ritual garb," or, more specifically, "a crown of oak leaves and grain and acorns with gold, bronze, and orange ribbons that hang down." It also said something about painting blue teardrops on our cheeks.

On the day of, I skipped the ritual garb and face paint but did dress in all black—which admittedly came off more Ninja warrior/ New Yorker than witch, but in my defense I had to attend Zia's school's homecoming soccer game/bake sale beforehand, and I didn't want to completely alienate the Upper East Side parents of her classmates by dressing in flowing robes and a pointy hat— which I figured was probably way off but was my only reference for "ritual witch attire." Well, other than the crown of oak leaves and grain, which I wasn't going to wear either, at least not to my daughter's school.

That morning, running late, I frantically baked a triple batch of chocolate banana muffins, figuring they could work for both events. They worked for neither.

That was on account of the dry, weighty, cement-and-sawdust-like quality the muffins took on, which was due to a combination of factors: the highly overrated gluten-free, vegan, no-sugar, low-fat recipe I tried, thinking it a safe route for any gathering of New Yorkers (witches or not), and my well-documented lack of baking skills. Luckily Zia managed to offload the "muffins" onto some fellow classmates who were on sugar- and gluten-free, vegan, Paleo, or severely calorie-restricted diets and actually liked them—or else they took a bite, spit it out, and tossed the rest to the pigeons. I then bought an impressive array of cupcakes at what turned out to be a high-stakes baking competition between the mothers at the two schools. The baked goods weren't selling well from either side because none of the adults attending this event would ever consider eating carbohydrates and sugar—even carbohydrates and sugar fashioned into elegant French pastries decorated in their child's school colors. So I basically cleaned up and, in an opportunist moment when our school's moms were looking the other way, got a couple of dozen show-stopping cupcakes at a half-price "everything must go" sale held by the opposing team. Later that day, when I sent Zia home with a friend, she asked me, "Mama, where *exactly* are you going again?"

I said—okay, whispered—that I was going to a dinner for witches, and while I was expecting her to ask, "Are you crazy?" Zia just said, "Okay. But be careful. If you do something to upset the witches, they might cast a spell on you. So be nice."

*   *   *

ONE THING I had to be cognizant of—while engaged in what I hoped was open-minded inquisition into the sometimes fringe and the spiritually diverse—was how difficult it is as an outsider to come to terms with what are easy to perceive as the odd behaviors and strange beliefs of "other people." This occurs even when those people would likely perceive our own odd behaviors and beliefs as equally peculiar.

From what I'd experienced so far, it struck me that we either unfairly characterize or mock the behaviors we don't understand—as I was clearly doing with witchcraft—or we engage in them blindly, full bore.

Which brings me to my family, with its roots in the overly superstitious Indian culture where astrologers and faith healers and spiritual gurus known as God-men—as well as numerous deeply held, irrational secular beliefs—are so prevalent that superstitions in India are viewed as a broad-based, contemporary social problem. As a first-generation Indian girl raised outside Chicago, part Indian, part American, part Catholic, part Hindu, part Jain, and wholly confused, I'd had a lot of trouble trying to come to terms with this.

When I was growing up, my parents engaged in all sorts of culturally typical superstitious behaviors that would have made sense if we lived in Delhi or in a village in Rajasthan—or if all my friends in Chicago were from India. (Try explaining to your second-grade, non-Indian, Catholic school classmates why your mother won't take the salt shaker from them or that the scissors are planted in the garden "to ward off rain.") And then, when I was in my thirties trying to get pregnant, Archana Bua (my aunt—my father's sister) called from India to tell me that she was engaging her pandit (Hindu priest) to pray on my behalf in order to, as she put it, "help." And while I found her effort endearing and I thanked her, I politely suggested that she stop, assuring her that my getting pregnant was something Atul and I would have to tackle ourselves.

Oh, but I was wrong. So wrong.

Archana Bua immediately scoffed off the ridiculous notion that baby making wasn't an intercontinental activity accomplished through prayer and superstition to be engaged in by extended family members and said, flat out, that she and her pandit would be continuing with their prayers whether I liked it or not.

She then told me that I was to repeat a specific mantra every morning and evening for the next 108 days and—get this . . . *drum roll*—refrain from having *s-e-x*.

"S-e-x" being a word that she both whispered and spelled into the phone.

Flummoxed, I refrained from suggesting that abstaining from s-e-x would make it exceedingly more difficult—okay, I wanted to say, downright f-ing impossible—to get pregnant. Instead, I bit my tongue and asked her to tell me what the mantra was so I could write it down.

Later I began to think about the fact that people engage in odd behaviors in the name of religion all the time and these are rarely scoffed at as "superstitions" but rather are taken at face value, considered pious, and revered and respected. I had to take to heart that we all have fundamentally odd religious and cultural behaviors and superstitions, and those of "other people" only seem odd to us because, especially in the case of a historically and commercially misrepresented practice like witchcraft, we have no accurate information about—let alone personal history with—them. In other words, I should lighten up about the goat heads and live chickens.

ALONG WITH ZIA'S recommendation to "be nice," this was a very healthy perspective for me to bring to the witches' potluck dinner—for the simple reason that if any spiritual practice was going to test my open-mindedness, it would be witchcraft. Or at least that's what I thought. It turned out that what I believed I knew about witchcraft was way off.

But in the subway headed downtown, it occurred to me that if Archana Bua was struggling with the s-e-x part of baby making, she was going to have a hell of a time if she ended up having a blasphemous, spell-casting heathen in her family. So I had to take a deep breath and remind myself to keep an open mind.

After all, along with the rest of my family, I engage in all sorts of ridiculous behaviors that outsiders would likely scorn.

* * *

TRADITIONAL WITCHCRAFT IS a polytheistic pagan religion that dates back thousands of years and has been practiced in varied forms around the world. Because it predates the modern religions, it is often referred to as the "Old Religion." In a thumbnail sketch, witches believe that, instead of our being at the mercy of an all-powerful supreme being, they can tap into a pool of energy to harness powerful mystical forces and put them to use in the form of specific spells either for evil (Black Magick) or for good (White Magick).

Unlike most modern religions, witchcraft had no central organization, no scriptures, and no sacred text like the Bible, Quran, or Torah. There was just a loose set of parameters and beliefs practiced by fragmented groups operating pretty much in isolation and on their own—that is, until the practice of witchcraft was outlawed in much of the world.

The rise of Christianity, followed by the Inquisition and the Reformation, led to widespread persecution of anyone suspected of practicing witchcraft. Although the exact numbers are not known, an estimated 50,000 to 80,000 predominantly female accused practitioners were tortured and executed around the globe. Which, of course, sent followers of witchcraft into hiding.

In 1484, when Pope Innocent VIII reported that Satanists in Germany were "meeting with demons, casting spells that destroyed crops, and aborting infants," he asked two friars to write what amounted to a "state of the union" on witchcraft. The work they produced, the *Malleus maleficarum* (*The Witches' Hammer*), told stories "of women who would have sex with any convenient demon, kill babies, and even steal penises."

And I thought goat heads were problematic.

WICCA IS A modern interpretation of witchcraft founded by Gerald Gardner in Great Britain after the repeal of the witchcraft laws in England in the 1950s. As it gained popularity there, it rapidly spread around the world, particularly to the United States. Any secretly practicing witches could now come out into the open—at least without fear of being put to death—and over time many people who felt spiritually disenfranchised found themselves migrating to Wicca.

Wiccans, just like their traditional predecessors, have great autonomy: there's no central authority and no official "book." Wiccans believe that the earth is their cathedral and that everything in the universe—living and nonliving—holds power, and they practice magick, which means that they cast spells to bring about personal empowerment, healing, and success. And that magick is the manipulation of energy, not the "magic" of commercialized Western tricks and illusion.

Since Wicca is diverse and self-directed, different practitioners believe different things, but generally Wiccans don't fear aging or death. They view both as natural transitions—death being a turning of the wheel to another realm, where they'll still be able to interact with the living. Since Wicca is egalitarian, every practitioner has equal access to the power of the craft; there's no hierarchy and no male dominance. There is no clear demarcation of the separation between good (God) or evil (Satan), but while Wiccans don't believe in "the devil," they do acknowledge both the polarity of male and female and that Gods and Goddesses have a good and a dark side.

Wicca is also a sexually liberal religion, accepting of all forms of sexuality; anything goes as long as it's between (or among) consenting adults. This openness has drawn in many who feel ostracized by other religions over sexual orientation or behavior; Wicca openly accepts those who are gay, bisexual, transsexual, polyamorous, or promiscuous without reservation or judgment, and some covens practice ritual nudity and sexual rites.

Wiccans don't recruit new members, collectively raise money, or believe that their way is the "only way." But this is not to say they have no guiding principles. Wiccans believe in what is called the Wiccan Rede—a precept to harm no one—as well as the Law of Threefold Return, which basically stipulates that anything they do, good or bad, will come back to them with triplicate force. That belief coupled with the Wiccan Rede heavily skews the use of a witch's power toward the positive.

It's a religious practice that does not involve dead chickens or severed goat heads or "This is why I hate you oil." And here's one random fact, just because it's my favorite: a baby witch is called a "witchlet."

OF COURSE I didn't know any of this when I went to the Eleventh Annual Mabon Ritual & Witches ThanksGiving Dinner, which turned out to be nothing like I expected or feared. I don't know exactly what I expected, but somehow I thought there would be something goth and Halloween-like or extremely dark, but the event was no different from any other family-style, church-basement type of gathering. Just think *really, really eclectic family*—because the openness and community of Wicca attracts a wide spectrum of people, especially in a place like New York City. In fact, it was the most diverse group I have ever broken bread with.

*   *   *

WHEN I ARRIVED at the center where the festival was held, I handed over my $15 cover charge to the "money witch" and then awkwardly attempted to engage in small talk with some of the other attendees. There were only about twenty people, and I couldn't tell how many of them already knew each other, but there wasn't too much interaction, and everyone—myself included—appeared slightly uncomfortable. I then noticed a grand-looking woman—short and rotund with long black and pink braids and wearing a crown—whom I recognized from the Facebook page as Reverend RavenHawk. When I went up to introduce myself, she embraced me in a big, Amma-style hug. That hug went a long way toward washing away my fears and made me feel welcome. As people straggled in, I continued to introduce myself, but I later confirmed that a lot of them were first-timers too, so the whole thing—at least at the beginning—felt more uncomfortable than communal.

But as uncomfortable as it was, there was nothing even remotely off-putting—no red-flag-raising witch paraphernalia or dark, ominous notes. And I was told that the blue teardrops we all would have painted on our cheeks were to symbolize the cycle of life; sadness over the loss of the sun, the solstice, and joy over the mother giving birth to the son. On hearing that, I felt badly about my preconceived, misinformed, erroneous notions.

We eventually all sat down at a long dinner table for a blessing before we ate. The food was then laid out down the center of the

table, with a makeshift altar in the middle. Since the rental agreement at the center didn't allow open flames, instead of burning wax
candles we had to use battery-operated ones, and instead of burning actual incense, we passed around a small plastic baggie with
herbs—that looked like weed—which everyone sniffed. Looking
back on it, knowing what I now know, objectively speaking, I can
imagine how intense this ritual would have been if conducted under the stars with real candles and real incense—and in the nude.
(Not that I would have attended; I'm just saying.)

Next up was chanting and a lot of off-key but wholehearted
singing, and then a witch named Opal Rose rang a bell, and another named Helena cast a circle with a prayer. Next we were each
given a small tealight candle to burn later in our homes, and a small
bottle of oil was passed around to anoint our candles with. We were
then asked to take turns saying what we were grateful for from the
past year and what we hoped for in the coming year.

HONESTLY? EXCEPT FOR the lack of a football game on in the
background, kids running around, and a drunk uncle snoring on
the couch, this felt like Thanksgiving dinner at any house in
America.

As for giving thanks, Reverend RavenHawk went first. She expressed gratitude for her health and said that in the new year she
hoped to lose weight and be sexier—a comment that made everyone laugh. After she finished, we went one by one, up one side of
the table then down the other, as each person expressed thanks and
hopes and fears. The themes covered both the good—people reported being grateful for family, love, health, and this community
that gave them a feeling of belonging—and the not so good. Some
of which was halting and staggering—in part because these reflec-
tions and admissions were very personal and being delivered, by
and large, to a group of strangers. A couple of people lamented lost
jobs and difficult financial times. One person was struggling
through gender transition; another had suffered the death of a parent; one was new to the city and didn't know anyone.

When it was my turn, I wasn't quite prepared to share anything deeply personal, so I kept my comments generic. I started by thanking all of them for welcoming me to their celebration so openly and then expressed gratitude for my health and that of my family. As for the upcoming year, I struggled to articulate something and then awkwardly mentioned that I was writing a book—I had recently decided to document my spiritual quest by writing about it—and hoped it would go well.

Later in the evening, a woman came up to me and asked about my book; when I told her, she said she'd do some spell work to ensure it would succeed. I was taken aback and grateful: it was such a kind, open, and unexpected gesture from a complete stranger—a witch no less. It also taught me a lot about my own misconceptions, as well as the real worldview and nature of Wiccans.

I have to say, the whole event resonated as nice. No demonic sex, baby killing, crop destruction, or penis stealing. Nobody cast an evil spell or sacrificed an animal; none of the stereotypes that I—or the church elders in the 1400s—erroneously associated with witchcraft were even remotely evident. And by the end of the night I had befriended two witches.

*   *   *

MARY, WITCH NUMBER one, was in her early thirties and lived in New Jersey. She was raised in a traditional Italian Catholic family, which meant going to church and getting weekly religious instruction. By fourth grade, she had discerned an overriding hypocrisy in the teachings of the Catholic Church and resented what she perceived as "bossiness" and male dominance within the religion. Even at that young age, Mary felt strongly that Catholicism was "not for her" and that she didn't belong—something experienced by many who turn to paganism and witchcraft.

In middle school Mary was drawn to films and TV shows like *The Craft*, *Practical Magic*, and *Charmed* and read the only book on witchcraft in her school library. When she asked her grandmother about the word *strega*—"witch" in Italian—she learned that it was a "bad word." Everything Mary experienced told her to keep her interest in witchcraft quiet. She told me that, even though she was straight, she felt a kinship with the gay community: she too felt she had to hide a fundamental part of herself for fear of being judged. "Even if we are all out of the broom closet, we're still secretly in there in some form. So we take comfort in each other's company, even if we are all really different, because we get to breathe a bit." Then, laughing, she added, "It's not like we all go to church on Sunday."

When she was about fifteen years old—in hiding and without access to other witches—Mary joined The Craft by performing a self-dedication ritual. That involved purification (taking a bath to represent a clean start), casting a circle, creating a sacred space in her bedroom where she set up a makeshift altar, invoking the elements (air, earth, water, fire, self), introducing herself to the Gods and Goddesses, stating her intent to get to know them and honor the earth, and then initiating the process of writing her own Book of Shadows.

Mary cast her first spell when she "charmed" a piece of jewelry —a guardian angel brooch—to make it a healing piece to give to her Catholic mother for a knee injury that nothing was helping. After her mother wore the brooch for a week, she said her knee was substantially better.

Mary never told her father she was Wiccan, but she told her mother and her fiancé and even some coworkers. Still in partial hiding, at her wedding she covertly integrated some pagan elements. Lavender wands (associated in Wicca with love spells) were part of the wedding favors, and she wore a piece of starfish jewelry to represent the five points of the pentacle and three small starfish in her hair to represent the Goddess in her three forms—maiden, mother, and crone.

Mary finds compelling the Wiccan religion's concept of creating one's own energy, its openness and the ability it provides her to choose her own path, and its lack of hypocrisy, misogyny, and rigidity. When asked about her spirituality by strangers, she says she is pagan, not Wiccan. If she says "Wiccan," people get confused; often they ask, "You're wicked?" To which she has to say, "No, I'm not a Broadway musical!"

The witches I met, like so many others in oppressed groups, have a great, self-effacing sense of humor.

PATRICIA—WITCH NUMBER two—half Cuban, half Puerto Rican, was raised Muslim in New York City; for years she wore a full Saudi head scarf and face covering, even covering her hands with gloves. She told me she really tried hard to embrace Islam, didn't resent the modesty of the hijab at all, and prayed five times every day. But she found her prayers unanswered and became increasingly disenchanted with Islam and Allah as she came to perceive— just as Mary had—hypocrisy in her childhood religion. But in her case she faced it from both the other women at the mosque and her own mother. When her mother threw her out of the house when she was seventeen and her fellow Muslims at the mosque gossiped behind her back about it, she felt unnerved and betrayed by her religion and went looking for something better.

Patricia found that something better in, of all places, Barnes & Noble—in a big book with a pentagram on the front. The book, full of spells, spoke of her power—power that Islam, as taught to her, said she would go straight to hell for using or even thinking that she had in the first place. Given that her fiancé, a Muslim man, said he didn't want her to go to college because there would be men there, it seemed to her that her fiancé and family were hiding behind Islam and claiming that "women can't do anything" and that "she had no rights." But witchcraft and that big book with the pentagram on the cover told her otherwise.

Patricia then found a group of witches on Yahoo! and signed up for an online witch school.

Then the school went bankrupt, and Patricia broke up with her fiancé, ditched the hijab, entered into a relationship with a woman, found the Wiccan Family Temple website, and began practicing witchcraft. Patricia, like Mary, has her own personal Book of Shadows. It contains her core rituals and spell recipes. But she rarely casts spells; she finds them draining, although she did cast a spell to help herself quit smoking—and it worked.

She was a long way from Islam.

AS DIFFERENT AS Mary and Patricia are, their attraction to Wicca bears a stunning resemblance. Both felt disenfranchised by their childhood religions, in which both perceived hypocrisy, gender inequality, and sexual repression. Both had to hide their practice of Wicca from others. Both say they won't push their religion on their children. Both have enormous respect for the natural world and believe in their own power and ability to channel it—along with a greater force culled from outside—to bring about positive change for themselves and the world around them. They struck me as smart, powerful, confident women.

* * *

HONESTLY, SPEAKING WITH Mary and Patricia and reading about Wicca, I was hooked, lined, and sinkered. On the surface, everything about it appealed to me: the openness; the acceptance and reverence for self and nature; the individual, private nature of the practice; the belief in personal freedom, gender equality, and the enormous power of the individual—constructs virtually nonexistent in mainstream religions.

I'd felt a sense of connection with other practices before. But every time I thought I was getting somewhere, finding a spiritual solution that just might be the perfect fit for me, I stumbled on a deal breaker—something that sent me running for the exit. Wicca also included a couple of those.

The first thing that I found disconcerting derived from my original fears: the concept of Black Magick, especially the idea that it existed, that it was a possibility, one potentially under my control or the control of other witches. That scared me.

Even with the Wiccan Rede—the edict to harm no one—and the Law of Threefold Return, Wiccans still acknowledge the existence and power of evil.

The second thing that I found disconcerting was the thought of having that much power under my control.

I totally understood Patricia's quit-smoking spell. I could see how going through the ritual of casting that spell was affirming for her and that it underscored and openly articulated her desire to break the habit—as well as primed her to follow through on her commitment. And I understood how that self-affirmation would give her strength in moments of weakness and was perhaps a large part of why she succeeded.

But I struggled with other spells. Even Mary's spell to heal her mother's knee was tough for me to believe. Patricia's spell theoretically helped her dig in and change her behavior in a manner that secured a desired outcome. But directing energy to repair a health problem—unless you could chalk it up to the healing impact of dopamine, an out-and-out placebo effect, or a coincidence—was harder for me to wrap my head around.

And then I read about other spells. Like casting a spell to raise the funds to pay a phone bill. *Seriously?*

Here's the recipe:

> Gather green candles, patchouli oil, money-drawing herbs, parchment paper, and green ink. Then light the candles and a charcoal block, sprinkle some herbs, draw a picture of the phone bill on the parchment paper, draw a box around it to signify that you have power over it, and then draw a big X through it, recite a prayer . . . and then within a few days some unexpected funds will present themselves to you.

Reading this, I was a little unhooked, unlined, and unsinkered.

NEXT UP: THE open sexuality.

In Wicca, sex is both considered natural and revered. It is viewed as pleasurable and necessary and respected as a life-giving, powerful force that can bring you closer to the divine. Which at first sounded so much better than the oppressive, shaming, narrow-minded view of sexuality found in most religions.

But when I read about skyclad, Wiccan rituals performed in the nude because being unclothed brings you closer to nature, and The Great Rite, a Wiccan ritual involving either real or symbolic sexual intercourse (i.e., plunging a knife into a chalice of wine) as a means to draw energy from "the powerful connection between the male and female"—liberal, well-meaning, open-minded me got uncomfortable, to say the least. While, as an adult, I found the honest, unencumbered, open attitude toward sexuality very appealing *theoretically*, as a mother raising a young daughter, I wasn't so sure.

So I circled back to Mary and Patricia and asked them, as two women who had been in male-dominated, sexually repressive religions, what they thought of skyclad and the anything-goes openness about sexuality. They both said they found the relaxed attitude and broad acceptance appealing—but that they didn't engage in either nudity or sexual rituals; nor were those things on their radar screens. They both reminded me that Wicca is a "pick and choose what you want" religion; both kept coming back to the fact that you're free to be your own type of witch—as long as it's a good witch.

Realizing that it was possible for me to be a Patricia/Mary witch—confident, independent, defiant even, respectful of nature, accepting of others, brave, and empowered, a witch who is not subordinate to male power and dominance but can harness her own power and the energy around her to create better outcomes—I pretty much decided that I could be a good but somewhat conservative and fully clothed witch.

So, like them, I could say a very nonjudgmental no to skyclad and nudity and no to Black Magick and yes to my own power and self-direction—within reason. I could teach Zia about the enormity of her personal power—that she's not completely beholden to, dependent on, and powerless before a supreme being. I could teach her to believe in the power of self, that women have power equal to men and are not subservient in the context of anything.

Not the workplace. Or religion. Or the universe.

I COULD TEACH Zia to respect and revere nature and the environment, to be in awe of her natural surroundings, to believe that she has special powers. That is Wicca.

Then, as I thought about it, I realized that I was already teaching her these things. In fact, I had been teaching her all those things since she was born.

So I went ahead and voiced all this to Zia on a pared-down level—and she told me that she already knew everything that I had just said.

I was thrilled.

And then she told me that she had already practiced magick and that it had worked.

And there I was, once again, just as flummoxed as when Archana Bua told me not to have s-e-x.

*   *   *

I ASKED ZIA to specify about the magick.

She told me that she was in the car recently with Atul. They were trying to get to the train station and were late, and Atul was anxious, so she just started using "pretend magick" to make the traffic light change and make a space free up in the next lane, then to make the solid line change into a dotted line and to get the traffic to move forward. She basically orchestrated their trip to the train station. She said that each time she wished something, it happened; by using magick she had moved the cars around, and Atul got to the train station on time. She told me that even her "pretend magick" was real.

I didn't know what to say.

BUT I REMEMBERED that when Zia was a toddler, we could get her to do anything by telling her the moon or the ocean was telling her to do it—we would even fake their "voices" and have them instruct her to eat her dinner or go to sleep. Then I remembered that when three-year-old Zia had first seen a photo of Atul's mother—who had died from breast cancer when he was fifteen years old—and had asked where her Amma (grandmother) actually was, I had completely abandoned our religious roots in Jainism and Hinduism and reflexively, but unknowingly, reverted to paganism. I had told Zia that Amma was now a star in the night sky. I even showed her which one, pointing sort of randomly toward the heavens at first, then settling on the brightest star I could find.

"There she is," I said without missing a beat. "That's Amma."

We were both overcome with calm as we gazed up at Amma. And Zia had smiled.

And in that moment I didn't care that I was no different from the early Romans, Greeks, and Mayans—or the witches. Or that I had tossed away centuries of intellectual advancement and reverted to pagan star worship.

To hell with all those scientifically grounded facts. This whole grandmother-as-a-star thing felt really, really good. And, honestly, a lot of this other Wicca stuff does too.

When we went back inside that night, I Googled "brightest star in the northeast" and learned that I had likely pointed to Sirius, the Dog Star. Then I told Zia that Amma chose to be the brightest star in the night sky so that Zia could find her easily among all the other grandmas.

Yes, I actually told Zia that her dead grandma was brighter than the billions of other dead grandmas.

I had not only reverted to paganism; *I had made it competitive.*

Which I now realize is okay because I can be any type of witch I want to be.

THEN ZIA TOLD everyone at her preschool.

It crossed my mind that I might have to apologize to the other parents for planting the idea that the stars in the night sky were iconographic representations of divinity and immortality and the promise of eternal life and for introducing a scientifically unfounded, ignorant form of neopaganism to a religiously diverse group of children—which, depending on your perspective, might be perceived as adorable and sweet or blasphemous.

And then I thought that I might need to apologize a second time for claiming the best star for my own family.

LUCKILY, MY CONCERNS were unfounded. Members of Zia's class began pointing to the night sky at their dead grandmothers. And just like their kids had, the other parents embraced the idea and went with adorable and sweet. No one tossed me into the East River to see if I would float or pointed out that star worship just might be the oldest form of outdated, scientifically disproven idolatry and was, by and large, practiced by only ancient civilizations—and modern-day witches.

It seems that even though the Europeans largely abandoned star worship and paganism in the thirteenth century, it is completely plausible to a group of young children. Even to a group of Internet- and smartphone-savvy future titans of America attending preschool in Manhattan.

And it was plausible to their parents too—a few even thanked me.

So basically Zia and I were already pagans. Not Wiccans, but close.

We've worshiped the stars, listened to the moon and ocean, and, just recently, asked some apples and strawberries for permission to pick them. As Zia grows I will continue to teach her to revere nature, to believe in the equal power of women and men, as well as the power of positive thought and self-directed behavior. I will teach her to respect the rights of others to believe whatever they want, even that in certain circumstances we can conjure up magick by tapping into the infinite pool of personal and cosmic energy—which can be very powerful if we want to quit smoking, get to the train on time, or maybe even heal our moms.

I'll just explain that we do it with our clothes on. At least most of the time. Which, by the way, is totally okay with all the other witches.

Then, just when I thought I had this straight in my head, I circled back: I was still really wrestling with the concept of unlimited personal power. Even power directed toward good.

To my surprise, I saw it as a potential burden.

IN MY MIND, praying to a supreme being to help pay your bills or help your mother recover from an illness is somehow more believable than having the ability to control those things yourself—that is, if you get the recipe right and can conjure up the right energy.

And when I articulated that to myself, it hit me. I don't really believe that I have that much power. And here's the kicker: I don't think I want it.

Part of me still wants to have blind faith. Not to believe in *me* and the powers that I can conjure but rather to relinquish myself, to have faith in a supreme being or supreme force outside my control. There is just something appealing about feeling small in a big universe and having that be okay.

As attractive as I find the powerful promise of open acceptance and the self-direction, self-determination, and self-actualization, along with the ownership of outcomes and reverence for nature and the cycle of life that Wicca offers, part of me still wants to be on my knees with my hands folded in prayer, worshiping someone or something that has supreme power over me. Part of me wants to relinquish responsibility for my fate—and my forever—to an all-knowing, all-powerful being beyond my control and, yes, maybe even beyond my mortal comprehension.

Wicca essentially puts everything on me. And on a good day, that's empowering. But when I feel weak and vulnerable and needy and face what the seventeenth-century mathematician Blaise

Pascal described as "this infinite abyss" that can "be filled only with an infinite and immutable object; in other words by God himself," I fall back on the fact that there is something insatiably enticing about being taken care of, being powerless and submitting to a force I don't need to conjure, one that is just *there*. As compelling as Wicca is, I find myself still wanting that outpouring of radiant warmth and infinite light, wanting to surrender to an incomprehensible otherworldly, omnipotent, omnipresent power that asks nothing of me but reverence as it promises eternity and the banishment of all existential dread.

After all this, part of me still wants the sky to part and a voice to thunder, "I've got this. It's not on you, Bhu."

IN THE END, the witches gave me something sacred: insight. Not just into Wicca but into me. So I guess after all this, I am half witch.

With a half witchlet.

Who still is looking for half-more.

Chapter 5

TEMAZCAL

Mexican Sweat Lodge, Tulum, Yucatan Peninsula

The closest thing to a sweat lodge that I had ever experienced was a hot yoga class I attended with my sister, Avanti, when I was visiting her in Chicago. During my stay she was midway through a thirty-day Bikram challenge that entailed daily, ninety-minute sessions held in a 105-degree studio with such appalling, ceiling-dripping, wall-sweating, mold-inducing humidity that I was quick to classify it as the Devil's work. Or to put it slightly differently, in my opinion a Bikram hot yoga class, at least from my limited experience of a single one—never to be repeated—is a quick visit to Satan's lair.

Bikram yoga, introduced in California by Bikram Choudhury in the 1970s, is, in my mind at least, a dastardly corruption of real yoga—which is a calming and deeply spiritual practice that wise old Indians with soft Buddha bellies have engaged in for thousands of years. Choudhury has distorted it into something that is, on the surface, only baby steps away from the original (you perform twenty-six regimented positions and two breathing exercises) and yet wholly different.

The Bikram studio I visited stank to high heaven. Simply entering the room left me on the brink of passing out from the toxic combo of extremely high heat and humidity, fermenting sweat, and a lack of oxygen that is a hallmark of Bikram yoga. Three minutes into the class, after performing only the first of the twenty-six positions—standing deep-breathing pose (*pranayama*), which required minimal exertion and entailed nothing more than placing my interlaced fingers beneath my chin with my elbows at my side—I nearly blacked out. I then had the common sense to lie down, which, while preventing me from both the humiliation of fainting and a potential head injury, left me, for the remaining eighty-seven minutes of the class, lying prostrate on the dank and, to my horror, carpeted floor, where I slipped and slid on my yoga mat in a pool of not only my sweat but also that of my classmates—which was rapidly being expelled from all their bodies and condensing onto mine.

As for any feelings of spiritual transcendence sometimes reported by hot yoga aficionados, rest assured: I had none. Unfortunately—while sopping up pools of perspiration as I alternated between holding my breath (to avoid the rank odor) and deep breathing while holding my nostrils shut (to remain conscious)—I had ample time to contemplate the absurd notion that anyone could rise to any form of enlightenment or feel a spiritual connection of any type in such unpleasant conditions. I rapidly concluded that any inklings of spiritual awakening born out of the Dante's inferno of a Bikram yoga class were most likely not spiritual at all but, rather, delusions induced by dangerously elevated body temperature, low blood pressure, and a level of oxygen deprivation normally associated with life-threatening activities like huffing or vaping household cleaning products.

A second plausible explanation did occur to me at a particularly unfortunate moment that day. The scantily clad man towering over me was in standing bow pose (*dandayamana-dhanurasana*), a stance that, gazing up from my position on the floor, not only gave me a disturbing view of his sweaty derriere and man parts but also provided a moment of crystalline clarity—in which I concluded that any spiritual revelations in conditions like these could be wholly explained, not by the strict discipline of mind over body, as Choudhury and his converts might suggest, but by the heavenly exhilaration anyone would feel when simply allowed to leave this offensive hellhole at the end of class.

BUT A LOT of people don't share my opinion. Bikram yoga has many followers. And Choudhury himself reportedly has, or had at one point, thirty-five Rolls-Royces and Bentleys and an empire worth $365 million. He teaches classes wearing only a Speedo and a Rolex and supposedly cured President Richard Nixon's phlebitis (blood clots in the legs). Bikram yoga is also popular with people who work on Wall Street—especially after the market tanks—and has a long list of celebrity clients: Kobe Bryant, Kareem Abdul-Jabbar, Madonna, Quincy Jones.

Just not me.

Well, not me and not the seven women suing Choudhury for sexual harassment.

That makes at least eight of us.

In one of those cases, Choudhury testified in court that he was broke.

The jury laughed.

Then he said that he had donated all those expensive cars to the state of California to create the Bikram Auto Engineering School for Children.

The state of California said that wasn't true.

The jury laughed even harder.

Then they awarded $7.4 million to a former employee who charged him with sexual harassment.

YOU MIGHT THEN wonder why I would even consider going to a traditional Mayan sweat lodge after my singularly appalling heat-sweat-stink experience in a Bikram yoga class. The answer lies in my interest in the tradition of non-hot-yoga-related sweating employed universally throughout time and across cultures—from Finland to Japan to Guatemala to Australia—as a means of achieving both elevated levels of spiritual enlightenment and improved health.

* * *

SWEAT LODGES WERE used as a means to transcend: to communicate with the spirit world as smoke and steam carried prayers and intentions (symbolically) skyward. And regardless of the reason for a visit, sweat lodges always had spiritual overtones: many cultures don't consider physical health as separate from emotional and mental well-being—as we tend to do in the Western world.

So what's not to like?

Obviously, the high heat. And after my Bikram experience, the heat scared me.

Here's why.

They get *really* hot. In fact, indigenous cultures in the Americas designed their sweat lodges using the same premise that the Italians use for their clay pizza ovens: if you want high heat, go with a dome with a small opening at the top and pack the outside with clay. The Mayans, in fact, built sweat lodges of clay; the Mexicans, out of terrazzo. Native Americans constructed a domed frame of supple ash and willow saplings, then covered it in animal hides, mud, or woven blankets and either built a fire inside or hauled in rocks heated for hours in a fire outside and poured water—often brewed as a special herb-infused "tea"—over them to create large quantities of steam. Traditional Mayan ceremonies often began with the burning of copal—a sacred tree resin—to make the tea to pour onto the hot rocks; the Navajo Nation used a "brew" of water mixed with needles from pinion and cedar trees that had been struck by lightning.

Engulfed in ritual, the sweat lodge was very central to all these cultures. And though each was slightly different, they shared many universalities. Those universalities were a big part of what I found so intriguing.

GIVEN THAT SCIENTIFIC studies provide rather compelling evidence of the benefits of high heat in treating disease, we should not be quick to dismiss indigenous practices involving both elevated body temperature and extreme sweating to treat ailments as baseless or absurd or primitive—even sweeping claims that lean toward the grandiose. Francisco Javier Clavijero, a Mexican scholar and historian in the 1700s, wrote that sweat lodges were successfully used to treat serious medical conditions such as "syphilis, lepra, pains in the chest and back, [and] spots and growths on the skin" and were beneficial for what he called "constipation of the pores" as well as for "those who need to get rid of thick and tenacious humors."

In modern times the high heat of saunas has been linked to better cardiac function and oxygen uptake, lower blood pressure, and improvement in the function of the endothelial cells lining the arteries—even in patients with congestive heart failure. And modern Western medicine also uses high heat—hyperthermia—in very precise and controlled ways, even in cancer treatment.

Couple this with the known benefits of chanting, meditation, and forming tight communal spiritual connections—all part of the sweat lodge experience—and those early health claims don't sound so farfetched. And considering the powerful evidence of a mind-body-spirit connection, it's also hard to remain completely skeptical about the potential for spiritual transcendence promised by both high heat and sweat lodges.

In fact, I started to think that many of these ancient civilizations—comprised of people with no interest in sweating to obtain ripped abs or glowing skin but on legitimate quests for greater health and well-being, oneness with nature, cleanliness of body and soul, greater self-actualization, and spiritual connection—may have been on to something.

It also didn't hurt that I came to the conclusion that I should be open to exploring the spiritual and healing nature of sweat lodges as I stood half naked on a beach in the Yucatan while covered in Mayan clay during a moment of bliss that itself bordered on spiritual—one rarely experienced in normal day-to-day life but that extended spa vacations have a tendency to birth.

* * *

I'D LEFT MY job at Google and was about to start a new position at a tech start-up. It was one of those all-too-brief interludes where I felt liberated from both all work-related responsibilities and the stresses of finding a new job. After a family vacation with Atul and Zia at a beach in Mexico, I spent an extra few days with two of my girlfriends, Deepali and Mridu, who'd flown down to join me. Which is how I happened to find myself standing on a beach, partially naked, covered in mud, and blissfully open-minded enough to block out my abysmal Bikram hot yoga experience and schedule a visit to a *temazcal*—a traditional Mayan sweat lodge.

BUT FIRST THE mud. As in, the slathering of Mayan clay all over my body. Because the clay—my prelude to the heat—was, in and of itself, compelling.

Not in a true spiritual or religious sense but in the context of the childlike freedom that a spa vacation with friends can ignite. Especially if it happens to include standing topless on a spectacular white-sand beach while in a glorious meditative state.

Now, when I first read about the clay ritual, I was (of course) mildly skeptical. After seeing the option for a "beachfront full-body Mayan clay treatment" on one of the spa menus in my hotel room, I researched the benefits of Mayan mud/clay bathing and found that it promises to "stimulate, detox, and energize the skin" and "refine wrinkles, exfoliate, and regenerate." It also "serves as a face wash and toner" and aids in "healing skin lesions and absorbing impurities." And as if all that weren't enough, Mayan clay is also a "fantastic hair conditioning treatment."

But then they lost me, as was inevitable, when they added a promise too big for me to believe: that Mayan clay is "a sedative for the central nervous system" and "balances the electromagnetic energy field of the body."

Also disengaging—at least to me—was an option offered by some of the local spas for clay-covered participants to dig a "nesting" hole in the sand and bury themselves like sea turtles. I'm serious.

Disappointed in such seemingly exaggerated (or ridiculous) claims and options—after all, they'd had me, credit card in hand, at "exfoliates and refines wrinkles"—I once again stumbled on a few of those scientific factoids that I always seem to trip over just when I'm deciding that something I might engage in has taken its claims too far. There is, of course, no specific evidence that nesting like a turtle promotes health or spiritual well-being; however, from what I read, clay may be a different story entirely.

Essentially, because clay has negatively charged ions, it bonds to anything with positively charged ions, rendering it effective at extracting bad things from good things. And not just dirt from facial pores.

Clay is used to remove toxins from milk and animal feed and for patients receiving chemotherapy, as well as for cleanup after nuclear disasters. The Russian government dispensed chocolate bars made with French green clay to residents after the meltdown in Chernobyl to help pull toxins from their bodies; it also relied heavily on Bentonite clay for the removal of radioactive contamination in the environment.

Reading this, I immediately threw my turtle-nest-digging-inspired skepticism to the wind and booked a full-body Mayan clay treatment on the beach. I figured that if clay could clean up radioactive contamination after a nuclear meltdown like Chernobyl, it just might do wonders for me.

There was one immediate problem, though. You cannot cover yourself completely in wet clay in a one-piece bathing suit.

Which shouldn't have been a problem, given that I was at a hotel that hosted a Bikini Boot Camp. Which is exactly what it sounds like.

Rest assured: if the US military wanted to get soldiers ready for war while looking good in string bikinis, this is where they would send them. This was indeed boot camp: all-day exercise classes that—I can attest from my comfortable perch on a lounge chair by the sea with drink in hand—were not for the faint of heart. This was hard-core exercise, and the clientele was made up of the fitness elite, a collection of super humanoids who arrived, not flabby and in need of work, but in fighting form. It was the type of place where you wouldn't be caught dead arriving marginally fit, eating carbs, or wearing a one-piece, mom-friendly bathing suit.

ENTER ME. I was at the Bikini Boot Camp hotel on a conditional visit—the conditions being no bikini and no boot camp. I had in fact sworn to myself that I would not wear—or even put pressure upon myself to wear—a bikini. Or participate in any form of extreme exercise.

I was there to experience the health and wellness aspects of all-day (non-Bikram) yoga classes, spa treatments, and healthy eating while spending some time with my best friends, whom, between the demands of work and family, I had not seen as much as I would have liked. In fact, I had insisted to Deepali and Mridu that I wouldn't wear a bikini "under any circumstances"—certainly not after having a baby and certainly not at a resort that attracts those interested in getting up at 0600 to have their already perfect bodies systematically rebuilt by military-grade trainers and fashioned into something that would make a five-star general or an aerobics instructor proud.

But here's the thing. I had secretly packed a bikini in my suitcase "just in case." And I put it on.

I had no choice because of the mud thing.

Then I (bravely) headed to the beach where I removed the top.

Solely for the purpose of facilitating the application of clay.

I CAN HAPPILY report that no one notices cellulite or a slight jelly belly when there are bare breasts to scrutinize. In fact, all the women in our particular group were topless, just like I was.

As was—surprise—the one, very happy man in our group, who happened to be straight and looking rather pleased with his choice of afternoon activity.

The women were taking this clay thing seriously. The man was just having the time of his life and smiling. A lot.

THE RITUAL ITSELF was led by Mindy, a woman from a local ayurvedic spa, who had been signing all her e-mails "Om, Mindy," which my friends and I condensed to "Ommindy."

Ommindy provided buckets of wet Mayan clay and instructed us to slather it all over our bodies and through our hair; then she led us to the edge of the water and instructed us to close our eyes so she could lead us through a guided meditation.

As soon as she said, "Imagine all the things you want coming true right in front of you," I was in heaven.

I happen to be very good at setting intentions—it's one of my favorite things to do—so I immediately squeezed my eyes shut and started listing all the things I wanted to come true in my life: for Zia and myself, my marriage, my parents and friends, and my new job. I then expanded the list of good intentions to include some more distant acquaintances and then moved on to somewhat loftier goals that began modestly but then took on a life of their own and mushroomed to include some of the aspirations usually addressed by organizations larger than myself such as the United Nations, the Mayo Clinic, and the Gates Foundation. A compilation of good positive thoughts that, as you might imagine because of its scope, took quite some time to complete.

WHEN I FINALLY finished, standing at the edge of the sea with my arms at shoulder height feeling that only good things could happen going forward, I opened my eyes and my face cracked—which was mildly disconcerting but normal nonetheless. The clay had completely dried (as it was supposed to), and as I squinted into the bright sunlight, I saw the rest of our group bobbing in the water, looking back at me and laughing. They, apparently, had all finished their intentions much, much sooner than I had.

The cat was out of the bag; I wanted more than most.

Which is not necessarily a bad thing.

*   *   *

THE *UPANISHADS*, A collection of ancient Vedic texts written between 800 and 400 BC, contain the highly philosophical thoughts of Indian sages on all things revolving around life, spirituality, and the universe. They serve as the fundamental teachings of Hinduism and state,

> You are what your deepest desire is.
> As your desire is, so is your intention.
> As your intention is, so is your will.
> As your will is, so is your deed.
> As your deed is, so is your destiny.

The theory is that focusing on intentions through meditative practice is a very productive way to clear your head, set goals, and provide direction. Doing so changes your behavior on both a conscious and a subconscious level, and that changes your outcomes in a manner that brings you closer to what you actually want to achieve. Setting intentions can be a powerful tool to help lead you where you want to go, whether that destination is relatively close by, say, a small thing like being more patient, or distant, say, a big thing like finding a spiritual home.

So, knowing this, when I saw the others laughing at me, rather than feeling self-conscious about how long I spent on my intentions, I just started laughing too. Then I ran into the water and swam around with my friends, washing off the clay.

When I got out of the water and dried off, I felt on top of the world. My brain was flooded with dopamine and serotonin, and if you consulted the spa menu, I had refined pores, fewer wrinkles, increased collagen, lustrous hair, and a rebalanced electromagnetic field. A set of conditions that left me open to—even eager for—new experiences. I then made arrangements through Ommindy to go with Deepali and Mridu to a traditional Mayan sweat lodge, an authentic *temazcal* just down the winding, sandy beach road.

WE OPTED TO pay extra for a private session. Ommindy told us the shaman who would be "hosting" us had recently held ceremonies for some celebrities. She said she wouldn't say exactly who, but heavily implied that it had been Cameron Diaz, then she hesitated and said it was possibly Drew Barrymore, perhaps, Reese Witherspoon, or maybe Madonna, and several less famous friends. Then she paused and winked and said, "I'm pretty sure it was Cameron Diaz."

But when we got there, the shaman was wearing blue jeans and a T-shirt and looked like any other guy you might see in a Mexican seaside resort town like Tulum, and I had to reset my expectations. I'm not sure what I'd been thinking, but I had presumed that "real" shamans—and certainly Cameron Diaz's or Madonna's shaman— would dress in full shaman regalia all the time, just like nuns wear habits and monks wear robes and the pope wears his pope outfit, like it's their skin. They dress that way not only because it shows their high level of commitment to their chosen spiritual path but also because the clothes are part of who they are. In my mind, occupations like medicine man, nun, monk, and pope carry a unique level of authenticity; they're not "jobs" with "work uniforms" that you put on and take off.

Oddly, I was more disappointed in Cameron Diaz (or Madonna) for going to a medicine man who wore blue jeans than I was in the shaman himself. He probably had a day job. Like line cook. Or lawyer. They had private jets and the Dalai Lama on speed dial.

As I worked myself into a huff over the issue of authenticity, the shaman sent us to view the sunset while he changed. At that point I was brimming with what Clavijero, the Mexican scholar from the 1700s, called "thick and tenacious humors." Ironically, that meant a sweat in a *temazcal* was just the thing for me.

Plus, the sunset was one of the most beautiful I had ever seen—a good thing given what happened next.

ONCE DRESSED, THE shaman looked authentic, and once we started, he seemed genuine—not at all like he was performing for "tourists." Before we entered the *temazcal* he smudged us with smoke—a symbolic removal of negative energy—and told us that if it got too hot we could leave at any point. The temperature was what I would call "exceedingly hot." So hot that in a typical ninety-minute session, you can sweat several liters of water, which, as you might imagine, is trying for the kidneys but good for detox.

The sweat lodge has been called a symbolic womb, and it certainly looked womb-like. First impression as I looked around? It clearly was designed to incubate something. Or possibly even cook something.

Sitting in the dark, I hoped whatever it cooked would be spiritual in nature and not my actual flesh.

UNFORTUNATELY, THINGS DID not go well.

A mildly annoying element got the whole thing off to a slow start. I hate to blame anyone specifically, but it was the uninvited Russian woman with her friends and her baby. She was the girlfriend of one of the local hotel owners and had "asked" if she and her friends could join us, at which point I flew from zenned-out-pores-cleaned-wrinkles-reduced-feeling-so-good-I-actually-wore-a-bikini-yesterday-Om-Anjali to pissed-off-somewhat-entitled-New-Yorker in no time flat.

I insisted that this *temazcal* was full; we had paid for a private session, and she and her entourage would have to come back another time.

Then in a conflated, East-meets-West contradiction, I folded my hands, bowed my head, and said, "Namaste." Which confused everyone. Especially me.

And it wasn't just the whole barging-in-on-our-girls-night-out thing; it was the baby.

Okay, it was partially the barging-in-on-our-girls-night-out-thing-and-we-should-get-a-discount-or-refund-if-we-don't-get-a-private-session. But mostly it was the baby.

Seriously? Who brings a newborn into what is essentially a smoke-filled pizza oven for people?

But the shaman pulled me aside and told me that he couldn't say no to this woman because of who she was. Then I wondered what Madonna or Cameron Diaz would do.

The Russian woman's friends decided to leave anyway after only a short time inside, but we remained stuck with her and her infant. And, as I said, it didn't go well.

For starters, as promised, it was hot. Really, really hot.

Hardly the eight-hundred degrees recommended for a crisp crust on a Margherita pizza but nonetheless hard-to-handle hot.

The smoke and steam inside were choking. And—surprise, surprise—the baby cried.

And cried.

And cried.

At times I had to lie down on the floor to breathe better. But the mom of the year wasn't the least bit concerned about all the things that I was thinking about, like her baby's oxygen intake or possible kidney failure due to dehydration—because she was busy texting. Yup, there was cell service in the authentic Mayan sweat lodge.

THE SHAMAN BEGAN to chant and then led us through guided meditation, facing, in turn, each of the four cardinal directions. He called in our ancestors, repeating *Abuelita, Abuelita* (an affectionate word for grandmother in Spanish), and at one point asked if anyone wanted to share a prayer. One of the Russian woman's friends—who had yet to leave—started singing "America the Beautiful."

Super earnestly.

I was pretty sure that this wasn't what Cameron Diaz's shaman meant by a prayer. Also, we were in Mexico. So the song choice made no sense at all.

Plus, the baby didn't like the singing. So she cried even louder.

For the record, Deepali and Mridu didn't like the singing either, or the Russian woman, or the crying baby, or the high-tech form of communication going on in the *temazcal*.

Deepali lasted all of twenty minutes before she left, saying she was claustrophobic.

Mridu hung in for maybe another ten minutes and then said, "I get the idea. I'll see you back at the hotel."

I said, "Wait."

She said, "I'll be in the bar."

I couldn't compete with that. So I stayed without my friends.

AFTER ANOTHER HOUR of crying, a miracle occurred: someone came and took the baby out.

But she didn't take the Russian woman or her cell phone. So I spent the next hour continuing to try to meditate to the glow of her iPhone screen and the sound of text message blips.

Then a second miracle occurred: her phone rang, and she left to take the call. Which meant that I was finally alone with the shaman.

At this point I had been in the *temazcal* for a couple of hours and may have sweated enough to have caused local flooding. But I was determined and encouraged by this turn of events, so I stayed.

It was time to get down to business.

The shaman chanted and prayed, I chanted and prayed, and it continued to be almost unbearably hot—but with an intensity conducive to deep concentration and altered consciousness in a surreal, time-warping kind of way. Finally I began to see the draw of this: the prolonged heat, the steam, the deep meditation in the dark, the rhythmic chants. I actually sank into intense, deep meditation.

WHEN I EVENTUALLY emerged into the pitch-black night, I had no idea how much time had passed. I made my way alone, slightly lightheaded, down the street and back to the hotel. When I stepped into the lobby, I found Deepali and Mridu talking with a member of the hotel staff about whether to come looking for me.

It was 11:30 p.m., five hours since we'd left for the sweat lodge.

I felt drained. I wanted to shower, drink a few gallons of water, and sleep for a long, long time.

I COULDN'T SLEEP. So I started thinking about the big picture of what I was attempting to do. And that led me to think about something I had read about Stephen Hawking and the theory of everything. And that led me to think about something entirely different: the overview effect, a phenomenon reported by astronauts in outer space looking back at planet Earth.

Before you conclude that I was suffering from random bursts of distorted and possibly psychotic thoughts brought on by heat stroke and dehydration (which perhaps I was), let me explain how Stephen Hawking and astronauts in outer space can shed light on what I was experiencing. Because thinking about the theory of everything and the overview effect that night, whether those thoughts were brought on by an electrolyte imbalance or heat-induced existential thinking, made me feel much, much better about being baked in a pizza oven with the Russian woman in Tulum.

First off, I started to think about smoke differently. I became intrigued by the universal symbolic use of smoke in religions for both communication and ascension. Smoke or steam, it is believed, can carry intentions and souls into the heavens. Since smoke is a tangible, visible medium with which to link the earth to the sky, it validates the possibility of transcendence; it's a symbolic metaphor for the spirit and the spirit rising. The concept of pairing intentions with smoke or steam as a vehicle for transport gave me comfort—even inspired a little awe. I had new respect for the universality of the use of smoke across almost all religions and spiritual practices—be it via candles or incense, peace pipes or funeral pyres. So I reaffirmed that, even in an unsatisfying experience like the one I'd just had, while I hadn't found all I was looking for, maybe I was finding some small things.

By then I'd had a number of interesting, thought-provoking experiences, and though they didn't deliver me to the core of what I was looking for, they did allow me to dance around the fringes. Those small experiences enticed me to continue. They were the sum total of what would, in my opinion, make this entire journey—regardless of the magnitude of any final conclusions I arrived at—more than worthwhile on its own.

That led me to think that, in the big picture of my quest, I had been looking for my own personal, spiritual version of what physicists like Sir Isaac Newton, Albert Einstein, Stephen Hawking, and others call the theory of everything—when maybe instead I should be happy with small things, like smoke.

Those physicists set out to find a way to perfectly link everything in the universe by uncovering one all-encompassing theory that explains it all. And while they've come up with Newton's theory of gravity, Einstein's theory of relativity, string theory, superstring theory, and M-theory, I was, on the spiritual side of things, fundamentally trying to do the same thing—admittedly on a much smaller scale and with a much smaller intellect. I was essentially looking for the singular, all-encompassing, mind-blowing, comprehensive truth that would anchor me to some all-consuming, self-altering sense of awe and confidence as I, too, spun through time and space.

I was looking for a theory of everything spiritual for Anjali and Zia.

And yet, so far, just like those physicists had failed to find a theory of everything in the entire universe, I had failed to find a theory of everything for my own spirituality. And that led me to think about being content with the small things that I did find.

And that led me to think about the astronauts.

Even if this was a feverish delusion brought on by over four hours in a sweat lodge—after all, I hardly ever think about Albert Einstein or Stephen Hawking or astronauts—it nonetheless made me feel much, much better.

* * *

WHEN ASTRONAUT EDGAR MITCHELL first saw Earth from the Apollo 14 spacecraft, he experienced an all-encompassing, life-altering feeling of overwhelming awe and a fundamental shift in awareness and spiritual clarity. Other astronauts have reported the same thing. And these weren't just the Earth-is-so-beautiful-I-can't-believe-I'm-here kind of career-capping revelatory moments; they were spiritually deep and transformational.

When Frank White interviewed astronauts in the 1980s, they often reported that seeing Earth from such a great distance led them to feel not only "awe" but also "a renewed sense of purpose." White called this the "overview effect." The astronauts said that the experience was "transcendent," or what Mitchell called a "grand epiphany accompanied by exhilaration."

What they reported sounded very much like a spiritual awakening. They consistently cited a renewed sense of wonder at and respect for being part of something bigger than themselves.

I SAW A parallel between what I was doing as I looked as an outsider from a great distance at all these spiritual practices. Like the astronauts looking back at planet Earth, I too was beginning to see the wonder of a grand overview. I began to see all the boundaries between these divergent belief systems and spiritual practices beginning to blur and disappear, just as the astronauts came to see the lines between countries and continents as profoundly artificial and irrelevant. Like them, I was blown away by the fact that there are far more commonalities than differences.

So it occurred to me that while I had been looking for an intense, singular state of certainty and knowing—a theory of everything—I may really have been seeking what the astronauts had: an intense, singular state of unknowing, of awe and respect for something so big that it is beyond understanding. I was beginning to think that just maybe it was better to accept that our capacity for understanding everything may be limited and that there will always be the unexplainable. In other words, to embrace that I-am-small-and-it-is-big perspective that so positively overwhelmed the astronauts.

And then this occurred to me: The natives of the Americas—the Aztecs and Mayans, the Navajos and Sioux and hundreds of other Indian nations—believed in a theory of everything long before Einstein or Newton or Hawking even started looking for it. They believed that mind and body, self and others, spiritual life and physical health, the present and future, life and death, the tree and the bear and the stars in the night sky were not separate but part of an interconnected continuum. They weren't looking for a mathematical theory based on physics; they had *faith*. They had both what Newton and Einstein and Hawking hadn't found—which physicists might never find—and what the astronauts had to travel to the moon to discover: they had a theory of everything and the overview effect.

That might not have been everything I was looking for, but it was something.

And then, just as the sun was coming up and I was feeling really good—like there was a forward-moving lesson here about being grateful for small bits of insight and appreciating the ability to see the commonalities and the big picture—I had a bad thought. When I considered my Bikram yoga experience in conjunction with this sweat lodge experience, I remembered the concept of plastic shamans.

"Plastic shaman" refers to those who claim to be medicine men or yogis or expert practitioners of a faith or spiritual practice when in fact they have little training and no authenticity and are just co-opting traditional cultural and spiritual practices and putting on a performance. At best, they are tourist attractions conducting staged events hosted by opportunists and charlatans; at worst they are dangerous. The harm posed by a plastic shaman can range from misrepresentation of a spiritual practice to actual death.

But I wasn't just worried about those two extremes—either that this sweat lodge was a total fraud or that my life had been at risk. I began to realize (sadly) that when you are not raised in a culture and thus don't internalize the nuanced belief system that underpins a practice as part of your systemic being, and then you undertake an isolated experience, like visiting a sweat lodge, it's hard for it to be as meaningful as it should be. So even if these experiences are authentic and the shaman is genuine, a single experience in isolation from the rest of the belief system provides no depth or context.

So, essentially, I had to worry not just about plastic shamans but also about plastic participants (e.g., the Russian woman and her baby) who can fall short and ruin the experience, as well as a plastic me because I lacked the cultural backdrop to receive all that it had to offer. So now I worried about being a "plastic" seeker and about how impossible it was to travel really far from what you know without potentially falling into the cheesy, embarrassing category of "spiritual tourist" or "cultural gawker." Then I began to worry that I was approaching this whole journey with wildly outlandish expectations.

And then?

To quote Britney Spears: Oops! I did it again.

I had another "plastic" experience in Cusco, Peru, and was once again a "plastic" seeker. For the third time.

But not on purpose.

But before I get to that, first I have to tell you about Fay and convening with the dead.

Chapter 6

THE "DIRTY" MEDIUM

Convening with the Dead,
Toronto, Canada, and Tribeca, NYC

A friend reached out to me saying that I absolutely had to e-mail a medium he knew named Fay. Mediums are conduits to "the other side" involved in what is described as "non-local information transfer." As in really non-local. As in so non-local that they talk with dead people.

We arranged for a call over e-mail. Right after "Hello," Fay told me she was a "dirty" medium, explaining that mediums usually "keep their vessels clean."

Luckily she clarified that the vessel mediums usually keep clean is their bodies. That means that, generally speaking, mediums don't do drugs, drink alcohol, or eat junk food. In her case, she said that she's vegan but drinks. After explaining this, she made a few jokes about tequila that led me to believe that she drinks *a lot*, but I said I was okay with that, thinking to myself that if I talked to dead people I'd probably also drink heavily—and stick to the hard stuff too.

Plus, I was thinking that if she could really talk to dead people, who would f-ing care if she drank, anyway?

So, in part to make her feel better, and in part because it was true, I told her that I was a dirty nonmedium and we should get together and do shots of tequila.

She laughed. I laughed. And we instantly hit it off.

Fay seemed funny and smart, and if you lopped off the "she speaks to dead people part," she easily could have been one of my friends. Plus, she refused to charge me. So that—coupled with the promise of tequila—made her pretty hard not to like.

Then Fay jumped right in and started asking me some general questions—if my parents were alive, how many siblings I had, if I had any children—and I was very intentionally guarded in my responses, giving simple, one-word answers and only first names, careful not to feed her any information that would make it easy for her to dupe me.

Even though I didn't want to be, I was really skeptical about this whole "talking to dead people" thing—especially over the phone. I was wondering why she didn't need to meet me in person or hold an item from a family member who had died, like I'd seen mediums do on television.

Just as I was ratcheting my skeptic's attitude into high gear, Fay announced that she had a strong image of a butterfly landing on her nose and asked if that meant anything to me.

I almost fell to the floor.

I somehow managed to say, "I associate butterflies with my friend Amani, who passed," while thinking *Maybe butterflies are a common-enough image associated with loss and grief and this was just a good guess* and *How the hell could she scam me so fast and so accurately when I have revealed so little information?* and *Jesus H. Christ, maybe she can talk to dead people!*

Then Fay said, "Amani stopped breathing suddenly. Someone was with her when she died. And he did something to her."

I tried not to react. Or overreact. Or breathe too heavily. Or pass out.

Next she asked, "Did she drown?"

Amani didn't drown but close enough. She had stopped breathing suddenly. Someone had been with her when she died. And he had done something to her.

Butterflies aside, Fay was three for four.

MY CHILDHOOD FRIEND Amani had died suddenly under unusual and suspicious circumstances when I was in law school. And there was absolutely no way Fay could have known that.

Amani died the day before she was supposed to visit me in Boston. She had been killed while visiting an acquaintance of hers, and it was unclear if her death was a horrible accident or a brutal homicide. I flew home to Chicago for the funeral, and the night before the service, completely distraught, I said to a friend, "I just need to know that Amani is at peace and that her family will recover."

That friend told me about someone she knew who'd been struggling with a lot of personal problems. In a moment of desperation, during a trip to the Amazon, he had fallen to his knees and asked the heavens for a sign that he should go on. At which point he had been engulfed in a swarm of butterflies.

My friend gave me a hug and told me to look for the butterflies.

That night, too distraught to sleep alone in my childhood room, I fell asleep on the floor of my parents' bedroom. When I woke up, the first thing I saw was a department store catalog on the floor; it had a giant butterfly on the cover. At the time this unnerved me, but I decided that it was nothing more than a coincidence.

Later, after the service, as Amani's body was being cremated and I was standing outside the funeral home huddled in collective grief and disbelief with my friends, a single butterfly flitted across the sky.

I lost my breath.

Broken and grieving, I flew back to school the next day and was in office hours with a professor at Boston University's law tower, when I glanced out the window and saw a butterfly flutter past.

Eleven stories up.

Butterflies started appearing everywhere.

Every time I thought of Amani, a butterfly appeared in one form or another—on the T-shirt of a child walking by or in a display in a store window. It was completely unnerving but also somehow reassuring.

THEN FAY SAID, "Amani is really glad that you didn't get that butterfly tattoo you were thinking about getting." I finally sat down on the floor. I hadn't told anyone that I had considered getting a tattoo of a butterfly in her memory—not even my closest friends.

Next, Fay told me that Amani visits me at my house and sends me butterflies. And she told me that she was at peace.

After a pause, Fay then asked if I was into design and fashion. While a few months earlier I would have said yes, my fashion status had recently shifted. I was now newly unemployed and writing a book and had of late formed a strong and quite possibly long-term and monogamous relationship with a pair of well-loved sweatpants, an old college T-shirt, and sneakers. But before I could answer, Fay told me that Amani said that I have to buy Zia a red Chanel purse when she turns sixteen, that Amani told her to tell me, "Just wait. You'll see. Zia will ask for the bag, and you'll have to buy it for her." Plus, "Don't be cheap, Anjali. Buy the red Chanel purse for Zia because I would have gotten it for her if I could have."

Red was Amani's favorite color. She was glamourous and into luxury fashion. A red Chanel bag was exactly what I would have scoffed at and Amani would have bought for Zia's sixteenth birthday.

At that moment, I was very, very uncomfortable. I didn't know what to make of any of this. I flipped back and forth between thinking *I am being played* and wondering *What has Fay not told me yet?*

Then Fay said, "Amani has two siblings but don't tell them about me," then added, "If they ask if you know a medium, then it's okay. Just don't bring it up because it could be hurtful to repeat any of this if they don't believe."

Then, just as I was trying to figure out how she came up with any of this, including the fact that Amani had two siblings, I remembered I wasn't even paying her.

If I was being scammed, I couldn't see the angle.

I was Demi Moore in the movie *Ghost*, watching in wide-eyed disbelief as a penny moved up the inside of my apartment door.

* * *

A FEW MONTHS later Fay e-mailed to say she was going to be in New York. We met for lunch at a restaurant downtown and she was not what I had expected.

Rather than disheveled and unkempt—which is how I imagined a tequila-drinking medium might look, since it was definitely how I would look if I spent my time downing shots while conversing with the dead—she looked like she worked at *Vogue*: slim and chic, wearing black Margiela jeans and Converse sneakers, and carrying a Prada bag.

We sat down in the restaurant, and when I realized she looked distracted, I asked if anything was wrong. Fay said, "There are so many spirit voices calling to me in here."

I leaned forward and innocently asked, "You mean dead people?"

She said, quite matter-of-factly, "Yes," adding, "Next time, we should go somewhere quieter."

When I asked what she thinks happens when we die, Fay at first said she didn't know. But later in our conversation she clarified a bit: "I do believe that we are visiting, that our bodies are our 'soul sacks,' and here on Earth we have to earn a backstage pass to the main event." She went on to say that we have to "wait well," with "activeness and kindness," and the here and now is the "waiting room." She also said, in a completely believable and comforting way, that she knows for certain that "love never dies."

Fay explained that in her line of work, "specificity is the key." She needs to "provide details that are specific and true so the client feels the pull of authenticity in that moment." She said that sometimes the people with whom we have a spiritual connection after they pass aren't those we were closest to in life. She also told me that she generally treats people who have suffered a major loss, often the loss of a child; those parents are experiencing "absolute horror," and hearing that their child is with a grandparent or family friend and is laughing gives the parent enormous, life-changing comfort and clarity. When she said that, I reflected back on both the specifics and the comfort and clarity she had already given me in a single conversation.

Fay went on to explain that she doesn't "see" but "senses" the people who cross over, and those who come to her don't comment about the day-to-day stuff like finances or jobs or "tell us" what to do. "In death they have earned a place of peace and quiet; we have to figure out that mundane stuff ourselves." She then said that there are two types of memories when someone passes: first, the ache of loss and missing the person, and second, what she called the "grocery store" moments, those everyday, mundane times when we find ourselves actually talking to the people who have died. "That's where 'mediumship' takes place."

Fay said, "The currency of the next life is the unconditional and authentic kindness we practice in this life. Especially kindness on bad days." She added, "Life is not meant to be easy," and that on the "other side," the blind can see, and the deaf can hear, and the sense of peace that I was feeling in the restaurant—and I was feeling a sense of peace—"was God."

Her specific mention of God surprised me, so I asked if she believed in God. She said that she believed "in Christ," reporting that she'd been raised Catholic and only lapsed from the religion during bad hangovers.

I laughed. She laughed. It felt like we were kindred spirits.

In fact, the entire time Fay and I were together, I was thinking of how there wasn't the slightest veneer of showmanship or sleaze to her. She was full of smart insights and compassion, she projected extreme confidence, and she had such a calming way about her that everything she had said felt genuine and heartfelt.

Then Fay blurted out, "I'm feeling a big pull over there," pointing over her shoulder. She then said that an *M* was coming to mind, after which she abruptly added, "Your husband's mother is here."

Atul's mother's name was Madhu.

Then a noise made me jump.

Fay laughed and said, "Don't worry. No one shows up in person when I do sessions." I laughed too, though I still glanced around the restaurant, half expecting to see Atul's mother.

Then Fay said she felt "a strong male energy" and asked if anyone male had passed when I was forty-one years old.

Alarms went off in my head, and my hands started sweating.

I gave her a tentative yes.

"Was he in the music industry and black?"

Holy f-ing shit! She's talking about Rich.

Fay was the David Blaine of dead people.

RICH NICHOLS HAD been in the music industry and was black and had died two years earlier, when I was forty-one years old. He'd been the longtime manager of the hugely popular hip-hop band The Roots, which is now the house band on *The Tonight Show with Jimmy Fallon*. I had met him at a tech conference a couple of years before he died, and we'd instantly hit it off. He'd tapped me to do a project with him, to which I'd instantly agreed. He was curmudgeonly and brash and absolutely awesome. He kept me in line too.

When he fell sick, I FedEx-ed him blessed water from John of God. He'd texted me, "I'm not drinking weird water from Brazil!" I'd texted back, "You have to! I carried it to New York all the way from South America!" Then, in utter Rich-like defiance, he told me that he'd had his wife pour it on his feet.

FAY THEN TOLD me, "Rich is fathering you through this work transition." Then she added, "You didn't know Rich well, but you knew him deep." Once again, there were the specifics: the devilish details that were too spot-on to be dismissed as a fortuitous guess or coincidence.

Fay then said, "Rich is singing the Stevie Wonder song *Superstition* right now." To which she added, "Oh yeah, and he says you have to lose ten pounds."

I was wholly convinced that Rich was here in the restaurant with us, singing like Stevie Wonder and mocking me for talking to a medium, all while slapping my hand as I reached into the breadbasket and twirled my forkful of carbonara.

Then Fay asked me if I had an aunt who had passed. To my tentative yes she asked, "Did she have three daughters?" I was back to *Holy shit!*

"She is in the distance, busy with her own girls, and she's not coming over." I looked around the restaurant expecting to see Atul's mother, a swarm of butterflies, Rich, and my aunt.

In the end I concluded that Fay was better than David Blaine; she was the Houdini of dead people.

BELIEVE ME, I didn't go into this wanting to believe. But when I left the restaurant, that calm feeling Fay had said was God stayed with me. As I walked back to my apartment, I was side by side with Amani and Atul's mother. I was with Rich and my aunt, and they were all looking over me.

At that moment I felt like I had hugged a friend who was wearing perfume and knew that the scent would stick with me for a long time, clinging to my skin and clothes and tugging at my memories as I went on my way. It was a faint and pleasant reminder that we don't lose people completely even in death and that I should be on the lookout for them, for the comforting aura and wake that trail behind those who are not entirely here but not entirely gone from our lives either.

LATER THAT NIGHT I told some of this to Atul.

He said, "You're crazy. There is no way she talks to dead people."

I said, "But . . . "

He said, "'But' nothing. Somehow she's guessing. Or you're telling her too much and you don't remember."

Honestly, I was annoyed. Really annoyed.

So I said, "Oh, and Fay said that your mother was in the restaurant."

Atul froze.

"And she told me that your mother told her that you are lucky to have me and she's grateful that we're married. And she thanked me for putting up with you."

Atul just stood in the doorway looking at me with a half smirk and raised eyebrow.

I thought I knew what he was thinking. Atul's mother died when he was fifteen, and I had told Fay that, so it was a really safe thing for her to have said.

I was waiting for Atul to say something smart back, like "She probably says that to everyone." But he didn't. He just looked at me and smiled.

And that made me realize something really, really important.

But before I tell you exactly what that is, I have to tell you about the spiritual placebo effect and the documentary film *Kumaré*.

*   *   *

VIKRAM GANDHI, AN American-born filmmaker from New Jersey who found himself disturbed by the self-help/self-improvement yoga/guru craze in America, traveled to India, hoping to find something more authentic. Instead, he found the same type of exploitive behavior. Back at home, he decided to expose this perceived fraud, so he grew his hair and beard, ignored all grooming tools, donned some loose, saffron-colored clothing, adopted a fake Indian accent and the gentle and wise spiritual demeanor of a swami, and in so doing created a fictional persona he called "Sri Kumaré." Then he headed out to do some participatory journalism, hoping to make a point.

Kumaré went to Arizona, presented himself as a famed guru from an Indian village he made up called Aali'kash, and quickly attracted a core group of dedicated followers. Despite what some have characterized as the "fraudulent, Borat-esque" nature of his behavior, Gandhi wasn't out to make fun of anyone or to gain financially. His motive was seemingly genuine: he wanted to demonstrate that we all have the power within ourselves to effect personal change and don't need any of the self-proclaimed gurus behind the $11 billion self-help industry to access it.

Kumaré's followers bought his schtick. They dedicated themselves to his teachings and adopted what he called "blue light meditation" and "mirror philosophy"—stuff he simply made up that involved the tried-and-true self-help staples of positive thinking and intention setting—to interesting results.

One woman lost seventy pounds. Others found kindness and confidence. Another drastically reduced her stress.

Gandhi had undertaken this deception not for the purpose of exploitation but rather to draw attention to the fact that so much of "all of this guru nonsense" is bullshit. He stated his belief that we are all "needy," that we "want direction," that we "want and are primed to believe." He ended up proving that believing in something—regardless of how genuine it is—changes our behavior. We become more powerful and can change our lives for the better ourselves.

Kumaré essentially became a handrail for people on the difficult climb of life. He helped them to tap into the inner strength they already had. You can call it what you want: chi, prana, ki. And even though Gandhi's Kumaré essentially engaged in fraud, it actually worked.

Thinking about Kumaré led me to reflect on a time when I was sitting on a friend's porch in upstate New York, drinking tea after meditating. On the armrest of my chair I saw a bug that was turned over on its back and flailing its legs. I watched it struggle for a minute, flipped it over with the edge of my spoon, and it went on its way.

That was all it needed, a nudge from a well-meaning stranger.

And that nudge changed everything—maybe saved its life.

THAT WAS WHAT Kumaré did. And Fay was likely doing it too.

We are all looking for someone—or something—to flip us over as we flail on our backs.

And when I realized this, the really, really important thing hit me.

Maybe it didn't matter if any of it was real.

Because, I realized—just as Kumaré's followers had—I felt better and more empowered with Fay's help than without it.

So what difference would it make if she had somehow faked it?

I liked having Amani with me. And I liked having Rich as a mentor, keeping me in check. And I liked having my aunt in the distance.

Even a staunch nonbeliever like Atul seemed to like hearing that his mother was pleased with his choice of wife.

It meant that we haven't really completely lost them.

So in the end, I had to consider if it really mattered whether Fay was legitimately "talking to the dead" or if she had Kumaré-d me; perhaps the gentle, positive manipulation of a well-intentioned stranger had simply flipped me over onto my feet as I was flailing on my back.

Because I had witnessed firsthand—just as Kumaré's students had—that there is an accessible force within us all. And no matter what we call it or how we classify it, no matter if it originates in something truly "divine" or in the subtle, deft manipulation of the truth, it can be a very real and very powerful force to improve our lives.

I was left to wonder whether what Fay did for me was really any different from what priests, ministers, rabbis, and other religious leaders do when they tell followers to trust in God or that God is watching over them and that everything will be okay. Because the simple truth is, I don't know if a medium can access the dead, but those religious leaders have no hard proof of their connections to God either.

I took away from the experience of "speaking" with Amani and Rich, with Atul's mother and with my aunt, the understanding that believing in something—no matter what it is—gives us strength, regardless of whether there is any real, proven, spiritual intervention at all.

But for it to work we must take a leap of faith.

The good news is that when we do so, we can tap into a pool of energy that we can leverage to significantly and dramatically improve our lives.

I will never know for sure if Fay or anyone else can actually talk to the dead, but I do know that believing they can has a powerful effect.

It is called the placebo shaman effect and serves as a source of superhuman strength for all of us.

The only prerequisite is that we believe.

It is not what I hoped to discover when I started looking for answers, but it appears to be true.

Chapter 7

MACHU PICCHU
AND AYAHUASCA

Cusco, Peru

Even though I fully admit that I was categorically and unabashedly stalking God, just for the record, I was not stalking Cameron Diaz. I say that only because it's highly probable that Cameron Diaz and I had gone to the same shaman and sweat lodge near Tulum, and now I was—by total coincidence and without any premeditated intent—about to follow in her footsteps to Cusco, Peru, and Machu Picchu.

I was scheduled to give a lecture in Lima, so Atul and I decided to make it a family vacation and fly from there to Cusco to take Zia to see the Lost City of the Incas. The clandestine plan in the back of my mind was that, while we were there I would, at some opportune moment, leave Atul and Zia hooked up to the oxygen tank in our hotel room (more on that later) and sneak away by myself for a day—or two—to meet with a shaman. As a route to self-discovery and my higher self, I intended to try ayahuasca, the ancient vision-ary "plant teacher" (okay, hallucinogenic drug) of the Andes. To-day, Peru has a robust ayahuasca tourist trade—promising visitors

109

a transcendent, transformational, some say "life-altering" spiritual epiphany.

In the weeks before we left for the trip, I Googled "how to find a shaman in Cusco," and up popped Cameron Diaz—and more Cameron Diaz.

I first told myself that this meant nothing; maybe a lot of celebrities go to both sweat lodges in Mexico and Machu Picchu in Peru. But when I started checking out the web links to Cameron Diaz, I realized that she wasn't just visiting the same places I was, she also appeared to be, spiritually speaking, just as uncommitted and confused (okay, just as unzipped and screwy) as I was. In fact, when I coupled what was clearly for both of us an affinity for spiritual exploration with what seemed to be a shared, similarly profound inability to make a binding pledge of loyalty to any one philosophy, it became apparent that, for all intents and purposes, Cameron Diaz and I were—at least in the God-seeking sense—sisters.

In any event, having not thought one iota about Cameron Diaz since Ommindy mentioned her name on my trip to Mexico, I stumbled on a YouTube video in which Cameron Diaz meets a shaman named Puma in none other than Cusco—the very city Atul and Zia and I were going to visit.

In this documentary Cameron travels with Puma, learning about his healing practices and Peruvian culture in general. They also tour Machu Picchu.

So, partway through the video I was thinking, *This is perfect. Puma is the shaman for me.*

And though they didn't discuss ayahuasca at all, clearly he could hook me up.

I mean, if he was good enough for Cameron Diaz, my sisterly sidekick grazing at the spiritual buffet, well then, he was good enough for me.

And I kept thinking that until just a few minutes later in the film, when Puma tells Cameron Diaz he'd been struck by lightning when he was six years old.

Puma said it matter-of-factly, adding that the event had been a significant, life-altering sign from above, or, as he put it, a "symbol of initiation." He basically explained that the Gods themselves had struck him with a bolt of lightning as a child to signal to his grandfather—himself a shaman—that he should train Puma as a medicine man.

Upon hearing this story, Cameron Diaz had looked alarmed. Mainly, I suspect, because at the time she was standing with Puma in a wide-open field. At this point, she asked Puma to ballpark how many people in Peru were, generally speaking, hit by lightning.

Puma basically said, "Lots of them."

Then he added something to the effect that whenever lightning strikes someone, it's a sign.

I was thinking to myself that surely God(s) could find a better way to communicate with us mortals than by striking six-year-old children with bolts of lightning. But it was pretty clear, from her worried expression and nervous tone, that at that moment, spiritual sister or not, Cameron was concerned more about her immediate situation.

And that made sense, because a lightning strike like that can stop your heart, blow the shoes off your feet, set your skin on fire—and fry your brain.

But since I had absolutely no intention of working with a shaman who had suffered a potentially significant brain-altering cosmic electrical event, I was back to square one. Shaman-less and headed to Cusco.

Yet, as I reflected on Puma's experience, I did envy the absolute certainty that lightning strike had given him—and his grandfather—about his life path. It occurred to me that this was one place where Cameron Diaz and I likely differed: I was open to a lightning strike from above.

At least metaphorically.

I sure as hell wanted my shoes blown off my feet and my skin set on fire; I wanted to be gobsmacked by faith.

AND THAT'S WHAT the ancient Incan plant medicine ayahuasca is supposed to do. It rewires your brain. It can be a short cut to faith and a direct route to God. For some people, ayahuasca is liquid, spiritual lightning.

So, as much as I was not into recreational drugs, I decided to try to find a shaman in Peru (other than Puma) to (maybe) try it; in my defense, ayahuasca's supposed to be both medicinal and absolutely no fun.

In fact, from everything I had heard and read, it is hell.

So that was my plan. I was going to stand in an open field, grab hold of the big-ass flagpole known as ayahuasca, and hope like hell to be struck from above.

But first I have to explain why I have friends who have their own shamans, and why none of them would return my e-mails.

IN CERTAIN CIRCLES—think highly educated, affluent, ahead-of-the-curve, trend-setting, tech-savvy, socially conscious, slightly bored, politically engaged, socially relevant, youngish, liberal professionals living in Brooklyn, the West Village, Silicon Valley, West Hollywood, and Venice Beach—shamans are like dentists, yoga teachers, and acupuncturists. Basically, everyone has at least one of each. In fact, these shamans are flown in to the United States, all expenses paid, from South America to hold ayahuasca circles with the same frequency that Barney's has shoe sales.

Okay, by "everyone" I mean a large contingency of hipster psychonauts—those who choose to use mind-altering substances to achieve clarity and deeper meaning in their lives. As Ariel Levy wrote in the *New Yorker*, ayahuasca is "the drug of choice for the age of kale." And as my friend Jeffrey, a chef in Manhattan, jokingly put it, "The shaman is the new drug dealer."

And ayahuasca certainly has its fair share of celebrity endorsers. Sting called it "the only genuine religious experience I have ever had." Tim Ferriss of *The 4-Hour Workweek* fame is a devout user, despite the fact that he says that it "completely fried his 'motherboard'" and gave him "grand mal seizures," along with "rug burns" on his face.

Like I said, it's strong stuff. And no fun at all. Ayahuasca causes vomiting, diarrhea, and hallucinations—both visual and auditory. Granted, it offers reportedly earth-shattering, mind-blowing self-awareness and spiritual clarity—but still, you pay a price to get there.

While many are drawn to ayahuasca to bring God and self together on intimate terms, South American cultures have also used it for centuries to treat all sorts of physical and mental health issues. And because ayahuasca affects serotonin uptake in the brain, today researchers are studying it as a treatment for depression, posttraumatic stress disorder, anxiety, and addiction. They are also investigating it for numerous other medicinal purposes, including to treat cancer and Parkinson's disease. Ayahuasca is even being given to prisoners in Brazil—murderers, rapists, and kidnappers—in a pilot program as a form of self-improvement therapy.

But as Tim Ferriss's rug-burned face clearly demonstrates, this is no party drug. To give you an idea of its wattage—and to frame it with a pop culture reference—a drug dealer in the TV show *Weeds* declared, "Peyote's a bicycle; ayahuasca, a rocket ship."

So, open-minded and intrigued (while at the same time reticent and petrified), I got the names of shamans from my friends and e-mailed a long list of them with the canned "We have a mutual friend/I would love to talk" message, followed by "I'm interested in trying ayahuasca and I hear that you do ceremonies, so was wondering . . . "

No one responded. For weeks.

Finally, when I was fairly convinced that the universe was giving me an emphatic "No Anjali! You should not try ayahuasca" message, one—and only one—shaman e-mailed me back. This particular shaman tersely instructed me to be "much more discreet when discussing the plant work." She directed, "In all of our correspondence, over email and phone, please do not use the names of specific plants. You can just refer to it as 'plant meditations' or 'circles' and I'll know what you're talking about. Thank you."

Basically, the shaman bitch-slapped me.

Here's the thing: Ayahuasca is legal in Peru. But it's illegal in the United States. So it was a well-deserved shamanic bitch-slap, and there was no way I was writing back to her. I'm a lawyer, for goodness sake, and ayahuasca is a Schedule I controlled substance, just like ecstasy and heroin—except during the religious ceremonies of two specific religious groups of which I was not a member. That makes taking it a Class A felony. One might assume that this was something that I would have Googled before putting it in an e-mail—but the prevalent use of the drug in my extended social circles in New York enabled that little detail to slip right by me.

So the bottom line is that I headed to Peru without a shaman connection. But I did manage to get struck by lightning—of sorts.

*   *   *

ATUL, ZIA, AND I flew to Peru, and I gave a lecture. We paraglided over the cliffs of Lima, spent a night in Cusco, took the four-hour train to Machu Picchu, stayed overnight there and explored the ruins, then trained back to Cusco—and like many understanding parents of young children who drag them to foreign lands, one night we eschewed the local cuisine of ceviche, alpaca, and guinea pig and ate at the Peruvian equivalent of Chuck E. Cheese's.

The city of Cusco—our home base bookending our visit to Machu Picchu—is 11,000 feet above sea level. As a point of comparison, that's twice as high as Denver, Colorado—the mile-high city. People who visit Machu Picchu have to acclimate first—and often do so in Cusco—or risk suffering altitude sickness. So when I made our hotel reservation in Cusco, I booked a room with oxygen. The option of having it pumped into the room sounded appealing until the reservationist said that "was for old people," so I went with option two: the tank.

Believe me, it was necessary. We all struggled with altitude sickness. We were out of breath. Our hearts raced. We felt lightheaded.

Zia vomited up her Peruvian Chuck E. Cheese's meal. Each time we went back to the room after exploring the sights, we'd lie on the bed together and pass the oxygen mask between us. It was weirdly, ominously apocalyptic.

But worth it.

CUSCO IS A World Heritage site. The old center of the city is breathtakingly quaint and architecturally stunning, studded with both pre-Columbian and Spanish colonial architecture—from cathedrals and temples and fortresses to ancient stonework and religious iconography. On our first night in the city we walked by a shaman shop—not hard to do in Cusco as they are everywhere—and, likely fueled by both the glass of wine I'd had at dinner and the altitude sickness, I felt compelled to go in.

The sign out front said all of the following:

Ayahuasca. Wachuma retreats. Shaman's Healing House. Ancestral Medicinal Plants & Ancient Healing Ceremonies. Offering to Mother Earth. Cleansing of negative energies. Coca Leaf Reading. Bath of Flowering. Natural Products. Travel Agency.

And they took Visa. And American Express. And Diners Club. And Discover Card. And cash.

Not blind to the obvious touristy and commercial nature of such an enterprise but lacking a connection to an authentic shaman recommended through friends and running out of time, I sent Atul and Zia back to the hotel without me and stepped inside.

* * *

THE WALLS OF the shaman shop in Cusco were lined with bright tapestries. There were herbal medicines for sale and two Peruvian shop keepers: a woman named Joanna and a thirtysomething guy who, I was told, was a shaman, wearing blue jeans, a white, long-sleeved shirt, and *mala* beads. He had fastidiously groomed facial hair and wore a fedora that made him look more like he worked in a recording studio in LA than in a shaman shop in Peru. He re-minded me of a Brazilian shaman I met years ago in the lobby of the Greenwich Hotel in NYC who had turned up dressed like a Brooklyn hipster in a brown leather jacket and a T-shirt with a pic-ture of Yoda from *Star Wars* dressed as a DJ on the front.

I guess there was a pattern. Just as I had in Tulum, I wanted my shamans in Peru to be old and wrinkled and in authentic shaman gear, not hip and hot, wearing Western clothes.

When I introduced myself to Joanna, she said, "The plant medi-cine was calling to you, and that's why you came into the shop." She then told me that ayahuasca allows you to communicate with "the universe," that "the active ingredient DMT has been called the 'God Molecule,'" and that "it's very important for healing depression, trauma, family and job issues, love, and overall health." She added, "Ayahuasca cures cancer too." And she was adamant about that. She said Western doctors don't pay attention to "plant medicine" be-cause there's no money in it—it's easy to get and cheap—and while I wanted to say that's not completely true, since roughly half of all drugs approved by the Food and Drug Administration in the last thirty years derive from natural products (think aspirin, morphine, quinine, penicillin, ephedrine, paclitaxel), I stayed quiet and lis-tened. She then explained that after you use ayahuasca, you'll feel very sensitive emotionally and full of gratitude; that ayahuasca teaches you to speak with your heart rather than your mind. She said that ayahuasca is "meeting you with you."

And here's where she really got me: she also said it helps answer the question "Why are we here?"

As we talked, Joanna explained that people come from all over the world to find the answer to that question, and she warned me that for ayahuasca to work, you have to do "the prep." You need to be prepared both emotionally and psychologically. And you need a good shaman.

I asked her about doing a ceremony, which involves a small group gathering in a designated location for the night, sitting in a circle, and drinking the tea under the supervision of a shaman. Jo-anna told me that one day, with one ceremony, would cost $300; two days with two ceremonies, $390; three days with three ceremo-nies, $550.

Honestly, at this point, I was thinking I should add a few days to my trip.

But then Joanna explained that, before you use ayahuasca, you should follow a recommended one-month *dieta*, a regimen to prep you for the experience—no pork, no coffee, no sex, no chocolate, no alcohol—which sounded pretty much like the posttreatment re-strictions John of God recommended, except that ayahuasca users can apparently have bananas, gassed or ungassed.

Hmmm . . .

When I told Joanna that I was interested but that I hadn't done the *dieta*, she told me that I could take a short cut: I could drink a large quantity of Peruvian volcanic water, which would make me vomit and give me diarrhea.

I told Joanna that I had diarrhea already.

She said I'd still have to drink the volcanic water and the process would take three hours. She then told me that the volcanic water costs $80—but detoxes you for one year.

I told her I didn't have $80 for water.

Joanna immediately dropped the price to $50.

I handed over the cash.

WHICH, UPON REFLECTION, was absolutely ridiculous. For a de-cision of this magnitude to be that price sensitive—I was saving thirty bucks—is downright absurd. Even I cannot vouch for my thought process at this point.

I could hear myself explaining to Atul, "I really wasn't going to do it, but she gave me a deal on water that would make me vomit!" But I couldn't think about that because Joanna had just asked the fedora-wearing shaman, who was repotting a peyote plant, to go get the volcanic water that had just gone on sale a minute ago.

So I sat down on a bench and waited. Joanna told me that the volcanic water was "Marcani" mineral water from the Quissachata volcano located roughly four kilometers north of San Pedro. When the shaman and his fedora reappeared a few minutes later, he was carrying a jerry can—one of those old military-style plastic jugs designed to hold five gallons of gasoline. He put it at my feet and then handed me a sixteen-ounce yellow plastic cup.

I was thinking that for fifty bucks I should have gotten a carafe and café table.

Next I was given a green purge bucket (vomit pail). As I contemplated what lay ahead, I noticed that there was, disarmingly, a roll of toilet paper sitting next to a bouquet of flowers on a nearby table.

This had started to feel more like a radical weight-loss spa treatment than a prelude to God: fly to South America, get altitude sickness, eat Peruvian Chuck E. Cheese's, have diarrhea, drink the volcanic water, vomit and have more diarrhea, hike into the jungle, drink the ayahuasca tea, have more vomiting and more diarrhea—this time with a whole group of people—hallucinate, face death, discover God and the universe in full force and encounter breathtaking, awe-inspiring, life-altering beauty, and, just maybe, bring home a new and improved you—and in the process drop some weight.

Or die.

Hmmm . . .

And yet, despite these grave concerns, knowing that my husband and child were asleep in a hotel down the street and that I could not, under any circumstance, do something this irresponsible on a whim, I went ahead and did it anyway.

FEDORA SHAMAN POURED me a glass of the water, and I drank it.

It was clear. And it tasted like the ocean.

As advertised, it caused severe vomiting and diarrhea. I was fairly warned.

I texted Atul from the shop at 10:45 p.m.: "I am drinking volcanic water to get rid of gastritis. Will be back to hotel in a few hours and pooping all night. See you soon. Love you."

He wrote back, "Ok. Love you."

It crossed my mind that when I felt better, I should consider whether it was a good thing or a bad thing that this text message seemed completely normal to Atul. It was as if I had said something completely mundane like, "Running late at work be home soon," not "I am drinking volcanic water in a shaman shop and will be pooping all night in our hotel room."

ALTERNATING BETWEEN SITTING and walking in circles to keep "things moving," I managed to drink three glasses of the water pretty fast, which I thought was a huge accomplishment until I looked down and realized that it barely put a dent in the five-gallon gas can. All the while, Joanna kept tapping my stomach and suggesting that I had a parasite, and the peyote planting, fedora-wearing shaman kept tapping my head and saying, "You think too much with this"; then he'd tap my heart and say, "You need to think more with this."

I was thinking that everyone seemed to be telling me that.

And then with my head in the green purge bucket, I had a flash that this was exactly what the Balinese medicine man Ketut told Elizabeth Gilbert in *Eat Pray Love*, when he drew her the picture of the four legs and missing head and said something to the effect of "Think with your heart, not your head." I then decided that every spiritual healer must say this to the weary, overthinking, burned-out Westerners who traipse around the world looking for salvation, which means that if we could just accept that—think with our hearts, not our heads—we could all save ourselves some trouble and just stay home. But overthinker that I am, instead of leaning into the whole think-with-your-heart-thing, I started to think with a mega dose of both affection and alarm about the Three Amigos I met in Lima.

So technically speaking, I was thinking simultaneously with both my head and my heart—which, while not perfect, might have been a small improvement. At least for me.

* * *

A LAWYER FRIEND of mine in New York who's Peruvian and has family in Lima had suggested that I meet her uncle for coffee when I was there. Her uncle Marco arrived at the café with two friends, all three of them successful Jewish Peruvian businessmen in their late sixties and early seventies who were absolutely lovely and adorably sweet as they spoke warmly about sacred architecture and Peruvian culture. They then went on to warn me about the dangers of young, untrained "fake" shamans—hucksters, they said—who were popping up everywhere and in it for money only, catering to tourists.

Like me.

They didn't say that, but we were all thinking it.

All three pounded home the importance of going to the right shaman if I wanted to try ayahuasca, agreeing that this would make all the difference, not only in terms of safety but also in the outcome of the experience across the board.

THE ENTIRE CONVERSATION with my Three Amigos in Lima had made me rethink the whole plastic shaman theory that I had come to after my realizations about Kumaré and Fay. I decided to refine it a bit to include a precondition: it doesn't matter if a shaman is "plastic" as long as the worst that can happen is relatively benign. Using a well-intentioned form of psychological manipulation to convince people of something comforting that helps them move on or allows them to tap into a pool of internal strength they didn't know they had is one thing. Administering potent medicinal hallucinogenic drugs is another.

Then, as all of this ran through my head while I vomited into the green purge bucket, I had an epiphany.

Not the spiritual kind.

The WTF-am-I-doing kind.

So, I sort of bitch-slapped myself and decided to go back to the hotel to be with my family. The next day I would take the train with them to Machu Picchu and forget about trying ayahuasca.

This came to me, in part, because I was thinking about the sage advice of my three grandfatherly and wise amigos from Lima and, to be perfectly honest, also in part because of another flash memory I had about a friend of mine named Noah.

Noah told me that he tried ayahuasca, and his giant revelation was that he should get circumcised.

That was his big takeaway.

In other words, while under the influence of ayahuasca, way out there in the middle of the Brazilian rain forest, Noah had a powerful vision about his penis.

I'm not sure why, but with my head in a vomit pail, that tipped it for me—the thought that I could go through with this and my religious and spiritual gain could be something not—in my mind, at least—significantly forward moving.

So at that point, elbow deep in the business end of crazy, it occurred to me that, even if I didn't actually die from the experience, I might have a dud of a revelation. I was only partway through the prep stage, and I decided that I'd had enough.

Several hours later, Joanna agreed.

She said, "This might not be the time for you." Then she warned me that when I came back, I had to make sure to get a good shaman, one who had "a government certificate."

In a nutshell, I chickened out.

But before I left the shop, I bought some herbs: palo santo wood sticks to burn for cleansing negative energy, sangre de grado oil for my "parasite" and gastritis, and muña oil to put in a cup of warm water as a tea to aid in digestion and relieve stress.

Then, loaded up with medicinal herbs and several pounds lighter, I walked back to my hotel, depleted and relieved.

And in many ways, more than a bit disappointed.

But that was before Machu Picchu and the lightning strike from above.

* * *

MACHU PICCHU IS spectacular. It's an Incan city spread out over five miles, built in the 1400s and abandoned in the 1500s, its occupants wiped out perhaps by smallpox (brought by European invaders), or civil war, or drought—no one is sure. It is now preserved in a beautiful state of partial ruin in what is called, for good reason, "a cloud forest" that is home to a vast number of species of orchids, butterflies, and birds. Many residents in the region believe in the spirits of the mountains (*apus*) even today, and anyone who has been to Machu Picchu will tell you that it inspires spiritual awe and reverence on a grand scale—and that the feelings it draws from within are indescribable.

On our final day in Machu Picchu, I got up early and headed out on a solitary hike under a dramatic sky, making my way in the light rain and fog along the trails to the Sun Gate (*Inti Punku*). At first, I worried that the weather would be an impediment, but the cloud cover only made the experience more ethereal and otherworldly.

I hiked for about an hour up the steep, windy mountain path, hardly passing another person on my way. When I arrived at a plateau with a great vantage point and a view out over the valley, I stopped to take it all in. I was tired from the day before and slightly breathless from the climb in the high altitude of the Andes. As I paused to rest, gazing in awe over the terraced green of the Lost City of the Incas, at the mountain peaks in the distance, and across the valley below, the cloud cover and fog rolled in and out, exposing only snatches of the view to me in fleeting but utterly spectacular glimpses. Isolated fragments of the majestic panorama were revealed to me one fractured, magnificent snapshot at a time. It was a theatrical game of hide-and-seek, a choreographed dance of earth and sky.

By the time I sat down on a rock to meditate, the fog and cloud cover had settled in dense and thick enough to completely obscure the view. I noted to myself that even though I could no longer see any of the magnificence before me, I knew it was still there. Sitting perfectly still, I had stumbled upon a metaphor for faith itself—to know with absolute certainty that something exists, even when you can't see it.

IN THE CONTEXT of this place, it seemed absurdly easy to whole-heartedly and with unyielding conviction completely dismiss the arguments of nonbelievers—the evolutionists and atheists and spiritually ambivalent. At the very least I felt compelled to acknowledge seventeenth-century Dutch philosopher Benedict de Spinoza's vision of God: that God is river and sea, mountain and sky, and that his handiwork is seen nowhere better than in the complex and grandiose laws of nature. Or to agree unequivocally with Thomas Edison: "When you see everything that happens in the world of science and in the working of the universe, you cannot deny that there is a 'Captain on the bridge.'" Or with Werner Heisenberg, who received the 1932 Nobel Prize in Physics for the creation of quantum mechanics, who concluded, "The first gulp from the glass of natural sciences will turn you into an atheist, but at the bottom of the glass God is waiting for you." It seemed impossible not to agree with all of them as I sat on my rock, eyes closed and heart open, engulfed by clouds and fog at what felt like the top of the world, knowing that just beyond my sight lay the ancient and sacred valley of the Incas.

As I continued to meditate, I felt wonderment at nature's beauty more intensely than I ever had before. I thought again of the overview effect that so overwhelmed the astronauts as they gazed back at Earth from outer space—that feeling said to overcome so many who see the expanse of the universe anew, not only from space, but also when looking out over mountain peaks and canyons at the beauty of our planet from afar. The perspective and vantage point of distance, the sheer magnitude and vastness and complexity before our eyes, can provide clarity and euphoric confidence as it instantly and categorically vaporizes any lingering uncertainty about the existence of God. Many who experience moments like these report that they know for sure that there is, in fact, a "Captain on the bridge."

For me, Machu Picchu was that vantage point, that high-up distant place. It was as if I was at the Gate of the Gods, the ancient city's *Amaru Muru* doorway, believed to be a portal to the spirit world where the mountains and rivers meet and form a powerful vortex of energy.

BECAUSE AS I was meditating on the mountain, I was struck by lightning. Not the electrical kind or the drug kind.

The God kind.

Or at least the closest I would come to the God kind on this journey.

It wasn't a discharge of 5 billion joules of cosmic energy, but it was a life-altering jolt—a bright flash and thunder from above.

I was Moses, who had gone into the midst of the cloud, and someone spoke to me. This is what I heard:

> I reveal to you the things you need to know in time. If I revealed to you my magnificence, or your own, all at once, it would be too much for you to handle. So I give you glimpses and then cover and reveal as you are ready to receive.

It didn't feel like a personal epiphany or the thoughts of a dehydrated, woozy, slightly hungover spiritual desperado. It felt like a spiritual intervention.

I opened my eyes and looked around. Nobody was there.

My skin had been set on fire.

Chapter 8

PATRICK THE HEALER
AND A *REIBAISHI*
Goa, India, and Kyoto, Japan

After I was gobsmacked by faith in Peru, where I found myself at the vortex of some type of otherworldly force, I came back to New York and found the city, unlike me, unchanged. Life went back to normal, except for the fact that I now had a lot more patience with myself and renewed confidence that I just had to keep doing what I had been doing—looking with grace and wonder for the answers I was seeking. Although truly believing that all the beauty and wonder of the universe would be too overwhelming for me to experience all at once, I was now genuinely shopping, so to speak, for those smaller insights.

But I was also travel weary.

So I decided that, for a while at least, I would find a way to continue my search from the comfort of home—which, luckily, turned out to be easier than I imagined. After all, thanks to the Internet, Buddhist priests and mediums who speak with the dead aren't the only things available for home delivery.

FROM DAY ONE, as I searched for my spiritual footings, Google had been my modern-day oracle—my conduit for a cosmic hookup. It was a high-tech stand-in for the ancient Indian *Asariri* (voice from the sky), *Ashareera vani* (person without body), and *Pythia*, the Greek priestesses of the Temple of Apollo at Delphi—all in one.

With the exception of the Internet's failure to help me find a shaman in Peru, Google was there for me and delivered. Just about everything related to God, spiritualty, energy healing, and oneness with the universe had a website or Facebook page populated with similar images, usually involving beams of radiating light, sated converts, and serene-looking prophets and healers who looked admirably contemplative—enviably lost in deep meditative thought, sitting in the lotus position, wearing long, flowing robes, projecting an aura of blithe immunity to the issues that drag down the rest of us—the unenlightened, wholly confused seekers like me.

Along with the pictures on their websites and social media pages, these healers and seers and the otherwise cosmically enlightened also had testimonials from satisfied customers and media links to feature stories in the mainstream press—and, of course, pull down tabs with e-mail addresses, phone numbers, FAQs, and disclaimers, as well as links to Google Maps, PayPal, and currency converters. What more could I ask for?

Before I left home to visit a healer or saint, I knew exactly where I was going, whether I could drink the water when I got there, and the nuanced dos and don'ts of each belief system. I had an international mobile data plan, phone numbers for local cab companies, and the locations of the nearest hotels, train stations, and ATMs—all facilitated by Google. When I headed out into the spiritual universe, I was—generally speaking—well informed and abundantly prepared.

Without the Internet, a lot of what I did would have been downright scary. But because I could read about the specifics, scrutinize the pictures, reserve a hotel room, and even arrange for a translator online, I wasn't overwhelmingly apprehensive about flying to Brazil to see John of God or to Peru to meet a shaman. So Google didn't just inform, it validated and legitimized, making me realize I wasn't alone in wanting to learn more about a particular practice or belief.

And Google shrank the world as well, making the Internet a spiritual universe unto itself. A medium like Fay in Toronto, an energy healer in Australia, or a faith healer in Goa wasn't off-limits or too much of a commitment in time and money because I could connect with him or her via Skype or text message, often immediately. Instagram and texting put tarot card readers and astrologers, people like my friend Ophi of the famed AstroTwins, only seconds away. Through the twin oracles of laptop and smartphone, I had access to the enlightened world in the palm of my hand.

* * *

PATRICK SAN FRANCESCO, aka "Patrick the Healer," is a popular faith healer in India who claims to have cured his own paralysis, a home full of lepers, his brother's terminal illness, and a patient whose heart had stopped beating—to name just a few.

When I first heard about him from my aunt, Rohini, I instantly responded to the confidence of his professional name: "Patrick the Healer." Just a first name and job description—like "Cedric the Entertainer." I was thinking to myself how I would love that kind of clarity in my life, but "Anjali the Lawyer" just didn't have the same ring.

Since we had relatives living in Goa where Patrick the Healer was based, I started hearing about him more and more, and the consensus of my family members was that he was "the real deal." Others say he's a self-promoting marketing genius, not a miracle healer, and quite a few go a step further, claiming he's an "outright fraud" and "charlatan" trafficking in grief and desperation, selling nothing but false hope.

It seems that it's always the same: the staunch believers are pitted against the staunch nonbelievers, with no way for the rest of us to discern truth.

Patrick the Healer charges for courses, training, and online meditation sessions, but he heals people for free. It's sometimes tough
for a consumer to tell the difference between generosity of heart
and a shrewd sales gimmick. But everyone agrees that Patrick the
Healer is a new New Age kind of guy. He says things like, "Talking
to God is a blast." He claims to "see colors" and "petals" around people's heads that contain clues about their lifespan. And he once gave
a three-minute talk in Los Angeles on dog biscuit recipes. These
random bits of information were hard to process.

IN A YOUTUBE video Patrick the Healer states, "We are all healers," that the body emits energy that we can find. Then he proclaims
that he's actually "closer to a plumber than an energy healer," stating that he uses a "tool box." He's big on metaphors.

> Fixing cells. Changing the configuration of DNA. Chiseling
> out the block in an artery. . . . I use something to drill into it.
> Something to chisel it away.

I was thinking that while my aunt might be impressed, Atul and
his fellow doctors would laugh out loud. *Changing the configuration
of DNA and chiseling out the block in an artery with energy and will?
That's absurd and ridiculous!*

But on the flip side, there's a whole field of bioenergy-based
healing and vibratory medicine—acupuncture, ayurvedic medicine, crystal therapy, therapeutic touch, Reiki, and qigong—based
on the metaphysical force of chi or qi (as it's called in China), prana
(in India), or ki (in Japan). So once again I found myself not believing and not not-believing either. I was always the skeptic straddling
the fence.

Maybe Patrick the Healer knows something we don't. Maybe he
can oscillate at a higher frequency than the rest of us. Who am I to
say he can't clear a blocked artery? Or maybe it's just a placebo effect. And so what if it is? That is, if it actually works.

So I asked Atul, "Doesn't any of this make you the least bit curious?" He immediately said no.

But after a few conversations with my aunt, it started to feel like I actually knew Patrick the Healer, like he was a kooky old family friend. And what I found most intriguing was that he could treat you over the phone or even via text message. And because of my positive experience with Fay over the telephone, my interest was piqued. And then, as if on cue, my aunt gave me Patrick the Healer's cell phone number and said, "Just call him."

I SENT PATRICK the Healer a message on WhatsApp.

And I must have believed it would be that simple because I was really disappointed when I got no response. I tried again, sending information about how I was connected to local Goans, even stating the names of the close relatives I had living in his hometown. "I'm Anil and Bina's niece (who live near Benaulim) from the USA!"

Still nothing. I upped my game.

I gave up texting and did what my aunt had suggested: I called him.

He didn't pick up or call back.

Even though I was leaving voice messages.

Then in moments that I am ashamed to say took on the demeanor of Glenn Close stalking Michael Douglas in *Fatal Attraction*, I started dialing his number again and again with no regard for what time it was. In my defense, according to his website, he was always traveling, and it was too time-consuming for me to try to keep track of what time it was in all the places he was visiting.

He never picked up.

I started obsessing about it. Not boil-his-pet-rabbit obsessing, but still.

I texted and called, again and again. I wondered if he recognized my number and was avoiding me. And because I texted him on WhatsApp—which lets you make long-distance phone calls and send text messages for free and displays a single checkmark to show that a text has been delivered and a second mark when the message has been read—it became clear that I was being ignored.

Every text message I sent had two checkmarks.

That second check—*Got it! Heard you! Don't care!*—felt more disconcerting than if I had been left in the dark thinking that maybe he hadn't actually seen my messages at all.

Damn it! I thought. How could a healer be blowing me off? I started acting like a jilted girlfriend. I had to stop myself from spinning out of control.

But technology had failed me in oddly confusing and conflated ways. The technology that gave me unbelievably simple access also gave me a false sense of closeness—even to people I didn't know at all.

HEADING OUT TO lunch with my friend Marina, as we were walking to the restaurant, I stepped out of the flow of traffic on a busy sidewalk to call Patrick the Healer again. Exasperated, Marina said, "That's the third time today!"

I ignored her comment, dialed his number, and said with the dismay of a teenager, "He isn't taking my calls!"

She sardonically asked me how long we had been dating. Then she asked if he even spoke English.

The look on my face said it all.

Marina then commented, "I'm going to stop taking your calls too if you don't stop sounding so crazy."

She had a point.

I'm Facebook friends with Questlove and follow Lady Gaga on Twitter, but I don't think either of them would take my phone calls. And I'm pretty sure I won't be having lunch with either one of them soon.

But that thread of logical thinking worked for only a nanosecond.

I UNRAVELED. I started stalking the whereabouts of Patrick the Healer online. At which point I realized that I was being a jerk. Patrick the Healer travels twenty-eight days a month to heal people. He runs a charitable foundation. He's a busy guy.

Then I found out he was going to be in Dubai, conducting workshops on what he calls "light healing." I thought about going.

At which point Atul suggested that Patrick the Healer was going to be in Los Angeles and that was much closer than Dubai. Or better yet, he said, I could do an online webinar. A four-hour meditation session with Patrick the Healer for the autumn equinox cost $30.

I thought flying to Dubai would make a bolder statement.

Atul disagreed. Plane tickets to the United Arab Emirates, he said, ran five thousand bucks.

AT THAT POINT I realized that Marina was right. I needed to reel—or real—it in.

So in the end I backed away. I didn't fly to Dubai or Los Angeles or even sign up for the online seasonal meditation session. I stopped calling and texting Patrick the Healer altogether. I officially snubbed him because he was avoiding me.

The oracle of Google had led me astray.

THEN, MONTHS LATER, when I mentioned this jilted-girlfriend routine to Fay in a follow-up call, we had a good laugh. But then she said, "Patrick the Healer didn't get back to you because you don't need healing."

That comment would have been a lot easier to slough off if everything else Fay had said hadn't been true.

Plus, she wasn't the first one to tell me that.

* * *

A YEAR EARLIER I had attended a work conference in Osaka, Japan, so I'd traveled to Kyoto for the weekend to meet with a *reibaishi*—which translates to something between a psychic, a shaman, and a medium. The Japanese translator I had hired for my trip, Tomoko, had recommended him to me.

The whole thing turned out to be weird.

I had bumped into an old work acquaintance at the conference, and he had tagged along with me to Kyoto. After a beautiful and serene meditation session in the garden of the monastery, the two of us, along with the translator, sat awkwardly in the *reibaishi's* apartment as he looked at me quizzically.

He had purplish-blueish-silver-tinted hair. He also lived in a nondescript apartment building. I had expected more of a *yamabushi*—a mystical Japanese mountain hermit—stripped of encumbrances and embracing the monastic life. Instead, the man sitting before me appeared to have been sucked in by the secular trappings of both L'oréal and Ikea.

First he asked, through Tomoko, if I was married to the guy I was with. I quickly replied, "No, he's just a random friend"—at which point my old colleague looked vaguely offended. Then the *reibaishi* replied, through the translator, "Good. It wouldn't last."

That just made the whole thing even more awkward, but before that feeling could settle in and take root, luckily the *reibaishi* asked why I had come to see him and what questions I had for him.

I asked what had by then become standard fare: "What should I be doing with my life? And will everything be okay?"

He raised an eyebrow and then closed his eyes, and his whole body began to shake.

As in his whole body vibrated like an unbalanced washing machine on the spin cycle.

Then he opened his eyes, looked at Tomoko, and nodded his head as he leaned to the side and said something in Japanese. She translated it to me as "Yes, all will be fine."

I almost laughed out loud. *That's it?*

Everywhere I went, it seemed that I got the same ridiculously simple, nondescript, nonactionable, and wholly uncomforting advice.

"Anything else I need to know?" I asked.

After a promising back-and-forth exchange between the *reibaishi* and the translator, Tomoko said, "No."

Then the *reibaishi* started laughing.

I guess he found my situation funny.

I HAD TRAVELED a great distance to get there, paid ¥10,000 ($85) for this private session, embarrassed myself in front of a colleague, and brought along a translator. So I pressed him.

When I did, the *reibaishi* commented that usually people came to him when there was a problem they needed help with. But, he said, I was obviously "fine."

I thought, *I want to be more than fine!*

He said that I "just had to keep doing what I was doing," that I "was here out of curiosity, not real need."

He repeated, "Normally people come to see me when something is wrong, when life is difficult, because they need answers before they can continue. You are fine. Just be happy. Don't think so much."

Ha!

How could he know that when I had told him almost nothing about myself or my life?

Then I reminded myself that he wasn't a therapist, he was a *reibaishi*—a psychic/shaman/medium—which meant that in theory he didn't need me to tell him anything in order to know stuff about me.

Before we left, he told me not to have any more children because the next one would be more like my husband. And then he cracked up again.

I didn't know if I should feel insulted or relieved.

But I wanted my ¥10,000 back.

* * *

SO FAR, FOUR people had told me that I didn't need healing: the Japanese *reibaishi*, Patrick the Healer, Fay the dirty medium, and Chade-Meng Tan, an engineer at Google with the job title Jolly

Good Fellow. He had basically said the same thing way back when I started this project. He taught a popular course at Google called "Search Inside Yourself," and after attending, I'd pulled him aside and asked about the meaning of life and how to go about building a spiritual foundation for Zia. Basically I was asking how I, a mere flawed and mortal woman aspiring to join the seraphim in the highest order of the angelic hierarchy, could possibly become a pillar of strength capable of holding up all the celestial bodies orbiting the heavens. But he'd taken a radical shortcut around my existential angst and simply said, "You're fine. Zia will be fine. Stop trying so hard."

At the time I had scoffed at that answer as too easy. It was very clear to me that I needed more.

But now, after having heard that refrain again and again, I parked that thought in the back of my mind.

Maybe I am fine and don't need healing.

And with Fay's help, I reluctantly moved on from Patrick the Healer of Everyone but Me and decided to join a laughing yoga group online.

They were far more welcoming than Patrick the Healer. They returned every one of my texts and calls.

And they promised to heal, not just me, but also the whole world. For free.

And they weren't upselling anything either. Or talking to dead people.

And they never once told me I didn't need to be healed.

Plus, I could do it without leaving home.

Chapter 9

LAUGHING YOGA

Mumbai, India, and Johannesburg, South Africa

Jolly Good Fellow Google engineer Chade-Meng Tan had so ex-
tolled the virtues of laughter that when I'd accosted him at work
one day with all my questions, he abruptly suggested that I change
my job title to Jolly Good Counsel and make a few people laugh.

At that point, I was left to wonder how I always seemed to find
myself brutally thrashing my way through the thick, tangled un-
derbrush of life with what felt like a machete as I kept bumping into
fellow travelers who were easily treading a seemingly unencumbered path to the same place with enviable, almost magical ease.

Then Chade-Meng had segued into an account of how on his
fortieth birthday, he'd met the Dalai Lama and that His Holiness
had given him a hug.

He effectively rolled right past my massive mountain of spiritual
distress and bewilderment by ignoring everything I had asked him.

Next, he told me that people asked him all the time what it was
like to hug the Dalai Lama.

At which point I just looked at him blankly.

He continued his story by saying that when they asked, he told them, "We hugged. It was nice. But he didn't call me again."

Then he laughed.

And I laughed.

While I had by no means completely forgotten about the enormity of my initial inquiry into the uncertain nature of existence that Chade-Meng had completely (but perhaps shrewdly) driven right by without even slowing down or glancing out the window to take a peek at, I'll admit I did feel a little lighter—like Atlas himself had swooped in and taken some of the weight off the shoulders of someone who had condemned herself to hold up the sky for eternity.

Then, the Jolly Good Fellow finished our conversation, not with the deeply spiritual discussion about God and the meaning of life that I was so desperately seeking, but with a golf joke, which he instructed me to tell my husband as soon as I got home.

A priest decides to blow off giving Sunday mass because he wants to golf. He lies to another priest, saying he isn't feeling well, and asks the priest to cover for him. The angel Gabriel sees this and is very upset and tells God, "God, you must punish this priest for lying and playing golf." God says, "Yes, I will punish him." The priest goes to play golf and gets a hole in one on the first hole. Gabriel is stunned. The priest hits another hole in one. And then another and another. Gabriel turns to God and says, "God, why are you letting the priest hit all these holes in one? You were supposed to punish him!" God says, "I am!"

Gabriel still looks confused so God delivers the punch line: "Who is he going to tell?"

When he finished, Chade-Meng laughed again.

I laughed too.

And when I told the joke to Atul, he laughed as well.

OKAY, I GOT Chade-Meng's point.

Lighten up, Anjali. Things will work out. Stop trying to be a Titan; just be human and be happy and trust the universe a little.

So in reverence for Chade-Meng and the Japanese *reibaishi*, Fay the medium, and, by default, even Patrick the Healer—and, if I thought about it, I could add to the list my mother, Atul, most of my friends, and even Norberto in Brazil, because they too had been telling me (in one way or another) that I was fine and should just focus on being happy—I joined a laughing yoga group.

Actually I joined two.

* * *

IN 1995 A physician in Mumbai known as the "Guru of Giggling" started laughing yoga clubs, where people get together and laugh; the first group had just five people. An offshoot of this movement, where people laugh over the Internet via Skype, began a few years later. Today, the laughter movement has become a global phenomenon with over 8,000 clubs in sixty-five countries. And it's called laughing yoga not because you are in downward dog or child's pose while laughing but because it incorporates pranayama—yogic breathing—into what are essentially "laughter exercises."

The concept behind both in-person and online laughing is to use the power of laughter to improve health and happiness—not just on an individual basis but also on a heal-the-entire-world level—a concept that I at first found ridiculous.

But there is some compelling science behind laughter therapy as a means of improving health. Laughter has the power to lessen pain, reduce stress-related hormones, boost the immune system, and raise good cholesterol. And there's evidence that it may improve cardiac health and lower heart attack risk in diabetic patients and is therapeutic in treating cancer patients.

The mechanism behind the health benefits of laughter is that stress causes shallow and irregular breathing, decreasing oxygen intake, while deep breathing (yogic breathing) increases oxygen intake. And the key to deep breathing is a longer exhale than inhale.

And here's the tie-in: laughing is the best way to achieve a deep and complete exhale.

In other words, deep breathing fundamentally improves our health, or as the Bible says, "A joyful heart is good medicine, but a broken spirit dries up the bones."

But there's more. Laughing yoga also creates a social network. And feeling connected to others, feeling part of a community, lowers stress and makes us live longer. So something like laughter therapy, which could seem silly, has a sound scientific basis.

But for it to work, there are parameters. According to the experts, you only get the full, health-improving benefits of laughing if you laugh fifteen to twenty minutes a day—every day. And the benefits require "sustained and robust" laughing—not a random giggle or brief ha-ha. Plus, the laughter must also be "mirthful"—as opposed to nervous, cynical, or cruel.

For those of you who, like me, assumed that the act of laughing would be simple, think again. There are over 150 different laughing exercises on the Laughter Online University website, with names like ants-in-your-pants laughter, constipation laughter, and—my favorite—the boss-quit-today laughter (they note on the site that cheering is allowed). Then, on YouTube, there are all sorts of videos demonstrating different laughs, such as the hot-soup laugh and the milkshake laugh.

In this context, laughing—something I considered spontaneous and natural—oddly presents as a skillset that takes practice, like playing the piano or knitting. And while I found all of this interesting from a health and well-being standpoint, I still wondered about the purported spiritual, global-healing aspect.

But then I reminded myself that humor isn't alien to traditional religions. The founder of the Jewish Hasidic movement, Baal Shem Tov, said, "Humor is the thing that ushers a person's mind from a place of constricted consciousness to a place of expanded consciousness." And numerous religious leaders, from Buddhists like the Dalai Lama to Catholics like Mother Teresa to Protestants like the megachurch preacher Joel Osteen, have incorporated laughter and humor into their religious practices.

But there's more here too, and it has to do with ancient Vedic tradition and pooled cosmic energy—which is where the heal-the-world component comes in.

THE LAUGHING YOGA movement has a basis, in part, in the "field theory of global consciousness" and what would come to be called the "Maharishi Effect." It dates back to 1500 BC and originated in India with Vedic rishis, who believed in a universal self (Atman or Brahma) as part of a collective whole, as well as with the Hindu scriptures (the *Upanishads*, *Bhagavad Gita*, and *Brahmasutra*), which taught that one could tap into the collective consciousness through meditation.

The Maharishi Effect predicts that by getting enough people meditating—or perhaps laughing—at the same time, we could, at least theoretically, cause a shift in global consciousness that would reduce violence and increase world peace.

And as ridiculous as this sounded when I first started thinking about it, it's not such a reach to believe that enough meditating or happy, laughing people could cut negative behavior off at the root. (Proponents of the Maharishi Effect even provide some oddly specific numbers on exactly how many engaged people would be needed to heal the world.) But ignoring the specifics of the math, it's certainly hard to argue with the fact that both bad and good behavior have a way of proliferating. Especially when you consider what psychologists call the "spillover effect," whereby our response to one isolated event spills over into another—say, a bad day at work that leads to road rage or a smile that becomes contagious.

But even if you don't buy into the global-consciousness part of the philosophy—or perhaps the highly dubious math—consider this: if there is a collective energy force that we can leverage through a widespread increase in positive behaviors (meditation, prayer, hugs, laughter), it could potentially "spill over" and offset negative behaviors (bullying, violence, crime). As much as there are vicious cycles, there are virtuous cycles too. So it's at least feasible that there could be something to the heal-the-world concept of laughing yoga after all.

*   *   *

THE INTERNATIONAL LAUGHING yoga community, which has groups all over the world, is, by self-definition, a welcoming group. And while I found the whole experience irrefutably and whole-heartedly downright weird, it was also enlightening. When I first made contact via e-mail with the laughing yoga group in India, I got back this: "Hey haha we laugh at 11 pm Eastern US time every night."

It was incredibly simple, and there was no fee. I just had to register with them and then sign on to an audio-only Skype call at the designated time. When I did, their logo—appropriately, a yellow happy face wearing headphones and laughing—popped up on the screen. People were typing short, upbeat messages. (Even though this group originated in India, they were all writing in English.) Emojis were a big thing—but there wasn't any actual speaking. The audio portion was reserved only for laughing, and no one laughed until we were told to begin the session.

THE FIRST STRING of group texts was completely benign, although a little awkward:

- Ho Ho Ha Ha! Good morning from India! (smiley face emoji).
- Hello Vinayak! Are we laughing soon?
- We are laughing in ten minutes.
- I am so happy now.
- We are happy because we laugh.

Having gotten the drift, I jumped in to introduce myself. "Hi! I'm Anjali Ha Ha from New York."

A woman from Texas popped in with, "Thank you I love you."

I was thinking, *Shit! Was that directed at me? What do I say—I love you too? To a perfect stranger? From Texas? On Skype?*

I started searching for an appropriate emoji, hoping that I could dodge her declaration of love with a wink face or flying turkey. Or maybe a beating heart. Or better yet, something confusing and completely random, like a purple frog.

I noticed that this group seemed to prefer emojis that danced or throbbed.

Oddly, despite the wide choice of appropriate emojis, I couldn't find one I liked, so I typed, "Hello ha ha thank you for having me ha ha."

It was the best I could come up with under pressure.

At this point Zia had woken up, and she came into the room and asked what I was doing. If I had been wearing bunny ears or a cape and goggles and attempting to fly, Zia wouldn't have passed judgment; she just would have wanted her turn. So I said, "I'm laughing online with people in India."

As predicted she jumped in with "Can I do it, too?" probably thinking it was no stranger than anything else mommy does these days. Zia then climbed onto my lap and immediately started picking out emojis.

Then we began, and the audio kicked in with a nonstop, overlapping stream of laughter paired with more emojis and random typed comments like "We are so happy because we laugh."

My laugh and Zia's laugh were completely fake and forced. It was surprisingly hard to laugh genuinely on command—especially with no comical stimuli.

Midway through, I started wondering about my laugh, realizing that it was out there in the universe, unattached to its owner, for the first time in its life.

Then I started to wonder if my laugh was attractive.

I know this sounds ridiculously self-conscious, but we rarely put just a single part of ourselves on display. I realized, *I am just a sound track of laughter.* The emojis suddenly took on great import as visual accessories for my audio laugh. I started clicking on even more of them to "dress up" my ha-has, like selecting the right jewelry to enliven a bland outfit.

The only problem was that I had to fight Zia for keyboard time.

Then I started listening closely to the other laughs and thinking about the people behind them and whether they actually looked as I imagined they would based on how they sounded. In other words, I started thinking too much and judging them.

There was a robust, hearty laugh, and I began wondering what that guy looked like. Then I started to wonder if maybe it wasn't a guy at all but perhaps a woman with a deep voice. Then I thought about the laugh that sounded like a baby. I was picturing a six-month-old infant in a bouncy chair laughing his or her head off, but the more I listened, the more I thought that it might be a weird old guy in his basement chained to a radiator.

There were no radiator emojis.

I realized that by thinking way too much, I was undoubtedly negating the whole health benefit of this exercise, and all that overassessment was probably a big part of why my laugh was still so fake ten minutes in.

So I told myself, *Just laugh, damn it!*

The whole idea behind this is to fake it until you make it—like the depression treatment where they tell you to get dressed up, go out and do something festive, and smile even if you don't mean it and might not want to. The point is to simulate and then jump-start happiness. Apparently it begins to feel possible to *really* be happy after *pretending* to be happy. In other words, happiness and laughter are contagious—just like yawning and rudeness and itchiness and negative thinking . . . and the flu.

AND IT WORKED—eventually.

Roughly halfway through, my fake, forced laugh became genuine. I became giddy; my eyes filled with happy/silly tears, and I was laughing mirthfully.

The same pattern emerged with Zia. She started out with a completely forced and fake laugh, but about halfway through she too became genuinely giddy. Then downright hysterical. Then she didn't want to log off.

Or go to bed.

I should have seen that coming.

Someone then typed, "Very good laugh today." Since we were at the end of the session, we sent "laughter energy" to central Italy, which had experienced an earthquake earlier that day. Then we sent laughter energy for peace in the world in general. Then someone asked if we could extend the session for ten more minutes, and the host—and Zia—enthusiastically agreed.

In the end we laughed for close to thirty minutes. It was definitely strange—not showing-up-naked-to-work strange but still uncomfortable and disconcerting. I felt self-conscious for most of it and could only think about how much more awkward this must be in person, when you have to look at each other. Then I thought that, as disconcerting as it was because I couldn't see any of the people I was laughing with over the audio-only Skype call, at least no one could see me either.

I suspect that in person the laughter is much more contagious—I smile, you smile. Plus, in doing the exercises, you engage with each other, doing things like looking deeply into each other's eyes and resting your heads on each other's stomachs—so it's far more intimate when done in person.

ON THE PLUS side, Zia and I had fun.

It was actually nice—like coloring or baking cookies or reading together. But when it was over, we were both wired, and neither one of us could sleep.

People apparently do this laughing yoga thing over Skype at work and in their cars and while cooking. I started thinking about trying it while on a plane, waiting to take off, or in a car in heavy traffic—say, during rush hour on the West Side Highway heading into New York City.

Just put my phone on speaker and laugh my head off.

Then I considered what that might look like to all the other drivers, who would likely be thinking, *How come that person is so happy when she should be miserable just like the rest of us? What is so freakin' funny?*

Then, when the other drivers were looking at me, I could just roll down my window and say, "Hey! I'm in a Skype group that gets together to laugh for twenty minutes, and we are sending out energy to heal the world. Want to join?"

The person in the other car would probably think I was a total nut job. And I am guessing I might get booted off a plane if I tried it there.

But those other drivers would probably be wrong. And the flight attendants, while perhaps justified in their concern, would have miscalculated too.

Because—weird math aside—maybe if enough people were happier and had lower stress, outcomes *could* change on a grand scale. Plus, there are certainly worse ways to spend your time.

NOT READY TO give up, the next day I joined a laughing yoga group in South Africa because the time of the session allowed me to laugh at midday.

It was the same drill. Open Skype. Wait for the call. Introduce myself over the chat box—again with no actual verbal talking. Just like with the India session, just about every chat box entry included a "Ha ha" or "Ho ho ho."

I typed, "Are you all in South Africa?"

Helgahaha said, "I'm in Norway! Ha ha."

Someone else typed, "Banana Kiwi Mango."

I'll admit, that made me smile.

Then someone else typed, "Ho ho. Germany is laughing too."

It turned out that in this session of the South Africa laughing group, only one person was actually in South Africa.

Just like the session originating in India, this one was an emoji love fest. Exploding bombs, red-headed girls, dancing cats and penguins and monsters and all manner of silliness, coupled with comments about healing the world. But oddly, at least to me, there were no jokes or other comedic stimuli beyond the emojis.

Someone typed, "We laugh so hard we become one."

When we started laughing, even though I'd eventually caught on in the previous session, my laughing still felt odd and forced this time too. Then, as I listened to the others' laughter, I noticed a deep male voice and, just like with the group in India, what sounded like a baby. *Another hysterical baby?*

I was thinking, *That can't be . . .*

Then the baby—or whoever it was (think radiator guy)—completely lost it. Total hysteria.

I was thinking, *I'll have what he's having.*

Just like when I laughed with the group in India, my laugh started out sounding fake and put-on, but this time, halfway through, I hit a real dry patch. I felt I couldn't sustain the fake laugh anymore, and since a genuine laugh wasn't coming, I thought about hanging up—but then reconsidered because I decided that would be too rude.

AND THEN IT happened.

Suddenly, I was spontaneously laughing hysterically. Practically in stitches. Right up there on a par with the baby in the bouncy chair or the guy chained to the radiator.

WHEN IT WAS over, I wondered about the deeper level of functionality behind this—about not just the immediate health effects laughing has on an individual but how this might impart some broader good. How does this shared experience impact our beliefs and behavior? Would I be in a better mood if I did this every day? Perhaps be nicer to strangers? Choose a different job? Give more to charity? Would it serve as a reminder of our connectedness and shared humanity?

After all, most of what I was doing and reading about in my quest for spiritual salvation seemed to involve tapping into some form of universal energy and connecting with others—in a manner that promised to change both personal and global outcomes. Think about it: Hugging Amma, Paramji's Para-Tan sounding, Wicca, the Mexican sweat lodge, the dirty medium and talking with the dead. This theme was recurring again and again as I tried more things. These practices weren't promoting servitude to and reliance on a supreme being. They involved redirecting some form of cosmic energy for personal and collective good, something I would have dismissed as hogwash when I started out on this mission—okay, probably total f-ing bullshit—but as I sat there laughing with strangers, I started to wonder.

The impact on my hormones? I got that.

The fake it 'til you make it? I got that, as well.

But the other stuff? Heal the world?

Honestly? I was actually considering that too.

CONSIDER THIS: THE only thing that "laughter critics" could come up with (other than that the whole practice is fundamentally strange) is that any benefits could be nothing more than a placebo effect. But that brought me back to Fay and Kumaré and a giant *so what?* The placebo effect works. It doesn't matter what we use to invoke it, as long as it doesn't hurt anyone.

After all, you'd be hard-pressed to find a downside to laughing more. Plus, it's free.

And, unlike Patrick the Healer, the laughing yoga folks take every one of your calls.

Chapter 10

BURNING MAN
The Playa, Outside Reno, Nevada

This is the part where Anjali hits the road again in search of God and self and answers and goes to the mind-bending, life-altering, clothing-optional, costumes-encouraged, drug-infested, epically strange, definitely unnerving, boundary-pushing social experiment in the desert known as Burning Man.

If you don't know, Burning Man is an annual festival/phenomenon held in a massive encampment called Black Rock City that rises from the white sand of the Nevada desert like a pop-up metropolis; a necklace-shaped, semicircular ring of temporary housing and camps centered on "the Playa," a vast, dry lakebed comprised of cracked alkaline clay.

It's a stunning civic and architectural feat built from scratch each year solely to host an eight-day event. When it's over, parts of Black Rock City are burned in ceremonial fires, and the rest is dismantled and removed without a trace, only to be rebuilt again a year later.

Essentially, it's a city made of magician's flash paper.

And temporary is a big part of the point.

DURING EACH WEEKLONG "Burn," Black Rock City hosts tens of thousands of attendees called "Burners." It's one part art installation, one part rave, one part human experiment, and a whole lot of crazy.

Burning Man is a unique amalgam of art, architecture, healing sessions, lectures, exotic machines, bicycles, tricked-out cars, music, elaborate costumes, and unabashed spontaneity, along with epic dust storms and boundary-pushing excess in all forms imaginable. The Burn has been called "a modern-day hippie drug fest" and "a hedonistic clearing of the head." And there's plenty of debauchery: widespread alcohol and drug use, nudity, and sexual exploits—even sex-themed camps, including the infamous Slut Garden and Orgy Dome.

If anything Burning Man is enigmatic. It is a universe unto itself. It's a pilgrimage and participatory theater overlaid with a hybrid, peace-loving *Mad Max* aesthetic. By design it calls for radical self-expression and self-reliance—two things that are definitely not my strong suits—and there is no commerce. The economy is based on gifting; everyone brings things to share. And in some odd ways it is utopic—if you happen to like hot sand, dust storms, and pyromania and lean toward the no-frills, avant-garde, and edgy.

But to many, Burning Man is much more than that. It's a culture and an identity, a chance to break free from convention and tinker with self—so much so that the experience is hard to categorize and so beloved that many hard-core Burners refer to the other fifty-one weeks of their lives as the "default world."

THE BURN BEGAN in 1986 when Larry Harvey and Jerry James built an eight-foot-tall humanlike structure out of scraps of wood, dragged it to Baker Beach in San Francisco on the summer solstice, and, in ceremonial fashion, doused it with gasoline and lit it on fire. As "The Man" burned that night, a crowd gathered on the beach, and from that experience "emerged a community."

For a whole lot of intangible reasons in the years that followed, that community felt compelled to do it again. And again.

The original eight-foot-tall burning man from Baker Beach has since evolved into a seventy-foot-tall effigy that dominates the Playa northwest of Reno and, just like its predecessors, is ceremoniously burned every year on the second-to-last night of the festival in what very much resembles a pagan tribal ritual. Burning Man has breathtaking artistry and elaborate structures, and at center stage a temple to honor the dead is commissioned, designed, and built each year. That temple is burned on the final day as well. It's a city that self-immolates.

Today Burning Man has a massive global following, attracting close to 70,000 annual attendees, including some high-profile people like Jeff Bezos and Mark Zuckerberg, along with many of my fellow Googlers, including the big guns—Larry Page (Google cofounder and current CEO of Alphabet, Google's parent company), Sergey Brin (Google cofounder and current president of Alphabet), and Eric Schmidt (executive chairman of Alphabet).

As much as Burning Man is about roughing it and radical self-reliance, some Burn in comfort. Keith Ferrazzi—the master networker and founder of the consulting firm Ferrazzi Greenlight—even started a lux-travel ecotourism trip for the C-suite crowd to attend Burning Man in a "certain style." Think Wolfgang Puck's sushi chef and $10,000 for the week.

It's a far cry from the more pedestrian canvas tents, yurts, and RVs that house the masses. There's a chopper for quick ins and outs, a generator, an Airstream decked out with a chef's kitchen, and a couple of water trucks—a supreme luxury in the baking desert sun. Other camps set up elaborate amenities or just signature themes as well: everything from trampolines, to organic juice bars, to meditation, to threesomes.

BURNING MAN COFOUNDER Larry Harvey has called the festival a "petri dish," a "churning scene of interaction," and an "audacious experiment." Drawing parallels with the salons and patrons that nurtured artists like Brunelleschi, Michelangelo, and Leonardo da Vinci, he's even compared the temporary physical and social structure of Black Rock City to the humanist academy the Medici founded in Florence during the Renaissance.

He has a point. The art on the Playa is exquisite. And it enjoys patronage.

Burning Man—the organization—provides some of the teams of artists and architects with stipends for a quarter of the cost of the structures and art projects on display, with the rest of the funds raised by Kickstarter campaigns and individual donations. At the end of the week, all of it is dismantled or burned, which makes the experience and artistry of Burning Man all the more wondrous—a metaphor for the transient nature of life and beauty and the importance of being "present."

While the festival attracts a core group solely for the hedonism and party, others come for something else. Burning Man is more than an art extravaganza set in a free-spirited, postapocalyptic campground; it also offers a chance to break free from all convention, to experience the radical self-expression and self-reliance that Larry Harvey envisioned. This dramatic severing from norms and normalcy promises to prime the brain to unleash the subconscious mind, to push that envelope of self, and to cultivate creative breakthroughs—the kind that just might lead to self-actualization and innovative ideas. The opportunity to tap into this inner energy source and the cognitive gold mine it promises plays a big part in why many in the tech community have viewed Burning Man as the ultimate place to "find answers"—and which is why I wanted to attend.

At its core, Burning Man promises to kindle those coveted and inspired "eureka" life moments as it rattles your creative cage.

OBJECTIVELY SPEAKING, ON the surface Burning Man is everything a religion is not. And yet there are spiritual components to it. Lots of them.

Burning Man has rituals, symbols, ceremonies, and temples and a congregation full of believers, as well as ten clearly stated guiding principles:

- Radical inclusion
- Gifting
- Decommodification
- Radical self-reliance
- Radical self-expression
- Communal effort
- Civic responsibility
- Leaving no trace
- Participation
- Immediacy

Unlike the Ten Commandments or the Five Pillars of Islam, these are more about taking care of the world—and taking the world in—than about being morally correct. But in the end, they serve a similar purpose: they provide comforting guidance and structure to the Burning Man community, along with something concrete to belong to and believe in.

Lee Gilmore, a scholar of ritual and new religious movements, has identified Burning Man as an "important site" in what she calls a "contemporary movement" involved in "reinventing cultural assumptions about what constitutes 'religion.'" And many Burners report having life-altering revelations about the cosmos and inner self—many of them deeply spiritual in nature. Some of them are generated by the abrupt break from convention, others by entheogens—those plants and fungi such as peyote, psilocybin mushrooms, and ayahuasca.

FOR SOMEONE IN my position looking for something spiritually alternative, Burning Man is intriguing for precisely those reasons. If spirituality and religion are about finding meaning and something larger to believe in, if they're about belonging to something bigger than what is here, if they're about ritual and ceremony and community, Burning Man is that for some people. For me, though, I never once thought that The Burn could become my spiritual foundation or fundamental belief system. Rather I wondered whether it could trigger one of those jarring, redirecting, spontaneous Aha! moments that open a pathway to transcendent and spiritual self-discovery.

Larry Harvey's goal in the social experiment of Burning Man is singularly profound: he wants to alter civilization by rebalancing "individual action and collective identity." And that's what religion is, in part. We ask, Where do I end? What part do I play in the larger community? In the universe? Across time? Are we, as is and in our flawed and temporary way, enough? These questions are really nothing more than iterations of those that I knew Zia would be asking:

> Why are we here?
> What is the meaning of life?
> What happens when we die?
> Is there a God?

BURNING MAN IS so hard to categorize and such a different thing to different people that it has been called a bricolage—an improvisational assemblage of odds and ends. And as I grappled to understand it and gathered the courage to attend, time and again I was reminded of the old Indian parable of the blind men and the elephant.

You've probably heard the story. Six blind men in India hear that a large, exotic creature called an elephant has arrived in their village, and they ask to be taken to it. When the men surround the elephant, each ends up exploring a different part of the animal. One man feels the leg, another the ear, another the trunk, and so on. As they all attempt to describe what this creature is, its sheer size and their limited perspectives lead them to different conclusions. That leads to disagreement and arguing as each insists that he is quite certain of his experience. Then a sighted man wanders by and hears the blind men arguing. He stops to tell them that, as hard as it is for them to believe, they are all correct —each has just experienced the elephant from a different, and limited, perspective.

This parable is the foundation for one of the core principles of Jainism—something called *anekāntavāda* (nonabsolutism). Followers of the Jain religion respect the beliefs of others in part because they have learned from the parable of the blind men and the elephant that their own perspectives—even about religious truths— are inherently limited.

And therefore inherently flawed.

Unlike many other religions, Jainism teaches that no single person can have ownership or knowledge of absolute truth. So if you believe and practice *anekāntavāda*, you have no choice but to respect differences. And respect for differences leads to greater harmony.

The list of subscribers to *anekāntavāda* includes Mohandas Gandhi, who relied on it to guide his views on religious tolerance, and me. I grew up hearing the story of the blind men and the elephant and then hog-tied myself to *anekāntavāda* as I traveled the far reaches of the spiritual world looking for answers.

I knew that, metaphorically speaking, Burning Man was an elephant. I knew that, because of its size and scope, everyone's experience at Burning Man is inherently different—and that if I went, I would have my own unique experience too. And that I would have to respect everyone else's and they mine.

Though I had wanted to attend Burning Man for a long time, I had repeatedly put it off, not because the experience would be hard to categorize or disarmingly unique but because I was afraid it would push my boundaries too far and challenge my comfort zones a bit too much—or that I'd just plain hate it and be stuck there.

And I was afraid of being uncomfortable with the nudity and the drugs.

As much as I wanted to open pathways and have a spiritual breakthrough—and as much as I had attempted to in Peru—I don't do drugs. And I don't do naked either—at least not in public.

Then I found myself at a dinner party in New York City, sitting next to an extremely tall, handsome, bearded white man named Michael who was dressed in an Indian kurta shirt, wearing *mala* beads, and smelling of palo santo. He was a highly successful entrepreneur and part-time shaman and married to a woman who was a model and a designer. (New York couples can be intimidating. Really intimidating.) He was also a Burner.

Given his attire, I mentioned to Michael that I was on a spiritual quest, and he invited me to come with him to his camp at Burning Man. The thing was, he explained, our meeting like this was too fortuitous to ignore. Burning Man was only a month away, and he happened to have one space left in his camp and a way for me to get a ticket, even though they had sold out months ago.

"You're coming," he said. "It's settled."

I was tempted—after all, kismet was at the core of many of my adventures.

And as I breathed in the palo santo and took comfort in his Indian guru garb and *mala* beads, I gave Michael a tentative "Okay."

That weekend my husband and I stopped by a party Michael and his wife had invited us to at their home, and I introduced them. "I am the man who is taking your wife to the desert for a week of nudity and drug use," Michael said to Atul, jokingly.

I was secretly hoping that my husband—the sane, rational medical doctor—would find the whole thing untenable and insist that I stay home. He didn't.

Atul thought Michael was great.

He thought his wife was great.

He thought the whole thing was great.

So I e-mailed Michael's friend—who happened to be the CEO of Burning Man—secured a ticket, moved my schedule around, called my friend Megha to make sure she was still going, and phoned to tell my seventy-year-old Indian parents in Chicago that I had a conference to attend over Labor Day weekend. With limited phone service and no Wi-Fi.

I left out the rest of the details. For the obvious reasons.

I then swallowed hard and tried to accept that this was it. That this was my year to Burn.

*   *   *

BUT FIRST THINGS first. I had to make travel plans and pack. I reached out to my Burner friends for suggestions and combined that information with extensive and mildly perplexing online research about what to bring. Each suggested list usually started out with something disarming, like "Definitely bring steampunk goggles and a kiddie porta-potty with disposable bags." Or "No matter what, don't forget beef jerky and a metal cup with your driver's license photocopied onto it. And NO sequins." Or "Whatever you do, make sure you bring two types of earplugs—Oh, and Christmas tree lights! Battery operated Christmas tree lights are really important!"

HERE IS SOME of what I settled on: battery-operated LED lights, a bike lock, a ski jacket, ski goggles and steampunk goggles (options are important), beef jerky (even though I had never tried it before), granola bars, one hundred tiny plastic spray bottles to fill up with water and scented essential oils (my gift to the Playa), sunscreen, lip balm, coconut oil, temporary tattoos from a birthday party favor Zia had lying around, comfortable socks, a headlamp, and drugs (just kidding—but obviously many people pack them).

I ordered most of this stuff on Amazon. As the deliveries piled up inside my apartment door and I contemplated how best to prepare for what was looking more and more like a hedonistic sleepaway camp for crazy grown-ups rather than a spiritual quest, my assistant, who was adjusting my work schedule and had surreptitiously made my travel arrangements, awkwardly whispered to me just about the worst news ever. She said, "Just so you know, Paul is going to Burning Man too."

I looked at her blankly. Then the conversation went something like this:

"Very funny."

"No, really, he's going."

"No, he isn't."

"Yes, he is."

"No, he isn't."

"Yes. He is."

Paul was my boss. (Since I knew Paul was a Burner, I should not have been surprised, and yet somehow I was.) He's the CEO and cofounder of the wildly successful company where I was currently the general counsel, and now he was going to see me riding a child's bike through the Nevada desert decked out in ski goggles and a headlamp, apparently wearing Christmas tree lights and My Little Pony tattoos on my face—and possibly, but not likely, high on some questionable substances. No one wants to think of his or her lawyer walking around the desert for a week dressed like that, let alone like option two—wearing pasties and pantless. Or sitting on a child's potty.

And I certainly didn't want anyone—let alone my boss—thinking about me that way either.

Which was probably exactly why I needed to go to Burning Man in the first place: to get myself fully out of my comfort zone—pasties, blinking tree lights, and all.

SO, I THINK, it's a big place. The dust is blinding. Paul and I will never even see each other. Right?

No such luck.

As if in some cosmic confluence of bad luck and dark humor, Paul and I were booked on the same flight.

> JetBlue Flight 81.
> 7:51 p.m. JFK to Reno/Tahoe.
> Tuesday, September 1st.
> Arrives at 11:08 p.m.

He's an entrepreneur, so Burning Man made him hip and cool. I'm a corporate lawyer, so it just made me pathetic and weird.

Trust me, nobody wants to bump into his or her lawyer at a hedonistic rave.

I BLAMED GOD for this; He, or She, or It had obviously made the universe way too small.

NOT ONE TO pack light, I brought, in addition to most of the stuff on the previous list, the following: eye mask, razor, gym shoes for plane, denim jacket, Manuka honey (chocolate would melt in the heat, and I have a sweet tooth), Ziploc bags, face wipes, flip-flops, Doc Martens boots, water bottle, hat, meal-replacement bars, travel pillow, Elizabeth Arden 8 Hour cream (large tube), travel towel, sinus rinse, bobby pins, rubber bands, hair jewelry, deodorant, baby wipes, Excedrin, cash, Benadryl, hand sanitizer, scarves to cover my face from dust, silver skirt, denim shirt, gold-fringe jacket, sweatpants to sleep in, sweatshirt, socks (two pairs for each day), four tank tops, four T-shirts (two black, two white), two long-sleeve shirts, yoga pants (a fresh pair for the flight to and from Reno), underwear, unitard, ballet leotard, scuba pants, leggings (three pairs), shorts, mumus (three), fanny pack, day backpack, and my Burning Man ticket.

I planned on fitting all of this into two medium-sized duffle bags. Ha!

THEN, INSTEAD OF exhibiting radical self-reliance, I demonstrated radical procrastination—as in leaving the actual packing until literally one hour before I had to leave for the airport and then almost missing my flight. While ill-advised in any scenario, this is especially so when your packing list includes things like a massive ski jacket, steampunk goggles, and a portable potty.

En route to the airport I realized that I had forgotten to pack said ski jacket, which was the only reason that everything else fit into the two bags, and then I came to the conclusion that none of the stuff I was carting with me made me feel the least bit self-reliant or self-expressive, let alone radically so.

Instead, it felt radically cumbersome and radically heavy. And I felt radically overwhelmed. And radically not me. And radically freaked out.

And I was running late. My flight was at 7:51 p.m., and according to Google Maps I wouldn't get to JFK until 7:27. If, after all this, I ended up missing my flight, there'd be a strong argument that I'd done so on purpose. (Legally speaking, all the evidence would point in that direction.)

BTW, I packed the ski goggles, the headlamp, and the LED lights but didn't bring pasties—there was no way I was wearing pasties—or a "kiddie porta-potty with disposable bags." Mainly because I was staying in an RV, not a yurt. The RV had a toilet and a shower.

As I looked out the car window, I thought, *Thank God I'm staying in an RV.* Then I thought, *Thank God Megha is meeting me at the gate.*

WHEN I GOT to the airport, I barely had enough time to check my bags and run to the gate. I found Megha waiting for me, and we quickly boarded the plane. As we headed down the aisle, I concluded that the rest of the passengers must also be going to Burning Man based on their attire—there were too many top hats (this year's theme was "Carnival of Mirrors") and too much ironic facial hair for a normal flight. And the smell, a challenging combo of BO, funk, and patchouli, didn't bode well for me, as we hadn't even taken off yet, and I was already nauseated.

Just when I was thinking that it couldn't get any worse, I saw Paul walking down the aisle. He had passed through the first-class section and was heading my way, eyeing the seat numbers.

I was in 19F.

I'm pretty sure Paul was assigned to 19E, which was one of the few empty seats left on the plane and the middle seat between Megha and me. I came to that conclusion because, after he eyed the seat and then saw us, he gave us a quick hello before flagging one of the flight attendants. She looked at his boarding pass, glanced at

19E, then found him an empty seat a few rows up. (Perhaps there is a God after all.)

WHEN WE ARRIVED in Reno, Megha and I made a midnight run to Walmart for last-minute supplies. Cigarettes (I don't smoke), almond butter, hot sauce, V8 tomato juice, a bag of grapefruits, and caramels. Don't ask. I have no idea why I made those choices.

We then spent the night at a motel near the airport, got the Grand Slam breakfast at Denny's, ate as if it were our last meal, then caught the Burner Express Bus to Black Rock City.

The bus smelled like pee and beef jerky. Way worse than the plane. Beef jerky smells of rotting cow. I resolved to never, ever eat it.

Then I remembered that I had packed some.

A WOMAN SAT behind me on the bus in full conference attendee mode. She had the 157-page Burning Man brochure open and was diligently using a yellow highlighter to mark things of interest.

I hadn't even bothered to open my copy of the booklet, but somehow just having it made me feel better about telling my parents I was going to a "conference."

We turned off the highway at a sign that read "Special Event Turn"—which seemed an understatement.

And they weren't kidding about the dust. Suddenly a dust storm engulfed the entire bus, rendering visibility near zero.

At the entrance the dust cleared, and in some biblical-sized miracle of cellular communication, I had full bars and 3G. I was weirdly disappointed. I was looking forward to being completely off the grid.

First impression: A dusty tailgate.

Second impression: I wanted to leave.

Third impression: I still wanted to leave.

Final impression: Seriously mind-boggling shit.

*   *   *

I HAVE TO explain about the virgins.

First-timers are supposed to ring a bell, get slapped on the butt, and then roll around in the desert sand. A baptism of sorts that's supposed to make you feel included. Somehow I avoided it.

I just got off the main Burner Express Bus, parted ways with Megha as she headed to her camp, climbed aboard a beat-up school bus that delivered me closer to my camp, and started walking the rest of the way as I struggled with my duffels. Michael had e-mailed me that our camp was located at the K-3 coordinates of the Playa grid, which, based on the map and under the circumstances, looked like a long walk from the drop-off point. Then a random guy on a bicycle rode up to me—everyone rides bicycles around Black Rock City—and offered to carry my duffle bags.

I was a bit unnerved.

And not just because he wasn't wearing any underwear. Which I only knew because he also wasn't wearing any pants.

In New York this would have been comical. Nobody offers to carry your bag on the street unless they want to steal it. Or they are crazy. Or hitting on you. And if they do, they're generally wearing clothes.

Then I remembered the gifting ethos—not to be confused with barter—and took him up on his offer. He rode next to me with no apparent interest in stealing my stuff. Or asking me out. Or negotiating the bag carry for a specific trade. He was gifting me this.

This currency of goodwill was going to be hard to get used to. So was the pants-optional thing.

When we arrived at my camp, I was thinking about the structural problems of riding a bike sans anything. He then gave me my bags, and I tried not to glance down as I spontaneously offered him a grapefruit.

Some people gift palm readings, others grilled cheese sandwiches, and others hallucinogenic drugs. I was apparently the grapefruit lady.

Pantless bicycle guy said, "Thank you," and took the fruit. It was an awkward exchange, at least on my end.

He seemed fine with it. I watched as he rode off with my grapefruit into the dust.

THEN I MET the RV.

The brochure from the manufacturer for this recreational vehicle should have said, "Sleeps seven uncomfortably."

I put my stuff inside and changed. Since I don't feel burdened by clothing and would not prefer to walk around scantily clad, I compromised and in a throwback to the sixties—and perhaps a nod to Paramji—decided that my version of radical self-expression would be to take off my bra. For the entire week.

Then I decided to cover my braless body with a mumu (technically it was an Indian caftan, which to the dismay of my husband I often wore as a nightgown). Which basically meant that the whole braless thing would only be known to me.

Which, practically speaking and under the circumstances, I was fine with.

I am apparently so uptight that my idea of going to Burning Man and engaging in radical self-expression involved removing a single item of clothing and then basically hiding that fact from everyone by covering myself in a floral cotton sack. Everyone else was elaborately styled or minimally clothed except for ski goggles, body paint, and maybe a feather headdress.

After landing in Reno the day before, I had texted my colleague Laura and told her that I forgot to bring a coat—everyone had warned me that the nights on the Playa were cold. Laura and her boyfriend were a few of the organizers of the camp Robot Heart and were big into Burning Man. Before we left New York, she had told me that they traveled with a whole trunk of clothes to dress up in. And don't think these are cheesy Halloween costumes. This is radical self-expression with radical effort, and there's a lot of peacocking. Laura texted back, "I have a coat you can use!" She biked over to my camp the day I arrived, carrying a massive, floor-length, white faux-fur coat. Wearing a mirrored minidress, she looked like a sexy human disco ball. I, of course, was wearing what amounted to the Indian version of a 1950s American housecoat, which was, I fully admit, a poorly executed attempt at self-expression, a fact that became patently clear when I saw Laura pull up on her bicycle. As I watched her, in my head I could hear the Bee Gees singing *Stayin' Alive* and had a flash of John Travolta in *Saturday Night Fever*— whereas she likely had a flash of a hopelessly unhip middle-aged Indian woman who looked a bit like Mrs. Roper from *Three's Company*.

Laura gave me the coat. It was white and fake and fabulous. I wore it all week. Over my braless, mumu-ed self. Just putting it on made me feel awesome.

NEXT UP: I met my RV mates.

If my RV mates had come with a brochure, it would have read, "Six thirty-year-old bankers who flew in from Hong Kong for their first Burn, traveling with enough Cheezits and beer to survive the apocalypse."

I didn't end up sleeping in the RV even once, a fact that led my Hong Kong banker roomies to conclude that I was up all night raving.

I hated to ruin my image, but on the last day I fessed up and told them that I had slept each night on a couch in our camp's meditation/healing dome and not in the beaver-licking tent (don't ask), usually tucked in by 11 p.m., using my long, white faux-fur coat as a blanket in the cold desert nights. When I explained this to them (and even though in my own way I was pushing some boundaries), I left out the part about my being wildly and dangerously braless.

My RV mates had a packed agenda—even on day one. They were heading out to TEDx Black Rock. When they invited me to join them, I agreed (mostly because I had no idea what else to do), grabbed my purple and silver Camara bike (which came with the RV and unfortunately was child-sized), and set out in the dusty, hot sun to go to an actual conference in the middle of the desert, which made me feel slightly better about what I had told my parents.

We biked down the makeshift road and past a trapeze act, then suddenly came into a clear, open space enveloped in dust. And as the dust slowly settled, I gasped out loud at the site around me. I was surrounded by a vast, stark landscape dotted with incredible sculptures and people dressed in all kinds of elaborate getups riding bikes around the deep Playa. Then the dust storm picked up again, and they were gone. Just like that.

I kept stopping for a few seconds to get my bearings. The next thing I knew, I'd lost the rest of my group. I was secretly relieved.

I found myself drawn to a sculpture in the distance and just started riding toward it. It disappeared in the dust as I approached, but then another appeared to my left. It was completely disorienting but mesmerizing at the same time. This happened again and again for the next hour as I wove across the Playa on my bike, drawn from one sculpture to the next.

I was starting to get the appeal of this place.

THE DAYTIME WAS whimsical, and Burning Man was beautiful in a stark, exotic kind of way. Later I rode around the Playa with Megha for a few hours, but by the time the sun eventually set, I was just wiped out. Everything kept going, of course, but by 10 p.m. I was feeling a bit overwhelmed by all of it, as well as out of place, like I wished I could go home. Like I didn't want to be riding a child's bike through big sand dunes in the middle of the desert in a long, white faux-fur coat.

I wanted to plot an early escape. Maybe find my way back to Reno in the morning, grab a hotel room and take a shower, then read for a few days until my flight home. Or better yet, book an earlier flight back to New York.

I was caked in dust, and my head hurt from all of it.

Plus, I started thinking about the fact that religious quests were always about denial, suffering, and being painfully spartan. Yet Burning Man was the exact opposite. It was all about extreme indulgence in the physical, tactile, sexual, creative, and artistic human experience—as if the plan here was to reach the same destination, some kind of enlightened place, by going in the opposite direction as everyone else. I headed back to my camp, locked up my bike for the night, looked at the door to the RV, had a flash of what it would be like to be inside with the Cheezits and beer all night—or worse—and then walked to the meditation dome and fell asleep on one of the couches, my head spinning.

The night had a torrid underbelly, and sleeping in the meditation dome was a plan to avoid the darker side of The Burn.

But I felt conflicted and confused.

Burning Man allows people to scratch an itch they can't reach in the default world.

I itched all over but didn't know where to scratch.

I SLEPT ON and off, awoken over and over by sudden bursts of music, sometimes techno and sometimes—bizarrely—Mariah Carey, which was disconcerting but summed the place up perfectly.

The next thing I knew the sun was coming up. I felt a bit safer in the light of day. But I realized that I wasn't scared of "them." I was scared of me.

I'D BEEN IN Black Rock City less than twenty-four hours and was already losing track of time. I felt like I'd been there for days—maybe weeks even. I left the meditation dome, walked back to the RV, and finally peed for the first time since I had arrived, clearly dehydrated.

I changed my clothes, kind of brushed my teeth, and grabbed a can of V8 juice. The RV seemed to be running low on water already, and it looked worse than I had imagined—like something blew up in the Dollar Store. There was stuff everywhere and an obscene amount of processed food and snacks, plus all sorts of clothes and costumes strewn about. These guys had come prepared for a nuclear war—and were not big on tidying up. And based on the number of empties I saw, they were almost out of beer.

Outside, Michael and a crew from our camp had prepared a full spread of scrambled eggs, bacon, croissants, tomatoes, and avocado for breakfast. Plus they had Sriracha—my favorite hot sauce.

As Burners say, the Playa provides.

ACROSS FROM OUR camp was an organic fruit and vegetable camp. Every day they trucked in fresh organic fruits and vegetables and handed them out to passers-by. Remember, there was nothing for sale; everything was gifted. For a single moment I thought I could get used to this bizarre alternative world. Then the lawyer in me started calculating the cost of all this gifting. And the sweeping liability.

After breakfast I joined a group of people I didn't know at my camp who were sitting in lawn chairs with cup holders. I still had my can of V8. It fit perfectly. But I didn't.

Someone offered to fill my V8 can with vodka and then offered me a joint. It was 10 a.m. I politely declined both. Sort of faking a hangover. The mumu helped—I didn't look the type.

I had grown up as one of a handful of people of color in a largely white elementary school. My sister and I had been the only Indian kids in our Catholic school. Staying on the fringes was familiar and comfortable to me. And the other kids liked it that way too. They let us come in but not get too close. That's how I felt at Burning Man. I was there, but I wasn't really one of them.

I WANDERED BACK to the healing dome and just hung out in front. Eventually I went inside and did an astrology session with a tattoo artist/yogi/astrologer from Williamsburg, Brooklyn, named John. Then I decided to go see a clairvoyant, who was about a ten-minute bike ride away.

Apparently she didn't know I was coming and was out for the morning. I decided to skip it and keep riding.

I ran into Megha, and we biked toward the Temple of Promise. En route, we saw more of the insanely incredible artwork. I was living for the moment—practicing the core values of immediacy and participation. I stopped to admire one piece of artwork after another, and Megha and I got separated.

I continued riding around the Playa, disoriented by the low visibility and blowing sand. When the wind finally died down and the dust cleared, I saw something that looked like it had been built and trucked in specifically for me. It was an old-fashioned phone booth—the kind that you step inside with a door that you pull closed behind you. Up near the roof on the outside of this phone booth was a sign that read, "Talk to God."

It was too damned perfect.

INSIDE A WOMAN wearing a band jacket and top hat that sported moose antlers was on the phone. But her outfit didn't faze me in the least. After all, she was talking to God. On the phone.

So I dropped my bike and walked over to the phone booth. No one else was around: there was just me, milling about, and the moose lady, chatting away.

As I was waiting for my turn, the magnitude of this opportunity hit me. When I visited John of God (JOG) and queued up to ask him the big questions, I had panicked, then fumbled and asked easier questions. And JOG had just waved me on my way.

This phone booth to call God standing in the middle of the desert was a manifestation of exactly what I had been looking for. And yet, as I stood in the midday heat with the wind whipping and the dust flying, having finally found it, I realized just how absurd it was to have been looking for it in the first place.

There wasn't going to be a hard line to call God. There would be no mystic or entity to connect me to some supreme all-knowing power, and there would be no simple, clean answers to my questions.

I decided that I should just get on my bike and ride away and not bother to wait my turn and go through the motions of calling some fake God on the phone.

So what did I do?

I waited my turn until the moose lady was finished. And then I called God.

MOOSE LADY FINALLY hung up and stepped out. As I sized her up, I was wearing a unitard and ski mask, so who was I to pass judgment on her antlers and band jacket? She smiled at me, then hurried off. I couldn't help but note that she looked fulfilled—sated even.

I stepped into the phone booth, closed the door, and picked up the receiver. Then, in an ironic tribute to Judy Blume, I said, "Are you there God? It's me, Anjali."

I half expected that, just like JOG, God would say nothing. Maybe even hang up.

But God said, "Hi." In English. In a high, squeaky male voice.

WHICH, FRANKLY, REALLY bothered me. If fake God had to be a guy, I wanted booming, confident, powerful. Or maybe the wholly convincing and spectacularly agendered voice I had heard in my head while meditating in the Andes.

I STARTED TO get nervous. I wondered what fake-phone-booth God thought of my voice. Maybe he thought my voice would be deeper.

Then, before I said anything back, for some reason I started to wonder if he could see me. Not in the omnipresent God way but in the creepy phone-booth guy way. So I looked around but only saw dust and sky.

Then I started to wonder, if phone-booth God could see me, what would he think about the unitard and the ski mask?

Then I wondered what God looked like. And what he was wearing. If he preferred the moose lady's band jacket and antlers to my getup.

Then I wondered if God was naked.

Or if he would like a grapefruit. And what he thought of all of this and of all of us, collectively? Not just the Burners but all humanity.

Burning Man does that to you.

Just as promised, it messes with your head.

AND THEN I went for it. I asked him full-on, "Why are we here? Is there more? Are you real?"

It felt surprisingly good. Once again, I was Dorothy in *The Wizard of Oz*. But I didn't want to pull back the curtain and expose him as a fraud. I wanted him to give me answers.

And I wanted to believe. Really, really badly.

JUST AS I was about to hang up the receiver and run before God had a chance to ruin the dopamine-fueled euphoria/confusion that had flooded my brain, the guy on the other end of the phone line said, "What do you think?"

AND THERE YOU have it. In the Reno desert in this magical, hedonistic, bizarre-o, Oz-like moonscape of Black Rock City, some guy pretending to be God asked me to answer these questions myself.

I had been looking for concrete answers and some irrefutable external validation, and "God" himself told me point-blank that I wasn't going to get them.

Either that or some guy with a high, squeaky voice, who may or may not have been wearing pants, who may or may not have been wasted, and who may or may not have wanted a grapefruit, had essentially told me that I had to find the answers within.

I THEN HUNG up, put on my ski goggles, got on my child-sized bike, and rode off into the desert to find the Temple of Promise.

* * *

YOU GO TO the Temple of Promise to honor those you have lost, and I had carried prayers with me. Some from friends and family and more than a few of my own.

It was a beautiful, serpentine, conical, seashell-shaped wooden structure with ribbed, vaulted arches that towered almost a hundred feet in the air at its opening, then tapered to a sliver of a tail that curved around to create an inner courtyard. Inside the temple there were strips of white cloth on which to write prayers and thoughts, and there were white sculpture trees to hang them on in the courtyard.

I walked through slowly, then copied my prayers down and tied them one by one to the trees.

They fluttered like leaves.

On trees that wept like willows.

It was beautiful and calming.

I wandered back through the temple even more slowly a second time, reading a few of the messages scrawled on the walls. Then a few more. And more and more. People were sending love and prayers and final words to those they had lost. Waves of deep sadness came over me.

Then I started to sob.

Reading those final notes of love and loss and unspoken words was crushing.

I wrote more prayers to distract me and quell my sobs. One for my friend Delphine. For her to be happy and healthy and not always worry.

I wrote one for Rena—another close friend—who asked me to whisper our dear friend and fellow Googler's name and tell him that she understands.

That friend was Google engineer and adventurer Dan Fredinburg, who was climbing Mount Everest just a few months before when a massive earthquake triggered an avalanche, killing him and eighteen other climbers on the mountain and thousands in the surrounding area.

Dan didn't just climb the biggest mountains, he took on all sorts of behemoth challenges. Like making the world a better place.

I was carrying a prayer from Dan's mom too. She asked me and other friends of Dan's to go to the Temple of Promise and tell him that she loved him.

Dan loved Burning Man, and that did me in.

I whispered Dan's name in the Temple of Promise.

I told Dan that his mom loved him.

The phone booth to God made this experience all the more con-crete and important.

Phone-booth God had told me to find the answers myself.

I was trying.

But I knew firsthand that there is no grief bigger than that which spills from a mother's heart.

THE BELIEF IS that the Temple listens. So I whispered those prayers and wishes and names of lost loved ones over and over again.

I looked up from time to time to take in all that was happening around me. Groups of people were huddled over photos in tears. Others were writing messages on the walls to loved ones lost. Little teddy bears were left in remembrance of children taken too young. Army baseball caps were left for those lost at war. There was heart-ache all around me. And it was palpable.

My grief came up again and again, in waves. For all the people I had lost over the years. For the losses that I hadn't processed com-pletely. *For my best friend from high school, Sarah, who died of can-cer right before the start of our junior year of college. And of course for my childhood friend Amani, who was killed on her way to visit me at law school. For my grandparents and aunts and uncles, whom I barely knew growing up because they lived so far away in India, be-fore Skype and e-mail made it easier to close the distance. And for my lost pregnancies.*

THREE OF THEM before I carried Zia to term. I hadn't been able to process the depth of those losses because miscarriage is kept under wraps, like a dirty secret. One you are expected to pick yourself up from.

"Just dust yourself off, and try again," they said.

Everyone well-intentioned but causing pain, pointing out the "bright side."

"The good news is that you can get pregnant. A lot of women can't. Just try again."

"How soon can you try again?"

As if this one, or the one before, or the one before that didn't count.

It's a bright side and a dusting off that doesn't allow you to grieve. But in the Temple of Promise, I found a place and the permission to do so.

I was overcome with harrowing sadness.

There is structure to grief. There is community to grief and purpose. We need closure. All the things that I was missing when I miscarried—I found them here.

Profound loss is never really over, but in the Temple of Promise it felt contained. Finished even.

ON SUNDAY THE Temple of Promise would be burned, and all of these intentions and prayers would go up in smoke in what could only be described as a communal funeral pyre.

A few days later, I would be there as the flames of all that loss licked the desert sky.

LATER THAT DAY I walked out the far end of the temple, squinted into the daylight, and put my ski goggles back on. My eyes were red and burning. I felt depleted. I walked slowly toward my bike and pedaled off into the dust again. I stopped when I saw a strikingly beautiful couple. She looked like a Victoria's Secret model. He looked like he had stepped out of a magazine ad just to join her in this moment. They were wearing matching white face paint, feather head-dresses, and red and white keffiyeh. She had on a white bikini and fur vest. He was shirtless and muscular with leather pants. It looked like a photo shoot, and they were full of joy, as I was crushed by grief.

I overheard them saying they lived in New York, like I did.

AND THERE IT was—the three of us standing side by side, feeling different parts of an elephant.

THE NEXT MORNING I woke up to a view of the sunrise. It was clear and still and beautiful. I dozed, then woke again and stumbled back to my camp—lured by the smell of bacon. This wasn't a dream. We were in the middle of the desert, and again there was bacon for breakfast.

So much for roughing it.

I met lovely people at breakfast, including a young Indian couple, Simran and Gaurav. Simran was a Bronx Science grad who worked in food tech start-ups but was also a Reiki master. Reiki is a Japanese practice developed by a monk, a touch-free "laying" of the hands that adjusts the energy fields of the body. Her boyfriend, Gaurav, was a former art director who had recently decided to become a consciousness rap artist under the moniker "OG 10K." I had no idea what a "consciousness rap artist" was, but he had a gold grill on his bottom teeth that said, "Om mani padme om," in Sanskrit. Once back in New York, they were planning to do a Kickstarter campaign to fund a business to make third-eye-activating spiritual grills out of amethyst. I kept feeling that it was no longer okay to be just one thing.

EVENTUALLY I DECIDED to go for a bike ride to the Playa to see more of the art. Again, I ended up in the middle of an intense dust storm. I was so suddenly enveloped that I decided I should just find my way back to camp, but getting there took ages. I could see only a few inches in front of me, and sections of the road were now covered in mounds of drifting sand. It was like biking through sand dunes on a beach.

I looked the part. I wore ski goggles to protect my eyes from the blowing sand and blinking lights so I wouldn't get run over by the massive art cars that roamed the desert, blasting music as the people on board handed out drinks. I felt like I was beginning to fit in.

I found my way to the refuge of the healing dome. Simran was there and offered to do a Reiki session on me. Though I was a bit ambivalent, I had nowhere else to go. And I felt safe there, so I accepted.

I kept opening my eyes to watch what she was doing, but each time I did she sweetly smiled and asked me to close them again. While she wasn't actually touching me, it was weirdly calming.

Afterward a woman named Lauren gave me a tarot reading. Even though she was a beginner, her reading was pretty spot on. I lingered in the healing dome with a small group; we talked about our time at Burning Man and our hopes and fears for our return to the default world.

Eventually evening fell, and we gathered around a campfire. Someone asked if I wanted to do mushrooms.

As in, magic mushrooms.

As in, one of the psychedelic drugs that promise to open pathways to spiritual awareness and revelations.

And there it was: what I was afraid of—me pushing the envelope. All my life I had feared mind-altering substances. And yet I acquiesced—just like that.

WELL, NOT JUST like that.

I knew something about psilocybin, the active ingredient in shrooms—and not just from Timothy Leary and the Grateful Dead. From researchers at Johns Hopkins School of Medicine, who reported that after they had dosed healthy patients looking for a spiritual experience with psilocybin in a controlled study, the recipients felt positive effects that were still present over a year later. Almost all reported that it was "one of the top five most meaningful experiences" of their lives, with almost half identifying it as "the single most meaningful experience" they'd ever had. They cited transformative increases in self-awareness and compassion.

I could go for that.

Plus, from what I knew, mushrooms aren't addictive, and shamans and medicine men have used them throughout time for healing. Plus, oddly, doing mushrooms here felt safer than doing ayahuasca in Peru—and at first I had been willing to (maybe) try that.

So I sat down with the group of complete strangers and ingested a small quantity—roughly an eighth of an ounce—of *Psilocybe cubensis* brewed in a tea of orange blossom water and honey and waited for my universe to expand and then open up to glorious, undeniable, sustainable transcendence.

It didn't.

The mushrooms just made me sleepy. Really, really sleepy.

No bright colors, no rainbow halos or sense of peace or greater connection to the cosmos, and certainly no heightened spiritual awareness.

What about in the weeks that followed? No Aha! flash of crystalline clarity. No prolonged sense of wellness. And certainly no God moment.

I kept looking but coming up empty.

THE NEXT MORNING I woke up in the healing dome again and headed back to the RV, where I found a note on the whiteboard for me from two friends from New York, Jeffrey and Satya, asking me to come to their camp by 9:50 a.m. for a surprise. So I rode over and found that not only had they made chocolate-chip and blueberry pancakes and eggs and bacon (what was with all the bacon?) for their camp but were also inviting me on a helicopter ride around the Playa.

Paolo, the chopper pilot, was on call for the wife of a wealthy Burner in case she felt like leaving or wanted to spend a few hours in San Francisco or Reno, to "take a break," and he was killing time by gifting other people rides above the Playa. And because the universe was a strange and generous place, Jeffrey and Satya decided to extend the invitation bestowed on them to me.

From up above, Black Rock City was breathtaking. This vantage gave incredible perspective to the magnitude of the effort that went into this place, as well as the massive organization and planning involved. But I ignored that; I thought about the fact that all of it would be completely gone in a few days.

We're here, then we're gone too. There is beauty in that. It's humbling and simple.

And it's exactly why we need to know that there is more.

AFTER WE LANDED the three of us took a long bike ride around the Playa to find friends and visit with healers and meet Marian Goodell, the CEO of Burning Man. When we found her, she was in full event-operations mode. She had a clipboard with highlighted documents and a walkie-talkie. She said she wanted to get in touch with me when I got back to the default world to talk about my impressions.

I wouldn't know where to begin.

THE NEXT DAY, I was laying on the giant trampoline in our camp when I looked up and saw two people dressed all in white emerge from a nearby RV. The woman was in full white lingerie, garter belt, corset, elaborate feathered gold headdress, and a white-leather bomber jacket. The guy was in a white-silk tux vest and pants and spats. They looked beautiful but were clearly looking around for someone, so I asked if I could help. They told me that they were getting married at sundown, and the photographer, who was supposed to be there, hadn't shown up. They explained that my camp was the initial meeting spot for the ceremony, which would be held at the temple. It was magic hour. I had a small camera back in the RV, and while hardly a substitute for a professional, I offered to help however I could.

As all the other guests started to assemble, Michael, who would be the officiant at their wedding, emerged from his yurt wearing an elaborate getup, including a gold turban.

The driver of the art car that would take us to the temple told us that his Playa name was Jyoti. Jyoti was my mom's eldest sister's name, and she had died a few years before in India. As I was thinking, *What are the chances of that?* I asked him the genesis of his Playa name. He said, "There's an app."

He pulled out his phone and asked me a few questions, hit some keys, and then proclaimed that my Playa name was Joy, spelled J-o-i.

Somehow that made sense to me, even though very little else about this entire Burning Man experience did.

The wedding was one of the most beautiful and touching ceremonies I had ever been to.

This place held nothing but contradictions.

I MADE IT to Saturday and the burning of The Man. Even though The Man had been towering over the Playa all week, I could not have been prepared for what was coming next. He was attached to a platform, lit with colored lights, and loaded with fireworks and would be doused with gasoline and set ablaze.

We stood several hundred yards away around the perimeter. A ring of fire dancers performed as tens of thousands of people jockeyed for a good place to watch.

This was it.

The Burn.

Art cars were driving around the Playa blasting techno music that enveloped us from behind. Then the fire dancers suddenly stopped, took grand bows, and wrapped up their performance.

A hush came over the crowd.

And then there was fire. Like I'd never seen before.

AS I WATCHED The Man burn, and the following day as I watched the Temple of Promise burn, I knew this to be true:

We are temporary.

And spectacular. In life and in death.

There is an irony to the juxtaposition of our extreme importance and our complete irrelevance.

And there *is* more and it *is* glorious.

I KNEW THIS to be true, too:

We are all blind men feeling our way around an elephant.

And while I envy the absolutists, for me there is no answer there. Finding a spiritual home will require *anekāntavāda*.

I LEARNED THREE more things in the desert as well:

For many of us, our spirituality will be like Burning Man: a bricolage, a tapestry of odds and ends, an assemblage of religious beliefs and spiritual practices pasted together in a recombining.

Finding God requires radical self-reliance.

And spirituality isn't something one can gift.

Chapter 11

VIPASSANA MEDITATION
Barre, Massachusetts

The goal of meditation in all its varied forms is a bit of Eastern-inspired DIY brain remodeling, the viability of which is based on *neuroplasticity*. The fact is that we can structurally change our brains—increase the thickness of the prefrontal cortex and grey matter as well as rewire our neural pathways—as we improve cognitive function and alter our mind-set and perspective through mental conditioning. While each meditative practice approaches that remodel a bit differently, Vipassana literally means "to see things as they really are." And the goal is to do just that—to see things as they are—through rigorous meditative practice in order to reach what is called "purity of the mind."

Vipassana, or mindfulness, meditation uses a technique taught 2,500 years ago by the Buddha—Siddhartha Gautama—as a way to train our minds to accept our thoughts and experiences without encumbering them with either positive or negative emotions. An itch, for example, isn't annoying as hell; it's just an itch. And an aching back is just that—nothing more. Framing things in this manner levels out the ups and downs of daily life, changes our focus, and paves the way to greater happiness as we achieve what Buddhists call equanimity, or even temperament. The idea in Vipassana meditation is to acutely self-observe—often to an excruciating degree—as a means of self-transformation.

When it's done correctly, three things will happen.

First, we'll feel calm and centered, which actually can lower our blood pressure and stress hormones. Second, the nonstop thoughts and ruminations that go on inside our heads—amusingly referred to as "monkey mind"—will cease, and we will achieve mental stillness. This marks the beginning of the end of both wanting and wanting things to be different. And third, from there our worldview, and therefore our behavior, will change.

A typical training course for Vipassana meditation is a ten-day retreat held in almost complete silence, with ten to twelve hours a day spent in mindful meditation. The premise behind the silence is that if we are enveloped in external silence, we'll be better equipped to cultivate what Buddhists call noble silence—the internal quieting of the mind that brings peace and calm and is the route to greater concentration and deeper awareness, which will eventually enable us to create our own "spiritual refuge."

HERE WAS THE problem with this for me: as much as I wanted the spiritual refuge of a still mind, ten days of silence is a tall order for a highly social extrovert and prolific talker like myself. I'm the kind of person who fills any awkward silence, even if that means reverting to nonsensical rambling. So much so that I've often speculated that, if under police interrogation, I would likely keep on talking until I had confessed, not just to the crime in question, but also to all the unsolved crimes in the country.

On the flip side, meditation was not a new concept to me, and I liked it. A lot.

I'd been practicing transcendental meditation (TM) for years—in fact, it's one of the few things that I've stuck with consistently. TM makes me feel calm and centered and helps me concentrate.

But TM is both effortless to learn and easy to practice—it takes only twenty minutes twice a day and can be done virtually anywhere—whereas Vipassana meditation is often described as painful mental and physical torture.

So the challenge for me was that, while I wanted to try a Vipassana retreat, I was afraid of the obvious: the physical and mental trauma of ten days spent in silence.

And it's not just the not talking. Vipassana meditation is taught in a silent bubble of broader isolation where you are away from family and work, with no music, television, computers, or cell phones. There's also no reading, writing, or eye contact either. And since you're cocooned with a large group of other people in an artificially silent environment, there's limited ambient noise as well.

In other words, this is no cabin in the woods where you're by yourself in silence that feels natural. It's superimposed group silence—which in my book had to be extra intense.

Zombie apocalypse intense.

But there was an even bigger problem. If I decided to do a silent meditation retreat, I had to consider that when it's quiet—as in really quiet, with none of life's normal distractions—I'd be alone not only with all my fellow meditators but also with the last person on earth I'd ever choose to be alone with.

Me.

Which is the entire point, but a hellishly scary proposition nonetheless.

To make matters worse, my only reference for Vipassana meditation was Julia Roberts in the scene in *Eat Pray Love* where she's sitting in the garden at the ashram in India as she's being eaten alive by mosquitos and isn't supposed to swat at them or even move. While she attempted to work through it, until she had mentally reduced this discomfort and suffering to "just" a swarm of mosquitos, I was scratching myself wildly the entire time on her behalf.

And yet, while on the surface the no talking and the solitude-practiced-as-a-team-sport scared the crap out of me, if I was to be perfectly honest, in a small way, it also had some appeal. After all, I live in New York City, which is constantly noisy in a very affronting way.

Plus, as a working mother, I have little refuge from the noise, so my life is, by its very definition, loud—often deafeningly so.

And, with our smartphones, we're never alone, and our minds are never quiet anymore, even at times when just a few years ago they would—or at least could—have been.

On top of all of that, if they gave Olympic medals for monkey mind, I would bring home the gold. That means it's not only noisy in my external environment; there's a racket going on inside my head all the time too. So, despite all my fears, I considered just how debilitating all this noise is and, in a moment of unbridled optimism and overblown confidence, signed up for a ten-day silent retreat, thinking, *If Julia Roberts could do it, so can I—after all, how bad can it be?*

I WOULD LIKE to report that my friends and family had a range of reactions when I told them what I was doing, but that wouldn't be true.

Most of them just started laughing. Hysterically.

Atul thought I had finally gone off the deep end and flatly declared that I wouldn't last. So I asked him how long he thought I could make it. With a note of urgency, he said, "You better find a twenty-minute retreat. I think you can handle not talking for twenty minutes."

You've got to love a husband with that much confidence in his wife.

And then he proceeded to tell me a long story about how even he wouldn't last more than two hours. Since Atul's even chattier than I am, I was mildly annoyed that he thought he would last longer than I would. I was—admittedly—being somewhat defensive, but I told him that I thought he wouldn't last longer than ten seconds. Then I said, "Go ahead. Try not speaking. See how long you last."

He said, "But . . . "

See? One second.

WHEN I TOLD Zia that I was going to a retreat where you can't talk for ten days, she asked, "How will you go to the bathroom?"

First, I thought, *Okay, at least she didn't laugh*, and then I tried to clarify, "I can't speak for ten days Zia, but I can go to the bathroom." She said, "How?"

Now I was really confused, and then I starting thinking, *If I can't even answer that simple question, how on earth will I tackle the big ones?*—which was unfortunately becoming the theme song of my life.

Luckily, Zia set things straight by clarifying: "How will you ask to go to the bathroom?" With great parental relief, I realized this was actually quite logical. In Zia's world of kindergarten, you have to ask permission before leaving class to go to the bathroom, which would actually pose a daunting problem at a silent retreat full of five-year-olds.

Then I told my friend Sally. Big mistake.

When she stopped laughing, Sally told me that years ago, on a five-day Vipassana retreat, she had her wife bust her out on day two. She had taken her contraband cell phone into a closet and texted her wife an SOS. To help her save face—obviously she wasn't being held captive by Buddhist meditators—her wife called the center, faked a family emergency, and broke Sally out of there three days early.

Sally told me quite emphatically that ten days was "pure insanity," especially for my first try. "You'll get the idea after a few hours. Don't torture yourself."

I said, "But I signed up already."

She said, "Trust me. Un–sign up."

I said, "But Julia Roberts did it in *Eat Pray Love*. And she's chatty and she shut up for much longer than ten days."

Then Sally said, "And she married Javier Bardem too."

As in, not going to happen, Anjali.

I was about to say that Julia Roberts didn't actually marry Javier Bardem or even attend a real silent meditation retreat—at least not the one in the movie—but decided that wasn't the point.

So I full-on panicked. Then I Googled all the mindfulness centers within driving distance of Manhattan that offered mini, truncated Vipassana retreats. While there were, alas, no twenty-minute programs, I did find a five-day program at the Insight Meditation Society in Barre, Massachusetts. I thought, *Perfect. Sign me up.*

And then I heard Paramji's voice in my head, and he was, once again, saying, "Not so fast, Bhu."

THERE WAS A waiting list.

I could understand a waiting list for the new iPhone or an elite college. But a waiting list to not talk for five days?

Really?

YEP. REALLY. I was number eight on the list. So I waited.

For weeks.

Then I got an e-mail saying that I had been bumped up to the fifth slot.

I sent an excited e-mail back saying that I would keep my fingers quietly crossed—which I thought was kind of funny—but got no response.

I then guessed that silent-meditation humor wasn't a "thing." (I was wrong, but more on that later.)

A week before the retreat I got an e-mail telling me that a slot had opened up, and I actually found myself fist pumping while yelling, "Yes!"—like I was holding the ball in the end zone at the Super Bowl. This wasn't because my competitive side was coming out but because of the abject fear that had been building in my head about what might happen if I actually went on the ten-day retreat I had scheduled—a reservation I still had time to cancel—undoubtedly to the delight and fist pumping of someone on that retreat's waiting list.

At the time, I was wholeheartedly convinced that this slot opening up was a sign from above, a cosmic acknowledgment that there was no way on earth I would be able to keep my mouth shut for ten whole days. After all, as so many of my loved ones had pointed out, even five days on a word-free-keep-your-mouth-shut diet was going to be a challenge for me.

But I reminded myself that before Vipassana there was transcendental meditation—at least for me.

* * *

TM IS PRACTICED two times a day for twenty minutes while sitting comfortably with your eyes closed repeating a (secret) mantra—a word or sound that has no meaning to you (say, *kirim* or *iem* or *shiring*)—chosen for you by a TM teacher and presented in a prayer ceremony. The concept is that as you get lost in the mantra, all the external and internal "noise" is blocked out and doing so allows you to "transcend." First, sinking deeper into the repetitious sound and vibration of your mantra and then into an altered state of consciousness.

TM was founded in India in the 1950s by Maharishi Mahesh Yogi, and it tipped mainstream—and leaned decidedly west—in the late 1960s when the Beatles met Maharishi in England and then followed him to his ashram in Rishikesh, India, to study. TM's appeal—both then and now—lies in its Eastern roots, its promise of spiritual connection, and its role as a gateway to what followers of TM believe is an "infinite field of creative energy."

The Beatles were disciples of the Maharishi for eight months in the late 1960s, at which point they had some differences and parted ways. But the end result of their TM experience was a prolific work of creative genius, namely the White Album, which is proof positive to many that TM does, in fact, provide access to a vast pool of creative energy.

TM has millions of followers around the world and is often taught in schools and to at-risk populations—like veterans dealing with posttraumatic stress disorder, prisoners, and the homeless—as a means of lessening stress and aggression and improving concentration. And there's significant scientific evidence that it's effective. The film director and screenwriter David Lynch was so enamored with the practice that he set up the David Lynch Foundation in 2005 as a nonprofit to raise funds and awareness of TM in order to teach it not just to individual clients but also to those at-risk groups for reduced fees—or free.

But while a whole lot of people swear by the technique—Jerry Seinfeld, Russell Brand, Martin Scorsese, Ellen DeGeneres, Lena Dunham, Clint Eastwood, Dr. Oz, and Howard Stern (and me)— TM has its critics as well. Some, like the state of New Jersey, find it too close to a religion. Others perceive it to be a form of hypnosis. Some even declare it to be psychologically dangerous. TM has also been criticized for its commercialization. Certain organizations charge what some deem excessive fees—between $1,000 and $2,500—"just" to receive a "secret" mantra and lessons on how to repeat it while sitting still. The Maharishi himself amassed a fortune—reportedly $3 billion, based on some sources, as of the 1990s. So, many of these critics think that, yes, TM might work, but any practice that involves clearing your mind and resting calmly for twenty minutes twice a day—say, going for a gentle walk or sitting on a park bench—would lower your blood pressure and stress too, and for a whole lot less money. And the truly pissed-off say, "I did it. Here's my secret mantra. Now go repeat it for twenty minutes. Lesson over. You just saved two grand."

Then there's this red flag about TM as well: according to the Maharishi University of Management—TM's mothership—by tapping into "the unbounded field of creative intelligence" that is "the source of everything in the universe," TM practitioners are able, at least theoretically, to access the unlimited universe of bliss and energy not only to produce works of genius like the White Album but also to allow the body to defy gravity in something called "yogic flying."

First stage: springing or an upward bounce.
Second stage: hovering. As in levitation.
And the third stage: actual flying.
Like Superman or a 757.
Some critics call it "butt flying." Most laugh.

ON TOP OF the potential for practitioners of TM to individually defy gravity and fly, there is something else called the Maharishi Effect, which you might remember from the laughing yoga chapter. The premise is that if a large international fleet of butt-flying yogis were to reach critical mass while simultaneously springing and levitating, they could—in a similar fashion to the laughing yoga practitioners—potentially generate a cosmic force of massive, aggregate, communal good chi.

Chi, of course, is the energy of the universe.

Enough good chi, in fact, to generate a force sizable enough to change the temperament of the planet.

I am not making this stuff up.

THE PUNCH LINE, of course, is—craziness aside—I love TM. Zia has been practicing it since she was four years old. And it's the one thing in all of what I've been doing on this quest that Atul was willing to try with me.

There's a zinger there too. Atul didn't learn and start to practice TM because as a medical doctor he understood the cardiac and mental health benefits—which are profound. For example, those who practice meditation, including TM, even at-risk groups like prisoners and alcohol and drug users, experience not only lower blood pressure and stress levels but also promising improvements in behavior. Over time those who meditate lose less gray matter and improve cognitive function. And doing just three days of mindfulness meditation has been shown to improve biomarkers for systemic inflammation—indicators of disease—a benefit evident even four months after the meditation ceases.

What does my husband, the interventional cardiologist, do when faced with this compelling scientific data on the comprehensive health benefits of meditation? Of course, he recommends it to his patients and learns and practices TM himself.

But, in his case, he practices solely for the purpose of improving his golf game.

He wanted to beat his friends. And it worked. Thanks to the David Lynch Foundation, my husband's 2011 biannual excursion to play golf in Scotland was his White Album. He won—for the first time. By a lot.

SO HOW DOES TM differ from Vipassana meditation?

In a television interview with David Frost, John Lennon said, "Maharishi said . . . that [TM] meditation is like dipping a cloth into gold. So you dip it in and you bring it out. If you leave it in, then it gets soggy. If you sit in a cave for the whole of your life, then you'll get a bit soggy. So meditation is like going in and coming out, in and out—for however many years."

And while that is decidedly true about TM—you dip in and out—the Vipassana silent meditation I was about to embark on is all about getting soggy.

HERE'S WHY. REPEATING a mantra for twenty minutes twice a day (dipping) is a whole lot different from practicing ten to twelve hours of meditation daily for five to ten days in physical and mental discomfort and almost total silence (getting soggy). The bottom line is that TM is relatively easy to master and Vipassana is freakishly hard.

And TM and Vipassana have other fundamental differences. Whereas TM is about completely suppressing all our thoughts in order to remove all distractions as a means of slipping into an alternative level of consciousness, Vipassana meditation is about facing our thoughts, examining them in excruciating detail, and then diminishing their power over us as a means of altering our perspective.

Unlike in TM, in Vipassana meditation there's no mantra; rather you focus intensely on being present and acutely aware. That hyperawareness is first cultivated by focusing on breath and breathing and then on what is called "body scanning." Body scanning involves moving your focus incrementally and sequentially from your toes to your head with intense concentration on each body part as you experience each sensation, both pleasant and unpleasant, in succession—for hours on end.

Beyond those distinctions, the similarities between the two meditative practices are evident. Both TM and Vipassana use a distraction device. In TM, it's the mantra. In Vipassana, it's hyperfocus, first on breath and breathing and then on "body scanning." But just as you learn to focus your attention on every detail of your physicality in the present moment, you then learn to apply the same interested-curiosity-with-no-judgment approach to each of your thoughts as they pop into your head.

In function, both are vehicles for "transport." In the case of TM, the end goal is to block out everything else in the world so you can access a deep sense of calm and that alluring infinite pool of creative energy. In Vipassana, the end goal is to find calm or stillness as well, but by confronting your physical sensations and thoughts head-on.

SO THEY ARE essentially two different routes to the same place.

For example, TM likely helped Atul's golf game because it trained his brain to quickly access greater concentration—an "unbounded state of restful alertness"—even when he wasn't meditating. And increased focus and concentration leads to all sorts of good things even more important than a lower golf score.

Here's why Vipassana meditation would also have likely helped Atul at golf. If he were mentally trained to accept and experience things for what they are—say, he just hit the ball into the rough—without attaching emotion and judgment to them, then instead of thinking, *What an awful shot, I suck at golf, and I'm never going to win*, he would be able to bypass that thinking completely and simply focus on his next shot. The idea is that dwelling on and assigning negative value to past performance can hinder our performance going forward. This means that while we can't change the fact—he hit the ball into the rough—we can change how we experience it, which in turn changes future behavior, responses, and outcomes.

A pretty compelling argument for meditation in one form or another, if you ask me.

*   *   *

THE IRONY OF having to tell everyone that I was going to a silent retreat wasn't lost on me. I had to contact (practically) everyone I knew to tell them I would not be contacting them. Then, worried about how no contact with Zia for five days would affect her, I prerecorded ten WhatsApp voice messages for her and sent them to Atul's phone: one for each morning and evening I'd be gone. I also left her two written notes for each day: *Have a great day! Don't eat too much ice cream! I love you! Don't eat too much ice cream!* When I got back home, Atul told me that Zia had been gobsmacked and dazzled—after all, she knew I was at a silent retreat. And when Zia asked Atul how I got her the "magic" voice messages each day, he told her that she had a "magic mama." (I have to say, that comment alone made this whole experience— and quite possibly my entire life—worthwhile.)

THE NIGHT BEFORE I left I couldn't sleep and was up late with pre-first-day-of-silent-meditation-school jitters. Then, in a late-night rookie move, I made the mistake of Googling "Vipassana" and "silent retreat," which yielded hundreds of first-person survivor accounts, both those posted on personal blogs full of typos and grammatical mistakes and quite a few in respected publications like *VICE* and *Slate.*

Everyone described the first couple of days as torture—everything hurt, everything was uncomfortable. And reading those accounts in rapid succession doused those night-before-the-first-day-of-silent-meditation-school jitters with gasoline and lit them on fire.

People reported becoming desperate. A few plotted escape strategies, and some even reported having disturbing psychological episodes—which of course only heightened my fears about being completely alone with my thoughts. The only good report I could find about the first few days came from a woman who wrote about how she distracted herself with elaborate sexual fantasies about one of her fellow meditators at the retreat—a guy wearing baggy blue sweatpants with whom she could neither speak nor have eye contact.

On the plus side, the consensus seemed to be that if you pushed through, by day three you started to settle in, and by day four you might actually be okay. By day five, you might be in deep meditation—but only if you're an early bloomer. Some suggested that on day six you might have sweeping epiphanies.

Then, according to the cyber world of survivors, the hard work and suffering paid off: day seven became otherworldly. Day eight even more so. By day ten you're in a state of blissful, serene peace that you never imagined possible. A few even reported not wanting to leave.

So, as I sat there in bed late at night staring at my computer screen, it became apparent that this presented a few obstacles for me. Mathematical obstacles.

By cutting my visit from ten days to five, I had basically signed up for the torture but lopped off my chances of reaching blissful, serene peace and epiphanies of otherworldly proportion. *Thank you, Atul and Sally.*

Feeling overwhelmed and mildly defeated, right before I fell asleep I listened to a dharma talk by Rebecca Bradshaw, one of the teachers I would have at the retreat, and it made me feel much better. Calm and optimistic even.

Rebecca has a very soothing and funny nature. She reminded me of my favorite art teacher in junior high school, who was a little bit kooky but so much cooler than anyone else I knew in the seventh grade. In this talk Rebecca recounted a story of a woman visiting the Rocky Mountains. While reading a Colorado Division of Wildlife pamphlet on what to do if you encounter a bear, this woman concluded that the advice was just as well suited for mindful meditation as for walks in the Colorado woods. Because, she said, "Thoughts were a lot like bears." As she continued reading the pamphlet, she substituted the word "thought" for the word "bear" each time it appeared. In doing so this woman came up with an endearing and comical perspective—that negative thinking and all those ruminations that we put ourselves through can be just as threatening as a grizzly.

Here's an excerpt:

> Learning about ~~bears~~ thoughts and being aware of their habits will help you fully appreciate these unique animals in the habitat in which they live.
>
> What to do if you meet a ~~bear~~ thought:
>
> There are no definite rules about what to do if you meet a ~~bear~~ thought. ~~Bear~~ Thought attacks are rare compared to the number of close encounters. However, if you do meet a ~~bear~~ thought before it is time to leave the area here are some suggestions:
>
> First stay calm. If you see a ~~bear~~ thought and it hasn't seen you, calmly leave the area. Stop. Back away slowly while facing the ~~bear~~ thought. Give the ~~bear~~ thought plenty of room to escape. Wild ~~bears~~ thoughts rarely attack people unless they feel threatened or provoked. Speak softly. This may reassure the ~~bear~~ thought that no harm is meant to it . . .
>
> Don't run or make any sudden movements. Running is likely to prompt the ~~bear~~ thought to give chase, and you can't outrun a ~~bear~~ thought.

As I fell asleep, I found comfort in the fact that there is silent-retreat humor after all, as well as in the fact that the goal of Vipassana meditation is to teach us how to observe our thoughts in a clinical and objective manner—to stare down the ~~bears~~ thoughts and remove their ferocity. And that made me feel optimistic. How wonderful would it be to encounter thoughts in the natural habitat of our minds—and be able to just walk away, not only unharmed but also empowered?

THE NEXT MORNING I frantically made a large number of completely unnecessary phone calls, e-mails, texts, and tweets, clearly gorging before the communication fast.

Then later that afternoon, walking to my car sipping the last cup of coffee I would have for five days, I noticed a friend's husband across the street. When I realized that, other than the garage attendant, he would likely be my last verbal contact, I started to head over to him—almost jogged, in fact—just so I could talk to him.

And then I realized that he appeared to be with another woman. I wasn't positive that I saw anything definitely incriminating, but something felt terribly wrong in my gut seeing him entering a hotel with his hand on this woman's shoulder—so I looked down and rushed past, praying he hadn't seen me.

Faced with the fact that I would now probably spend the entire five-day retreat worried about whether I should tell my friend what I had seen, I recognized that I was face-to-face with a very threatening ~~bear~~ thought that would likely leave me swinging from vine to vine with my monkey mind in overdrive.

As it dawned on me that unless I called my friend right now, I couldn't tell her for the next five days, once again something Paramji had said flashed through my head: *This is not on you, Bhu. Mind your business.*

That statement was instantly liberating—shockingly so—in that it became perfectly clear that I would be well on my way to a better life if I could just learn to do three things:

1. Back away slowly while facing a ~~bear~~ thought.
2. Mind my own business.
3. Shut up.

LATE FRIDAY AFTERNOON:
ARRIVAL

The three-and-a-half-hour drive turned into five because I was an hour late leaving my apartment, and there was massive traffic on I-95. En route I stopped for a Big Mac because, in my effort to leave the city on time, I had skipped lunch. Then I had to stop to chuck the garbage since showing up at a Buddhist retreat with a McDonald's bag in tow seemed reprehensible. Or at least ill-advised and uncivilized. Possibly even sacrilegious, even though it was a Big Mac sans the meat. Growing up, that's what my sister and I ate whenever we went to a McDonald's, and it was a habit I'd stuck with on the rare occasion McDonald's was my only option for food.

It was basically a bun. Okay, a sesame seed bun with special sauce, lettuce, cheese, pickles, and onions.

That missing beef was a powerful metaphor for my childhood. The fast-food chain Wendy's had a television commercial where a little old lady goes to a competing fast-food restaurant and, peeking under the bun to find a woefully inadequate patty, asks, "Where's the beef?"

For an Indian girl with vegetarian parents trying to embrace American fast food, it's in the trash.

AT ORIENTATION I met a woman who came to the center twice a year. She gave me the lowdown like we were twelve-year-olds at summer camp. She said I should sneak food into my room for the evenings in case I got hungry. Then she gave me specifics on what food items were easiest to hide in a napkin. (Later I saw her stashing a slice of bread in her bag.)

Then someone handed out the schedule. Just as promised it was pretty much nonstop meditation for twelve hours each day.

Mixed in with all that meditation, the teachers explained, were yoga, guided meditations, and short group sessions where we were allowed to speak and the staff checked in to see if anyone had any problems or questions. And as I looked around the orientation room, I noted about a hundred other attendees. I thought, *I'm nervous. I've never been removed from all the grounding and distracting identity markers of family, friends, home, and career.*

THAT EVENING WE had the first of the dharma talks given each night at 7:30 by one of the retreat teachers, in which he or she shared spiritual insights from the teachings of the Buddha. This particular talk was given by Rebecca Bradshaw—the same teacher who had given the "bear thought" talk that I had listened to the night before online. This one was about setting intentions; she encouraged us to just "let it happen." To allow yourself to "be you." Nothing more. It was lovely.

Next, the staff led us through some chants before we officially began our silence. They also described *Anjali mudra*, a hand posture commonly used in yoga for the opening and closing of class as well as in some postures. *Anjali* is a Sanskrit word that means "to offer" or "to salute," and *mudra* means "seal." *Anjali mudra* is meant to look like a lotus, the idea being that it might bloom one day. I took this as a divine sign that I was in the right place. And that one day I might bloom too.

WE BEGAN OUR five days of silence following the dharma talk. I was in my room by 9:30 p.m. Before bed I ate a stashed clementine and drank a cup of ginger tea.

Then I made my bed. We had to bring our own twin-sized bedding from home, so I'd brought Zia's favorite hot-pink striped sheets. It felt like I had a little piece of the person I loved most in the world with me as I embarked on finding myself.

SATURDAY: DAY ONE

Comforting pink sheets aside, I didn't sleep much. I kept tossing and turning, worried that I'd sleep through my alarm. The irony is that you can't sleep through an alarm if you don't actually sleep.

On a positive note, the 6:00 a.m. meditation was nice, apart from some upper back pain, but I found a position with a couple of pillows and a chair with a back that seemed to do the trick. It allowed me to subtly shift and lean back when sitting upright got to be too much.

At the end of the session the teachers asked if anyone wanted to give up his or her cell phone. I was using mine as a clock and alarm, so I wanted to keep it.

Okay, that's only partly true.

Honestly, it was a whole separation thing I had with my cell phone.

But they made a big ceremony of it. Holding up an oversized envelope, Rebecca suggested that people ceremoniously drop their cell phones into it, explaining that she would deposit it in a giant wicker basket at the front of the room. When the first person stepped up and dropped her phone in, it had all the drama of the choosing ceremony in *Divergent*. All three teachers and a number of the other students bowed their heads to the cell phone–less fool, saying, "Sadhu sadhu sadhu." *Well done well done well done.*

In all, only one other person gave up her cell phone.

Two out of a hundred.

As I clutched my phone, I was thinking, *For a silent retreat, there's a lot of talking.*

AT BREAKFAST THE food was simple but delicious. But meditative eating felt really uncomfortable. I chewed slowly and started counting as I stared straight ahead. There was no conversation and no eye contact. Just plates rattling and chairs moving. It didn't feel comforting, just weird—like eating in a library. The impact of the silence was profound; I became hyperfocused on every sound.

At registration the evening before, we'd been assigned yogi jobs. They ranged from chopping vegetables to cleaning the bathrooms to sweeping the front porch. My job was smudge patrol.

Mr. Clean Magic Eraser for forty-five minutes each morning.

I felt kinship with Julia Roberts in *Eat Pray Love* again. She had scrubbed floors at the ashram in India; I scrubbed walls in Massachusetts. We were practically sisters.

Two attendees spoke to me during work time. One told me that she'd already done the area I was smudge patrolling. I was thinking, *That's hardly the point. Idiots like us are on waiting lists for silent meditation retreats, which means that someone has always just done the part we both just cleaned.* The other woman asked me where to get the Mr. Clean Magic Erasers. I wanted to say, "At Target, forty miles up the road," but didn't. I was thinking, *They really don't get it.* This isn't about cleaning. It's about service and NOT TALKING.

I found myself getting pissed off. I was thinking, *Respect the silence.* I was actually enjoying not talking.

And EVERYONE was talking.

But it was barely three hours in, so I tried to reserve judgment.

In case you didn't notice, my mind was anything but still; there were ~~bears~~ thoughts everywhere.

BY 9:30 THAT morning I found myself desperate for some alone time. As quiet as this was supposed to be, there were still ninety-nine other vaguely silent people here with me, and I wanted some space. It was right after our first big sitting meditation and instruction. I decided to skip the next session, which was the first walking meditation, and have a cup of tea alone in my room. I craved the stillness. We live in a culture where being still is either impossible or perceived as laziness. So we run around in circles, confusing motion with accomplishment.

I went back to my room and did nothing.

Hoping for no motion and big accomplishment. Unfortunately I still encountered a lot of ~~bears~~ thoughts.

AFTER LUNCH, I took a ninety-minute nap and slept through both a walking meditation and a sitting meditation.

I worried that this was avoidance.

But I woke up in time for yoga, and I made myself go.

WHEN A SPIDER crawled up my arm in the middle of a downward dog, I refrained from letting out a yelp. I didn't kill it either. I simply gently scooted it off my arm.

Unfortunately, it landed on my neighbor's yoga mat.

Since I couldn't talk, I couldn't apologize. I also couldn't warn her. And since neither of us could make eye contact, I couldn't alert her or acknowledge my mistake with my eyes. In that moment I realized that, even more than deep conversation, I missed subtle, basic human communication—a smile and nod of the head, acknowledgment of others, simple manners, being polite.

When she saw the spider, she did the same thing—sent it flying onto her neighbor's mat. I saw where this was headed.

The afternoon and evening rolled on. Sitting meditation. Walking meditation. Mindful eating. Sitting meditation . . .

I was having trouble focusing on my breath—that's the first stage in Vipassana. Breathe in. Breathe out. Concentrate on dissecting the process; parse how the breath feels at each incremental stage of the inhale and exhale. And do it for hours.

How could it be so freaking hard to breathe? I'd been doing it rather successfully without any thought whatsoever for my entire life, and now I felt like I might suffocate. Or hyperventilate. Or hold my breath and pass out.

And there were ~~bears~~ thoughts everywhere.

DURING WALKING MEDITATION, I focused on moving my feet. Literally, I said, "Move foot, move foot," over and over again in my head as I trod a path back and forth for forty-five-minute stretches. Thankfully, time passed quickly during the walking sessions, although the day itself seemed to drag on forever.

Being mindful and hyperaware of the present—counting each chew and breath and step—without the distraction of external stimuli was completely warping my sense of time. By day's end I thought, *I feel like I have been here for my entire life.* I heard Sally's voice in my head: "You'll get the idea after a few hours. Don't torture yourself."

I thought, *Be present. Don't look for happiness in acquiring things. Happiness comes from letting go.*

I get it. Can I go home?

SUNDAY: DAY TWO

Up at 5:30 a.m. for a 6:00 sitting meditation.

I turned on my electric toothbrush. Realizing halfway through brushing my teeth that it was electric and noisy, I said, "Oh shit!" (loudly), before I turned it off, hoping that no one realized it was me.

Who says, "Oh shit!" at a silent retreat?

I TOOK 249 breaths in the first sit, every one of them flawed.

Then I decided that smudge patrol was boring and tedious—an old lady's job. Why wasn't I a floor mopper or pot washer? Something demanding and physical?

Then I realized I wanted those jobs because with them I'd know when I was done.

There is no "finished" on smudge patrol. There were white walls with tiny, barely perceptible smudges everywhere.

Then I realized I was wishing things were different.

Damn it!

I WENT TO meditation right before lunch. I was incredibly, deeply still for the first time.

Until I felt an itch on my nose.

I contemplated the itch like I was supposed to.

I got comfortable with the discomfort, saying to myself, "So this is what an itch feels like," just as I'd been instructed. I stepped back. Became curious. Thought about it objectively.

BULLSHIT.

That was a lie. I was not comfortable. Not one bit. It was a Himalayan itch. The biggest f-ing itch in the world.

I scratched. Almost ripped my nose right off my face. It felt wonderful.

Except it meant that I was weak.

The truth? In that moment, I didn't care.

FOR THE WALKING meditation in the afternoon, I took a hike on the trails. I counted my steps like a human Fitbit. The loop through the woods down to the pond ran about a mile.

Lap one: 2,432 steps.

Lap two: 2,567 steps.

Shorter stride? Miscounting? Insanity?

No clue.

To my dismay, the forest I was walking in was full of ~~bears~~ thoughts.

THERE WERE TWO men in a canoe fishing on the pond. As I approached I wasn't sure what to do. If they engaged me, should I say something?

Luckily, they didn't.

But when I got to the road, four people were packing up their truck after a fishing trip. They shouted out to me, "Hi there! How's it going?"

I froze, then said, "Hi." Then I gave them two thumbs-up and hurried past.

Another person walking his dog down the road said hello to me too. I just smiled and gave a little wave, and then scurried past with my head down, avoiding eye contact.

He was wearing baggy blue sweatpants.

I CONTINUED BACK to the retreat center, where not speaking was the norm.

I worried that a word or two would jinx my progress.

LATER THAT DAY, during the 3:45 p.m. sitting meditation—breathe in breathe out breathe in breathe out—a sudden feeling of intense fear washed over me. It radiated across my chest and for a flash was absolutely terrifying. I knew that I wasn't supposed to run—you can't outrun a bear thought—or assign any emotional value to it, so I went back to focusing on my breath, and it disappeared.

Interesting. It seemed to work.

I KEPT FALLING asleep during meditation. I would have thought it was just exhaustion, but I knew that at this point I was well rested. They say exhaustion can be a way to avoid the feelings that are bubbling up. So when I brought it up during the group session, Rebecca suggested that I try to take note of what happens right before the tiredness sets in, that I think about what is happening in that moment and get curious about it.

The pattern seemed to be that I was having a memory of being a child. Unclear what age. Maybe eight or nine? Or maybe younger? More like four or five. And then I would get drowsy, almost narcoleptic. Then jolt awake. It was unsettling.

Then I told Rebecca that I was a little surprised by how much talking there was in general. That I was prepared for stone-cold silence for five days, so the retreat was easier than I had expected, but I also wished there was even more quiet. She explained that the ten-day retreat does quiet down, and people fall more into silence, but since many beginners go on the shorter retreats, the silence takes longer to settle in.

Next, a guy named Terry blurted out that he had broken two of the precepts already, and he was clearly tortured by guilt. I was hoping he'd done something fun, like hit on a staff member or smoked a joint back in his dorm room, but his big confession was that he had picked up some ants surrounding a piece of food on the floor and thrown the food and ants in the garbage. His second offense—brace yourself—was that he had taken an extra piece of fruit at lunch to eat later that evening in his room.

I was thinking he must have spoken to the same woman I did who recommended keeping contraband food. But then I felt badly about that clementine—as well as the lifted apple, pear, and cookie waiting for me in my room.

After Terry confessed, a woman named Irene—who seemed a bit tightly wound and said that she was a serious practitioner of Buddhism and, to give some heft to this statement, told us she had lived in Asia for three months—launched into how she found herself judging everyone around her for breaking the rules.

Her timing was really bad, what with Terry's confession worthy of a *Dr. Phil* episode a few moments before. She told us that she held herself to a very high moral and ethical standard. I didn't think she was directing her comments toward Terry, but he looked even more racked with guilt than before.

Then Rebecca told us a story about a time when there were cockroaches in the center, and it became a huge problem because no one would kill them. So the roaches overtook the facility, and it got so bad that finally someone said, "I'll take the bad karma and kill the roaches."

Then they held a prayer circle the night before the very un-Buddhist extermination and asked the roaches very nicely to leave.

"A last-ditch effort," she said, "before plan B."

I was relieved that Rebecca told us that story, not just for Terry but also for me. There is some irony to all of this, and some practicality too—Terry and I took some food, and I said hi to a couple of people, and someone else decided to kill some cockroaches.

And guess what? The sky didn't come tumbling down.

THEN REBECCA ASKED if anyone would be willing to volunteer to ring the bell at the end of the next meditation. When no one raised a hand, mine shot up. I felt I had an easy yogi job—other people had to clean bathrooms and heavy pots and pans. Plus, I had contraband food in my room, so why not?

Rebecca said, "Great. You can do the after-dinner sit. Just bring your pillow up on the stage and lead the meditation."

I said, "Wait, what? I thought I just had to ring the bell."

My cool junior high school art teacher just looked at me and said that you can't ring the bell if you aren't sitting up front leading the session.

I WAS SO worried about being on time that I went into the room about fifteen minutes early and put the cushion/chair setup that I had been using to help with back pain right up on the main stage. I made sure that it would be comfortable and then, in a preemptive strike, I went to pee one last time.

I then sat, center stage, and looked around as the room slowly filled up. I was too "in the moment" to notice whether anyone seemed surprised to see me up there, but I felt that this leadership position was giving me some serious Vipassana cred.

If that was a thing. Which I suspect it wasn't.

Either way, I had it.

I CLOSED MY eyes for a few minutes right before 6:15 to set the tone. And then I proceeded to open my eyes and fidget for the next forty-five minutes.

Everyone in the room was absolutely still. Apart from the leader.

I was leaning forward, then leaning back. Moving my legs, moving them back again, shifting the clock a bit with my toe to make sure that it was in my line of sight each time I moved. I was so nervous that I would screw up that I ended up opening one eye to check the clock every couple of minutes for the whole session. All I could think about was how in the book *Eat Pray Love*, when Elizabeth Gilbert was the key hostess, she had an epiphany that transported her "through the portal of the universe to the center of God's palm."

Literally, Elizabeth Gilbert saw God.

Me? I wiggled.

FINALLY, AT 6:58, with only two minutes left before I was supposed to ring the bell three times to signal the end of the session, I closed my eyes, centered myself, and got still, thinking, *I've got this.*

Then I opened my eyes. It was still 6:58.

Closed them again. Opened them. It was still 6:58.

This was not possible.

So I waited for what felt like an hour, then opened my eyes again just as the clock turned 7:00 p.m.

I was on.

I picked up the wooden stick to lightly tap the bowl. *BONG!*

As in, HUGE *BONG!*

I said, "Crap," under my breath.

What meditation leader says "crap"?

Apparently the same one who packs an electric toothbrush and says, "Oh shit!"

Then I thought that maybe since I was sitting next to the damned thing, it wasn't that loud to everyone else?

I hit it again. Even harder. *What is wrong with me?*

I hit it the third time. Harder still.

And then I looked up to see the entire room full of meditators had put their hands in prayer position—*Anjali mudra*—and bowed to me in unison.

I bowed back.

Then there was a giant awkward pause while we all looked at each other until I realized that they were all waiting for me to get up before they could leave—so I tried to gather my things quickly and quietly to make my way off the stage.

WHILE THIS WAS the worst sitting meditation I had done, bar none, it was the one I would remember the most. Even if I didn't get in an actual minute of my own meditation, the fact that I was able to hold space and provide support for ninety-nine other people was humbling and powerful.

I ended up doing it two more times—the sitting-up-front-leading-ninety-nine-meditators-while-trying-not-to-fidget-or-hit-the-gong-too-loudly thing.

It was an honor. Really.

MONDAY: DAY THREE

I took a two-and-a-half-hour afternoon nap. I was so tired. And the spinach lasagna for lunch was delicious but made my exhaustion worse. I skipped one sitting and one walking meditation and, on top of that, slept through yoga too.

I was okay with it.

A Nepali monk once told me that it was totally fine for me to sleep during meditation because I was a mother and needed my rest.

Okay, I feared that he was lying to make me feel better and that I was avoiding the hard work of just being awake and still—and facing the bears thoughts.

After I woke up, I went to walking meditation, but instead of walking I sat on a bench with a cup of tea to watch the sunset. It was an absolutely gorgeous evening, with a perfect cloudless sky. People dotted the lawn around me, walking in almost comically slow motion. Rebecca called it the "depressed walking zombies." And there it was again: silent-meditation humor.

Behind me, I saw Kyle, an older Trinidadian man whom I remembered from the group session on our first day. He had told us that he had never meditated before in his life and had just decided on a whim to come and "check it out."

He reminded me of my father-in-law. A bit of a lovable mad professor vibe.

Kyle was doing his walking meditation on the path behind the bench I was sitting on and was singing to himself—loud enough for me to hear but not loud enough so that I could make out what song he was singing. I broke into a big smile.

Kyle didn't seem to get the rules of this place. Or perhaps he did and was breaking them just a little bit. That thought endeared him to me even more.

If they had detention at the Insight Meditation Society, Kyle would be in there with Terry and me.

Dinner was just a light bowl of soup with half a slice of bread, a kiwi, and half a pear. I chewed slowly, eyes straight ahead. The meal was incredibly satisfying. Then, when I got back to my room, for the first time during the retreat I was really tempted to check my e-mail and messages. In fact, I was emotionally hungry to do so.

Full confession: I'd almost checked e-mail a couple of times by accident. Just out of habit when I checked the time on my phone. And each time it happened I was flooded with anxiety. But in this moment, I felt, for the first time since I had gotten there, deep discomfort over how disconnected I was from my life. A life I loved.

DURING THE EVENING dharma talk Rebecca told us a story from the *Samyutta Nikaya*—part of the "Kindred Sayings" of ancient Buddhist scripture—about the Buddha's response when asked how he was able to cross a river during a flood.

"When I came to a standstill, friend, then I sank; but when I struggled, then I got swept away. It is in this way, friend, that by not halting and by not straining I crossed the flood."

NOW THERE'S ONE for the Temple of Me.

It reminded me of what Chade-Meng Tan (the Jolly Good Fellow at Google) had told me. He'd said that I was worrying too much about finding Zia a spiritual home. That I should just teach her compassion and kindness and the rest would come. He essentially told me that I could neither frantically swim nor aimlessly float to get to where I wanted to go. I would get there with just the right amount of effort.

Then Rebecca ended the talk by saying that those things that bug us—those are our teachers. Bow to them.

I wanted to bring her home with me.

TUESDAY: DAY FOUR

I really would've preferred to sleep in, but I got up for the 6:00 a.m. sit.

I started with TM, which felt confusing to do so early in the morning. Almost aggressive and too focused. So I switched to mindfulness meditation after about twenty minutes and settled into it quickly. And then stuff started coming up. That feeling of dread and anxiety again. The anxiety coming from the center of my chest, my chest tightening as it traveled up. It was a sense of dread that felt like pressure on my chest and stifled my breathing, which became panicked and shallow. I could see the headline: "Cardiologist's wife dies from sudden cardiac arrest brought on by a ~~bear~~ thought attack at a silent meditation retreat."

When the gong rang, signaling the end of the session, I couldn't move for a few minutes. After the hall was empty, I opened my eyes and slowly made my way to breakfast.

Despite not feeling hungry at all, I managed to eat a full meal. Hard-boiled egg, half a bagel and cream cheese, yogurt, granola, half a banana.

I felt overwhelmed—and stuffed.

Everyone was sitting in the dining hall, looking straight ahead, glum. This place was getting depressing.

I was feeling glad that it would be over tomorrow. It was raining outside, and that just added to the heaviness I felt.

Then I remembered that I had originally signed up for the ten-day retreat and had later worried that those five additional days would have been the breakthrough days. But now I didn't care. I wanted to go home.

When it was time for Mr. Clean smudge patrol, I hid in my room with a cup of tea, avoiding everyone. I needed to get up and get going but didn't want to. I figured that I had a bullshit job anyway. Who would notice if one of the smudge patrol didn't make it today? Then I felt guilty for not doing my part, so I headed on down, knowing that when I left the next day there wouldn't be a smudge left in this place.

My job on smudge patrol was the perfect metaphor for what I was doing here. En route to knowing myself better, I had to scrub out everyone and everything else.

LATER, THE GUIDED sitting meditation got intense for me. Things came up. Bad thoughts that I would normally block out. Or slap down. Or never have in the first place.

When Rebecca checked in with me at the end, she told me that I was doing it right, but I said that it felt wrong because it hurt.

I guess it was supposed to hurt.

Note to self: I was doing an excellent job of hyperfocusing on every nuance of how I felt and facing the ~~bears~~ thoughts—the good, the bad, and now the ugly.

REBECCA HELD A *Metta* meditation session later that evening. The goal of *Metta* meditation is to focus on loving-kindness. You first send that loving-kindness to yourself and then radiate it to others.

It reminded me of what Paramji had said: We have to love ourselves before others can love us. And that love has to be unconditional.

But I found trying to give loving-kindness to myself hard, and that same sense of fear washed over me as my chest tightened again. I followed Rebecca's instructions to think back to myself as a child and ask how I would keep that child safe and happy and peaceful.

A photo of myself came to mind. I was sitting with my mom and sister in the grass, probably at about seven years old. Half my teeth were missing, and I was wearing denim shorts overalls and a red T-shirt. My hair was in two lopsided pigtails, and I was smiling this crazy, goofy exaggerated smile. I looked exactly like Zia.

Where is that kid now?

Then the tears started.

Rebecca suggested that if we were struggling to instead think of someone whom it was easier to send kindness and love to. Of course Zia came to my mind immediately. Her joyful playfulness, openheartedness . . . essential goodness. My love for her was so pure and so deep and so joyful that it was easy.

And then the tears were happy.

I wished I could love myself like that, that I could get back to that lopsided, pigtailed version of myself. Then I realized that Zia reflects back to me the very best version of myself I could ever hope for.

Rebecca told us to envision a cone of light in all corners of the world, spreading peace and happiness. I envisioned Zia standing with me in the center and beaming her love and goodness all around her. That was easier than picturing myself doing it.

Zia wants to sparkle the world.

She is human glitter.

LATER REBECCA CONTRASTED the simple purity of this type of meditation with Americans' love of shopping. We voraciously consume, trying to fill our spiritual needs with things from the mall. She said that we don't need to fill the void with "stuff" or to keep "shopping around" for answers. We have everything we need inside ourselves.

This resonated deeply with me. I decided that I just needed to be still for a while and let the answers bubble up, that they'd been there all along but I hadn't been listening enough—or still enough—to hear them.

LATER, I TALKED with Jesse, an assistant teacher, and told her about the strong emotions I was experiencing. She said facing our thoughts and finding self-awareness was the point.

Then at the late-evening sitting, everything shifted, and I had a deep feeling of joy. I had a big huge ear-to-ear smile that I couldn't get off my face.

I was thinking, *This is what life should feel like.*

WEDNESDAY: DAY FIVE

It was over. I'd made it.

Before we left, the staff talked about the practice of *Dana*, generosity. They said we'd been in a river of generosity during the past five days and encouraged us to keep that current going when we got home. And since Vipassana retreats are often free or inexpensive and supported by donations, they asked us to support the center and the teachers—who aren't paid to be there—which I was happy to do. Then, when they asked who could offer rides to fellow meditators, I felt guilty but didn't raise my hand. Luckily two other people offered rides to New York City, and only one person needed one, so I was off the hook.

I felt both relieved and bad about my lack of generosity. But I'd been enjoying the silence, and I wanted to keep that going for the ride back. I didn't want to have to make small talk and *be* someone.

Then it hit me: I'm not the last person on earth I'd want to be alone with after all.

WHEN I GOT to my car, I turned on my phone, scanned my e-mail and messages, and realized that I hadn't missed a thing. That it's okay to turn off—not just our phones but everything. So I turned my phone off again.

I drove back to New York on I-95 in heavy traffic, which took six hours. As I reflected on the past five days, I saw that all the spiritual experiences of the past few years had common threads. The shamans using entheogens like ayahuasca and DMT, the extreme sweating in the *temazcal*, the jarring jump start of Burning Man, and the calm of meditation were all avenues to an altered state of consciousness that opens pathways to creativity and enlightenment and spirituality. The collective energy promised by Hugging Amma was just another iteration of the collective good chi promised by TM's yogic flying and laughing yoga and tantric sounding's tapping into the energy of the universe. All these practices and beliefs were routes to the same city; they were vehicles for "transport" for seekers to tap into a collective, cosmic, and infinite *more*. Not necessarily a monotheistic supreme being but something godlike nonetheless.

ON THE WAY home a few practical things stood out to me:

- I should engage in behaviors that are kind to my body and mind, not punishing but nurturing.

- I should feed my body lovingly and eat mindfully—and stop when I'm full; I'm not a compost bin.

- If I'm judging others, it probably means I need to be softer and more forgiving of myself.

- I should face the ~~bears~~ thoughts and not allow them to defeat me. Doing so will change my life for the better—and give me control and power.

As I approached the city I was thinking that the world doesn't come crashing to an end if we bow out for a few days. Zia was fine. Atul was fine. Work was fine. No friends or family had crushing, unaddressed needs. Five days on this earth can pass without my tending to the needs of anything or anyone else.

BUT MORE THAN that I knew this:

- Stop and face the ~~bears~~ thoughts; you can't outrun them.

- Don't push hard, but don't stand still either; find the right amount of effort.

- Laugh and be noisy.

- Then take some time to be still.

Then, as she heard my key in the door, Zia thundered down the hallway and leapt into my arms—beautifully noisy.

I like noise. It forms a physical community of joy and camaraderie.

And I like stillness. It connects us to ourselves. Improves perspective.

We just need to balance the two.

Conclusion:
Here I Am at the
Closing Argument

Lawyers love closing arguments. It's our chance to wow the judge and jury with a singularly compelling and dramatic summation. To drive home with absolute conviction the irrefutable fact that the case we have outlined points to only one possible conclusion: that we're right, and we've proven that beyond a reasonable doubt.

If I were in court and you were sitting on the jury, and I had argued a case for the existence of God and eternity and otherness, a case in which I had presented compelling evidence from my own route to salvation, one where I had achieved the highest order of spiritual oneness with the universe, this would be my chance to revisit the facts and remind you of their merits. It would be my final opportunity to proselytize and win you over to my side.

When this spiritual quest of mine began, and through a good portion of the process, I expected that in these concluding pages, I'd be doing just that. I expected that I would have experienced one of those indelible, glorious eureka moments of Einstein-esque proportion. Back then, I fully anticipated that I would have had a spiritual revelation that would have brought me to my mortal knees in thanks and reverence and astonishment and that I would be summing it up for you, right here.

I fully expected to *close* you.

In fact, when I started out, I assumed that I would have uncovered something akin to a mathematical proof of spirituality—a white-light moment of radiant, spiritual clarity. I was convinced that, if I just looked hard enough, the concrete proof of God and eternity and otherness would reveal itself to me. And I really thought that I would be able to say to my daughter and to you, "Here it is. And guess what? It is glorious!"

But that didn't happen. At least not in the way I had expected.

I DID LEARN that I couldn't find something as big as a spiritual home in a short amount of time, no matter how hard I looked. I had given myself a year, then two, then three, and then settled quite comfortably with the fact that it will likely take me a lifetime to find what I am looking for—which means, just possibly, it might be never.

And I am now okay with that.

A year in, I also realized the magnificent power of the human brain to release neurotransmitters that can produce feelings that are wholly and undeniably spiritual and positive and connective—even personally transcendent and creatively powerful. But as wonderful and awe inspiring as that is, I also learned that those dopamine rushes and endorphin highs brought on by hope and meditation, or by exercise and prayer, or by group singing and religious services, or by tapping into the subconscious brain in any number of ways are, for me at least, not necessarily indicative of God or eternal life, even though they may make us feel that they are.

But that doesn't make those transcendent states any less curious or life changing—or desirable.

It took even longer for me to realize just how personal a quest like this is and that no one can take this journey for another person. Not even a well-intentioned mother hoping to find a spiritual home for her infant then toddler then preschooler then school-age daughter.

I know now that I can only do for my daughter what my parents did for me: I can give her the foundation but not the house.

That lesson was hard to swallow, but once I did, it felt right. A spiritual home is something that we all have to find for ourselves. And I'm okay with that now too.

But even after my moment on the mountain top in Peru, I still can't tell you, and I can't tell my daughter, if there's a God or why we are here. Or what the meaning of life is. Or what happens when we die. And if I were asked today what my religious affiliation is, just as I would have before I set out on this quest, I'd hesitate, not sure what I should say. Desperate to provide a definitive answer, there's a chance that I would revert to my childhood religious roots and say, "Jain."

But in my heart I would know, just as I had as a girl, that that's not quite right.

WHEN I SET out on this spiritual adventure, I didn't know that I am what religious scholars and researchers call a "None." The classification "None" isn't an acronym or clever play on words. It is simply the painfully uninspired name statisticians have given to people who answer "None" when asked about their religious affiliation.

In 2014 there were 56 million Nones in the United States; as a group, we are growing in number. Nones represented just over 15 percent of the total US population in 2007, close to 20 percent in 2012, and 23 percent in 2014. That's a growth rate of roughly 53 percent in only seven years. Nones skew young too; over one-third of adults between eighteen and thirty-three in the United States reported being religiously "uncommitted."

I know better than most that not having a religious affiliation doesn't necessarily mean that Nones aren't spiritual. In 2012, 58 percent of Nones reported feeling "a deep connection" to nature and the earth, and 37 percent self-defined as "spiritual." It also doesn't mean that we don't believe in God. As much as 68 percent of the religiously unaffiliated Nones in the United States believe, with some degree of certainty, that there is a God. In fact, 30 percent were "absolutely certain" that God exists.

Knowing this gives me comfort; I have a lot of company.

WHILE THE SUM total of what I'm revealing here might suggest that I haven't made all that much progress since I began looking for my spiritual footings, I know for a fact that that's not true.

I'm now not only better informed but also fundamentally changed by what I experienced.

I know this, in part, because of one story that I haven't told you yet. And while it is normally not admissible to introduce new evidence in a closing argument, I decided to do it here anyway.

This story has to do with an experience I had early in my quest—with John of God (JOG), but only in the most indirect way. I didn't really recognize its full meaning and profound significance until I reflected back on the events a couple of years later. And that, in and of itself, says a lot about how much I learned about myself, about our collective spiritual nature, and about the divine simplicity of our humanity.

*　*　*

IN THE WEEKS leading up to my trip to South America to visit JOG, I mentioned my plans to some friends and then to a couple of colleagues at Google, thinking that a select few might want me to "put in a word for them"—just in case there was something real to this whole JOG thing. Then I mentioned my upcoming trip to my neighbor and the guy who works at the coffee shop I go to each morning. After that I told the checkout lady at Whole Foods, my doctor, and a stranger who sat next to me on the subway. I told each of them where I was going and why. I mentioned my skepticism and curiosity and offered to carry their three wishes to JOG along with my own, explaining that anyone traveling to The Casa could be a proxy for others and save them the trip.

To my surprise, my inbox overflowed. Friends told friends who told friends. Those friends apparently told strangers, who told more friends and strangers, who in turn told their neighbors and the guys who made them their morning espressos at their local coffee shops and the checkout ladies at their supermarkets, until it seemed in the days before I departed for The Casa in

Abadiânia that there was no one in the free world who did not have my e-mail address.

In just looking at the flood of messages in my inbox, I felt like a traveler who had offered in earnest to carry packages to friends and relatives back in the home country, only to realize that I didn't have enough room in my luggage. There were so many people and so many wishes.

But when I went back and re-read the e-mails, a few years later, I became intrigued. I noticed that they shared three commonalities. The first of which was rather curious.

Almost everyone sent me meticulous details about how they could be reached.

I had instructed them—or their friends had instructed them— to send, along with their three wishes, a photo, name, and date of birth. But they gave me full addresses with apartment numbers and zip codes. They even sent their photographs covered in elaborate arrows and circles, with comments like, "That's me on the left!"

Apparently all of them wanted to make sure that in the unlikely event that JOG granted their wishes, they wouldn't be delivered to the wrong address or wrong person.

Even if they didn't believe, they were hedging their bets.

THE SECOND COMMONALITY was just as curious but far more humbling. Profound even.

Virtually everyone—the stranger on the subway, the guy at the coffee shop, the lawyer down the hall, the Jew, the atheist, the Muslim, and the devout Catholic—asked for essentially the same three things.

Okay, there were a couple of outliers. One guy's first wish was for a job as a director of photography on a feature film. Then there was the woman in her forties who wanted a fourth child. And, yes, a couple of people asked for cash. But when I eliminated the hand-ful of anomalies, the similarities were staggering.

Every single person asked for good health for themselves and their families.

Almost universally, they next asked for happiness.

And then love. In that order.

> Health.
> Happiness.
> Love.

Sometimes they wanted a specific health issue fixed—a heart condition or loved one's stomach ailment. But more often than not they just wished for good health in general.

When it came to happiness, each phrased it slightly differently, but all wanted the same specific subtype of happiness too:

> The kind of happiness that sinks in and sets down roots in your soul.
> The kind of happiness that could sustain us even if we were to lose absolutely everything else.

Next, they all wished for romantic love.

Everyone asked for the kind of soul mate that we read about in epic, romantic novels. The kind of love that stays with us to the end of our days.

It struck me hard that, by and large, all these friends, and friends of friends, and strangers were looking for the same things that I wanted for my daughter and myself: a simplified version of the hu-man needs identified by social scientists like Abraham Maslow and Manfred Max-Neef.

No one asked for answers to the "big" questions. They didn't ask for proof of God or the meaning of life or a route to immortality.

Even when they could have asked for absolutely anything, they all asked for health, happiness, and love.

THE E-MAILS HAD a third commonality as well. Each ended in the exact same way. Instead of thanking me for carting these wishes all the way to Brazil, everyone said:
"Please don't tell anyone."

SO I DECIDED to tell everyone. Right here on the pages of this book.
Not because I am untrustworthy but because the fact that we have so much in common was important for me to hear. And I think that it just might be important for all of us to hear. Especially now.

I'M THE FIRST to admit that I'm not a statistician and that the data that I accumulated in my inbox and just reported to you here is more qualitative than quantitative, more anecdotal than scientific. It is, as anyone who works with data will tell you, hardly a statistically significant or demographically balanced sample. But nonetheless, I find myself thinking about those e-mails every time I worry about not being able to answer those big questions.

> Why are we here?
> What is the meaning of life?
> What happens when we die?
> Is there a God?

I remind myself that the shocking, humbling, endearing, unifying, commonality of our humanity is that, above all else, even when we have a chance to ask for anything at all, the vast majority of us want the same three things, and it's not answers to the big existential questions of God and eternity. It's assurance of something much simpler than that—we want health, happiness, and love.
That's it.
And with few exceptions, this is true no matter who we are, what name we give our God, or which religion, if any, we call home.

When we get past those internalized labels that marginalize and separate—race, gender, sexual orientation, nationality, and, yes, even religion—the truth is, we all want the same things.

Even the Nones.

Then I note that apparently most of us want these three things so badly that we will e-mail a stranger—even a spiritually confused None like me—and ask her to carry these simple human wishes halfway around the world just in case there is the remote possibility that those wishes might be granted by someone who is not a god. Let alone our God. Someone who is not even a member of our chosen religion. Someone who, on paper, seems like a fraud.

Perhaps if we can all see that what we want is so simple and more the same than different, we will all be able to find a peaceful spiritual home here on earth. That spiritual home that has proven so elusive for people like me, even as it is so well defined and so certain for others.

WHEN I THINK about the last few years and my spiritual quest, I now realize that even today, in a world fractured by religious, ethnic, political, philosophical, and racial divides, it comes down to this:

We are all the same.

And that means that in the end it doesn't really matter if I know the answers to those big questions, or what spiritual home I settle into, or what specific route to health, happiness, and love I take.

And that, I am certain, is the most important lesson of all.

Notes and Further Reading

INTRODUCTION

xv **There is compelling evidence:** Justin Barrett, *Born Believers: The Science of Children's Religious Belief* (New York: Atria Books, 2012).

xvi **Amma has a global reputation:** Jake Halpern, "Amma's Multifaceted Empire, Built on Hugs," *New York Times*, May 25, 2013, http://www .nytimes.com/2013/05/26/business/ammas-multifaceted-empire -built-on-hugs.html.

xvi **Amma supports a network of charities:** "Who Is Amma?," AmmaNY.org, http://www.ammany.org/charitable-activities.php.

xvii **Hugs release oxytocin, the "feel-good" hormone:** Paul Zac, "Trust, Morality—and Oxytocin?," TED.com, July 2011, https://www.ted .com/talks/paul_zak_trust_morality_and_oxytocin.

CHAPTER 1

1 **The church advises Catholics to not practice yoga at all:** Michelle Arnold, "The Trouble with Yoga: A Catholic May Practice the Physical Postures, but with Caveats," *Catholic Answers Magazine*, May 16, 2012, https://www.catholic.com/magazine/print-edition/the -trouble-with-yoga.

2 **A faith healer not sanctioned by the church:** Ronald L. Conte Jr., "Claims of Miraculous Healing: True or False? An Evaluation of the Claims About John of God, a Medium from Brazil, Who Presents Himself as if He Were Catholic," November 29, 2010, http://www .catholicplanet.com/apparitions/false194.htm.

2 **Even though this sounded completely ludicrous to me:** "About John of God," Johnofgod.com, http://johnofgod.com/about-john-of -god.

3 **Dr. Oz was consulted by ABC's *Primetime*:** "Is 'John of God' a Healer or a Charlatan?," ABC News, February 10, 2005, http:// abcnews.go.com/Health/Primetime/story?id=482292.

3   **Oprah reports of her near collapse:** Oprah Winfrey, "Oprah's Visit with John of God: You Are Exactly Where You Need to Be," Oprah .com, http://www.oprah.com/spirit/oprahs-experience-with-john-of -god-oprah-on-lifes-journey.

5   **You can't clip below the waist:** Deuteronomy 25:11 https://www .biblegateway.com/verse/en/Deuteronomy%2025%3A11.

CHAPTER 2

18   **Doing so liberates our souls and delivers us:** Pravin K. Shah, "Concept of God in Jainism," Jain Study Center of North Carolina, http://www.fas.harvard.edu/~pluralsm/affiliates/jainism/jainedu /jaingod.htm.

26   **"vibrational frequency of each Bija (seed) mantra":** "Para Tan Sound Healing with Mantra Shakti and Essential Oils," Tantric Goddess Network, http://tantric-goddess.org/para-tan_healing.html.

26   **Add that to the fact that the chanting:** Yu-Feng Zhou, "High Intensity Focused Ultrasound in Clinical Tumor Ablation," *World Journal of Clinical Oncology*, January 10, 2011, https://www.ncbi.nlm .nih.gov/pmc/articles/PMC3095464; Joel Weidenfeld, "Top 10 Amazing Uses for Sound," Listverse, November 14, 2012, http:// listverse.com/2012/11/14/top-10-amazing-uses-for-sound; Robin McKie, "High-Power Sound Waves Used to Blast Cancer Cells," *Guardian*, October 31, 2015, https://www.theguardian.com/ science/2015/oct/31/ultrasound-cancer-research-hifu-bone-trial.

27   **simply attending religious services more than once a week:** Shanshan Li et al., "Association of Religious Service Attendance with Mortality Among Women," *JAMA Internal Medicine*, May 16, 2016, https://www.ncbi.nlm.nih.gov/pubmed/27183175.

28   **Note that the "without sex" part:** "The Sound of Love with Shri Param Eswaran," IFC Tantra the Art of Conscious Love, http://www .tantra-ifc-the-art-of-conscious-love.com/para-tan_healing.html.

CHAPTER 3

43   **Researchers have found that Parkinson's patients:** Nicholas Bakalar, "Expensive Drugs Work Better Than Cheap Ones," *New York Times*, January 28, 2015, https://well.blogs.nytimes.com/2015/01/28 /expensive-drugs-work-better-than-cheap-ones; Christopher Goetz, MD, "The Placebo Effect, How It Complicates Parkinson's Disease

Research," Parkinson's Disease Foundation, summer 2012, http://
www.pdf.org/summer12_placebo.

44 **And this placebo effect doesn't just work:** Joseph Walker, "Fake
Knee Surgery as Good as Real Procedure, Study Finds," *Wall Street
Journal*, December 25, 2013, https://www.wsj.com/articles/fake-knee
-surgery-as-good-as-real-procedure-study-finds-1388009383.

44 **There are all sorts of other routes:** V. N. Salimpoor et al.,
"Anatomically Distinct Dopamine Release During Anticipation and
Experience of Peak Emotion to Music," NCBI PubMed, January 9,
2011, https://www.ncbi.nlm.nih.gov/pubmed/21217764.

44 **Since we all want to feel good:** Steve Sussman et al., "Drug
Addiction, Love, and the Higher Power," NCBI PMC, March 16,
2011, https://www.ncbi.nlm.nih.gov/pmc/articles/PMC3185195.

44 **And of course, religious and spiritual experiences:** "The Three
R's—Religion, Recognition, Reward," Neuro Research Project:
Neuronotes, June 26, 2012, https://neuroresearchproject
.com/2012/06/26/the-three-rs-religion-recognition-reward.

48 **I was looking for the God Effect:** Patrick McNamara, "The God
Effect: Religion Spawns Both Benevolent Saints and Murderous
Fanatics. Could Dopamine Levels in the Brain Drive That Switch?,"
aeon, August 11, 2014, https://aeon.co/essays/the-dopamine-switch
-between-atheist-believer-and-fanatic.

CHAPTER 4

61 **Wicca is a modern interpretation of witchcraft:** Janet Farrar and
Stewart Farrar, *Witches' Way: Principles, Ritual and Beliefs of Modern
Witchcraft* (Custer, WA: Phoenix Publishing, 1986).

69 **"and then within a few days some unexpected funds":** Scott
Cunningham, *Wicca: A Guide for the Solitary Practitioner*
(Woodbury, MN: Llewellyn Publications, 1989).

74 **But when I feel weak and vulnerable:** "Blaise Pascal: Finding God in
Revealing Fundamental Truths of Life," League of Everyday
Doxologists, http://www.doxologists.org/blaise-pascal.

FURTHER READING

Wigington, Patti, "The American Council of Witches." ThoughtCo.
February 19, 2016. https://www.thoughtco.com/american-council
-of-witches-2562880.

CHAPTER 5

79 **Well, not me and not the seven women:** Robin Abcarian, "Sex Harassment Scandal Rocks the Peace of Bikram Yoga World," *Los Angeles Times*, March 28, 2013, http://articles.latimes.com/2013 /mar/28/local/la-me-ln-sex-harassment-scandal-bikram-yoga-20130328.

79 **Choudhury testified in court that he was broke:** "Jury Laughs at Hot-Yoga Guy," *Lowering the Bar*, January 27, 2016, http:// loweringthebar.net/2016/01/jury-laughs-at-hot-yoga-guy.html.

79 **Then they awarded $7.4 million:** Christopher Coble, "Bikram Yoga Guru Loses Sexual Harassment Lawsuit," FindLaw.com, February 11, 2016, http://blogs.findlaw.com/decided/2016/02/bikram-yoga-guru-loses-sexual-harassment-lawsuit.html.

81 **Francisco Javier Clavijero, a Mexican scholar and historian:** Dr. Horacio Rojas Alba, "Temazcal I/III: The Traditional Mexican Sweat Bath," Instituto Mexicano de Medicinas Tradicionales, Tlahuilli A.C., Tlahui-Medic. No. 2, II/1996, *Tlahuilli*, http://www.tlahui.com /temaz1.html.

81 **In modern times the high heat of saunas:** Takashi Kihara et al., "Repeated Sauna Treatment Improves Vascular Endothelial and Cardiac Function in Patients with Chronic Heart Failure," *Journal of the American College of Cardiology* 39, no. 5 (March 2002), http:// www.onlinejacc.org/content/39/5/754.

93 **White called this the "overview effect":** Frank White, *The Overview Effect: Space Exploration and Human Evolution* (Boston: Houghton Mifflin, 1987); "The Overview Effect: Cosmic Consciousness and the Big Picture," posted by Justin to World Peace Through Technology, December 21, 2013, http://peacetour.org/overview-effect.

93 **The astronauts said that the experience was "transcendent":** Edgar Mitchell, *The Way of the Explorer: An Apollo Astronaut's Journey Through the Material and Mystical Worlds* (Franklin Lakes, NJ: New Page Books, 2008).

FURTHER READING

"Hyperthermia to Treat Cancer." American Cancer Society. http://www .cancer.org/treatment/treatmentsandsideeffects/treatmenttypes /hyperthermia.

Rath, Heather. "The Mexican Temazcal: An Experience in a Maya Sweat Lodge." The Travel Word. April 25, 2011. http://www.thetravelword .com/2011/04/25/the-mexican-temazcal-an-experience-in-a-maya -sweat-lodge.

Whitaker, Julian, Dr. "Health Benefits of a Sauna." Dr. Whitaker. https:// www.drwhitaker.com/health-benefits-of-a-sauna.

CHAPTER 6

97   **Mediums are conduits to "the other side":** Julie Beischel, PhD, et al., "Anomalous Information Reception by Research Mediums Under Blinded Conditions II: Replication and Extension," NCBI PubMed, January 7, 2015, https://www.ncbi.nlm.nih.gov/pubmed/25666383.

105   **Despite what some have characterized:** Kathryn Shattuck, "Vikram Gandhi's Documentary 'Kumaré,'" *New York Times*, June 1, 2012, http://www.nytimes.com/2012/06/03/movies/vikram-gandhis -documentary-kumare.html.

CHAPTER 7

110   **In this documentary Cameron travels:** Gus Holwerda, dir., *The Unbelievers* (Lawrence Krauss, JJC Films, 2013), http://www.imdb .com/title/tt2636522.

112   **And ayahuasca certainly has its fair share:** Katie Bain, "Ten Celebrity Ayahuasca Users," *LA Weekly*, November 22, 2013, http:// www.laweekly.com/music/ten-celebrity-ayahuasca-users-4169438.

112   **Sting called it "the only genuine religious experience":** Sting, *Broken Music: A Memoir* (New York: Dial Press, 2005).

112   **Tim Ferriss of *The 4-Hour Workweek* fame:** Biz Carson, "This Silicon Valley Angel Investor Loves a Drug That Gave Him Hours of Seizures," *Business Insider*, September 8, 2016, http://www.business insider.com/tim-ferriss-ayahuasca-2016-9.

113   **Ayahuasca is even being given to prisoners in Brazil:** Simon Romero, "In Brazil, Some Inmates Get Therapy with Hallucinogenic Tea," *New York Times*, March 28, 2015, https://www.nytimes.com /2015/03/29/world/americas/a-hallucinogenic-tea-time-for-some -brazilian-prisoners.html.

114   **I'm a lawyer, for goodness sake:** Centro Espírita Beneficente União do Vegetal (http://udvusa.org) and Santo Daime (https://en.wikipedia .org/wiki/Santo_Daime).

123 **At the very least I felt compelled to acknowledge:** Benedict de Spinoza, *Ethics* (London: Penguin Classics, 2005).

123 **Or to agree unequivocally with Thomas Edison:** James D. Newton, *Uncommon Friends: Life with Thomas Edison, Henry Ford, Harvey Firestone, Alexis Carrel, and Charles Lindbergh* (San Diego, CA: Harcourt Brace Jovanovich, 1987).

123 **Or with Werner Heisenberg:** "Talk: Werner Heisenberg," Wikiquote, https://en.wikiquote.org/wiki/Talk:Werner_Heisenberg.

FURTHER READING

Campos, Don Jose. *The Shaman & Ayahuasca: Journeys to Sacred Realms.* New York: Divine Arts. 2011.

Frood, Arran. "Ayahuasca Psychedelic Tested for Depression: Pilot Study with Shamanic Brew Hints at Therapeutic Potential." *Nature.* April 6, 2015.

Gable, Robert. "Risk Assessment of Ritual Use of Oral Dimethyltryptamine (DMT) and Harmala Alkaloids." *Addiction.* February 2007. https://www.ncbi.nlm.nih.gov/pubmed/17207120.

Robinson, Melia. "Silicon Valley's New Craze Is Flying to Peru to Take a Psychedelic You Can't Legally Get in America." *Business Insider.* December 6, 2016. http://www.businessinsider.com/entrepreneurs-awakening-ayahuasca-2016-11.

Veeresham, Ciddi, Dr. "Natural Products Derived from Plants as a Source of Drugs." *Journal of Advanced Pharmaceutical Technology and Research.* October–December 2012. https://www.ncbi.nlm.nih.gov/pmc/articles/PMC3560124.

CHAPTER 8

128 **He says things like, "Talking to God is a blast":** Bertie Da Silva, "Patrick San Francisco Is a Santa Claus Healer Out to Have a Blast, Finds Bertie Da Silva," *Telegraph* (India), April 21, 2012, https://www.telegraphindia.com/1120821/jsp/entertainment/story_15875702.jsp.

128 **Fixing cells. Changing the configuration of DNA:** "Patrick San Francesco—Healing ~ Talks ~ Workshops," video posted to YouTube by Patrick San Francesco, February 18, 2013, https://www.youtube.com/watch?v=-9PRMPAvlWU.

CHAPTER 9

137 **Today, the laughter movement:** http://www.worldlaughterday.com.

137   **But there is some compelling science:** "Laughter Therapy," Cancer
Treatment Centers of America, http://www.cancercenter.com
/treatments/laughter-therapy; P. C. Strike and A. Steptoe,
"Psychosocial Factors in the Development of Coronary Artery
Disease," *Progress in Cardiovascular Diseases*, January–February
2004; J. L. Bellert, "Humor: A Therapeutic Approach in Oncology
Nursing," *Cancer Nursing* 12, no. 2 (1989): 65–70; L. Erdman,
"Laughter Therapy for Patients with Cancer," *Oncology Nursing
Forum* 18, no. 8 (1991): 1359–1363; B. Trent, "Ottawa Lodges Add
Humour to Armamentarium in Fight Against Cancer," *Canadian
Medical Association Journal* 142, no. 2 (1990): 163–164; H. Williams,
"Humor and Healing: Therapeutic Effects in Geriatrics," *Gerontion* 1,
no. 3 (1986): 14–17; D. B. Leiber, "Laughter and Humor in Critical
Care," *Dimensions of Critical Care Nursing* 5 (1976): 162–170;
B. Saper, "The Therapeutic Use of Humor for Psychiatric
Disturbances of Adolescents and Adults," *Psychiatric Quarterly* 61,
no. 4 (1990): 261–272; M. Gelkopf, S. Kreitler, and M. Sigal,
"Laughter in a Psychiatric Ward: Somatic, Emotional, Social, and
Clinical Influences on Schizophrenic Patients," *Journal of Nervous
and Mental Disease* 181, no. 5 (1993): 283–289; J. V. Basmajian, "The
Elixir of Laughter in Rehabilitation," *Archives of Physical Medicine
and Rehabilitation* 79, no. 12 (1998): 1597; P. Hunter, "Humor
Therapy in Home Care," *Caring* 16, no. 9 (1997): 56–57; R. A. Dean,
"Humor and Laughter in Palliative Care," *Journal of Palliative Care*
13, no. 1 (1997): 34–39; J. W. Balzer, "Humor—A Missing Ingredient
in Collaborative Practice," *Holistic Nursing Practice* 7, no. 4 (1993):
28–35; K. Herth, "Contributions of Humor as Perceived by the
Terminally Ill," *American Journal of Hospice Care* 7, no. 1 (1990): 36–
40; J. Mallett, "Use of Humour and Laughter in Patient Care," *British
Journal of Nursing* 2, no. 3 (1993): 172–175; M. J. Balick and R. Lee,
"The Role of Laughter in Traditional Medicine and Its Relevance to
the Clinical Setting: Healing with Ha!," *Alternative Therapies in
Health and Medicine* 9, no. 4 (2003): 88–91; N. Cousins, "Anatomy of
an Illness as Perceived by the Patient," *New England Journal of
Medicine* 295, no. 26 (1976): 1458–1463; "More on the Humor-
Health Connection: New Study Finds Anticipating a Laugh Reduces
Stress Hormone," American Physiological Society, http://www.the
-aps.org/mm/hp/Audiences/Public-Press/Archive/08/10.html.

138　**"A joyful heart is good medicine":** Proverbs 17:22.

138　**The founder of the Jewish Hasidic movement:** Renee Garfinkel, PhD, "Laughter and Spirituality: Does Your Faith Have a Sense of Humor?," *Psychology Today*, July 26, 2013, https://www.psychology today.com/blog/time-out/201307/laughter-and-spirituality.

138　**And numerous religious leaders, from Buddhists:** "What the Dalai Lama and Patch Adams Have in Common: Laughter, and Compassion, the Best Medicine," Buddha Weekly, http:// buddhaweekly.com/laughter-the-blissful-state-of-non-thinking.

139　**The laughing yoga movement has a basis:** "Maharishi Effect," Maharishi University of Management, https://www.mum.edu/about -mum/consciousness-based-education/tm-research/maharishi-effect.

139　**The Maharishi Effect predicts:** John S. Hagelin, "Is Consciousness the Unified Field? A Field Theorist's Perspective," Maharishi International University, https://www.mum.edu/wp-content /uploads/2014/07/hagelin.pdf.

139　**Proponents of the Maharishi Effect even provide:** Bob Roth, "Maharishi on 'The 1% Effect'—How Just a Small Percentage of People Can Change the World," TM Blog, May 11, 2012, http://www .tm.org/blog/maharishi/maharishi-on-the-1-effect.

139　**But even if you don't buy into the global-consciousness part:** Sally Peden, "An End to Terrorism and War: New Peace Government Proposed by World Renowned Quantum Physicist," The Miracle Times, http://www.themiracletimes.com/September-03/John_ Hagelin/John%20Hagelin.htm; "Transcending: The Fastest Way to a Better World," Transcendental Meditation, http://transcendental -meditation.be/transcending-is-the-fastest-way-to-a-better-world.

142　**In other words, happiness and laughter are contagious:** Sigal G. Barsade, "The Ripple Effect: Emotional Contagion and Its Influence on Group Behavior," Yale School of Management, Working Papers Series OB, August 2001; Trevor Foulk, Andrew Woolum, and Amir Erez, "Catching Rudeness Is like Catching a Cold: The Contagion Effects of Low-Intensity Negative Behaviors," *Journal of Applied Psychology* 101, no. 1 (January 2016): 50–67; Henning Holle et al., "Neural Basis of Contagious Itch and Why Some People Are More Prone to It," *PNAS*, September 19, 2012, http://www.pnas.org/content /109/48/19816.abstract; Gerald J. Haeffel and Jennifer L. Hames, "Cognitive Vulnerability to Depression Can Be Contagious," *SAGE*

Journals, April 16, 2013, http://journals.sagepub.com/doi/abs/10.1177/2167702613485075.

CHAPTER 10

151   **Lee Gilmore, a scholar of ritual and new religious movements:** Lee Gilmore, *Theater in a Crowded Fire: Ritual and Spirituality at Burning Man* (Berkeley: University of California Press, 2010).

152   **Larry Harvey's goal in the social experiment:** Larry Harvey, "Following the Money: The Florentine Renaissance and Black Rock City," *Burning Man Journal*, March 10, 2016, https://journal.burning man.org/2016/03/philosophical-center/tenprinciples/following-the -money-the-florentine-renaissance-and-black-rock-city.

173   **From researchers at Johns Hopkins School of Medicine:** Maia Szalavitz, "'Magic Mushrooms' Can Improve Psychological Health Long Term," *Time*, June 16, 2011, http://healthland.time.com/2011/06/16/ magic-mushrooms-can-improve-psychological-health-long-term.

CHAPTER 11

185   **The Beatles were disciples of the Maharishi:** Allan Kozinn, "Meditation on the Man Who Saved the Beatles," *New York Times*, February 7, 2008, http://www.nytimes.com/2008/02/07/arts/music /07yogi.html.

186   **Some, like the state of New Jersey:** *Malnak v. Yogi*, US District Court for the District of New Jersey, 440 F. Supp. 1284 (D.N.J. 1977), October 20, 1977, JUSTIA US Law, http://law.justia.com/cases /federal/district-courts/FSupp/440/1284/1817490.

186   **Certain organizations charge what some deem:** Lynn Stuart Parramore, "Transcendental Meditation: How I Paid $2,500 for a Password to Inner Peace," AlterNet, March 31, 2013, http://www .alternet.org/economy/transcendental-meditation-how-i-paid-2500 -password-inner-peace.

187   **Over time those who meditate lose:** Sara W. Lazar et al., "Meditation Experience Is Associated with Increased Cortical Thickness," NCBI PMC, November 28, 2005, https://www.ncbi .nlm.nih.gov/pmc/articles/PMC1361002; Mark Wheeler, "Forever Young: Meditation Might Slow the Age-Related Loss of Gray Matter in the Brain, Say UCLA Researchers," UCLA Newsroom, February 5, 2015, http://newsroom.ucla.edu/releases/forever-young-meditation

-might-slow-the-age-related-loss-of-gray-matter-in-the-brain-say
-ucla-researchers; Mark Wheeler, "Evidence Builds That Meditation
Strengthens the Brain, UCLA Researchers Say," UCLA Newsroom,
March 14, 2012, http://newsroom.ucla.edu/releases/evidence-builds
-that-meditation-230237; G. Pagnoni and M. Cekic, "Age Effects on
Gray Matter Volume and Attentional Performance in Zen
Meditation," NCBI PubMed, July 25, 2007, https://www.ncbi.nlm
.nih.gov/pubmed/17655980; Marjorie Bernier et al., "Mindfulness
and Acceptance Approaches in Sport Performance," *Journal of
Clinical Sports Psychology* 4, no. 4 (December 2009), https://www
.researchgate.net/publication/266408608_Mindfulness_and
_Acceptance_Approaches_in_Sport_Performance.

192 **In this talk Rebecca recounted a story:** Rebecca Bradshaw, "Mindful
Awareness of Thoughts and Emotions," Dharma Seed, July 29, 2016,
http://dharmaseed.org/teacher/143/talk/35461.

203 **"through the portal of the universe":** Elizabeth Gilbert, *Eat Pray
Love: One Woman's Search for Everything Across Italy, India and
Indonesia* (New York: Riverhead Books, 2006).

206 **"When I came to a standstill":** "Saṃyutta Nikāya 1: Connected
Discourses with Devatas: 1. Crossing the Flood," Sutta Central,
https://suttacentral.net/en/sn1.1.

FURTHER READING

"How the Beatles Learned Transcendental Meditation—and What They
Thought About It." *Transcendental Meditation*, December 10, 2014,
http://tmhome.com/experiences/interview-lennon-and
-harrison-on-meditation.

CONCLUSION

215 **In 2014 there were 56 million Nones:** "America's Changing Religious
Landscape," Pew Research Center, May 12, 2015, http://www.pew
forum.org/2015/05/12/americas-changing-religious-landscape.

215 **In 2012, 58 percent of Nones reported:** "'Nones' on the Rise," Pew
Research Center, October 9, 2012, http://www.pewforum.org/2012
/10/09/nones-on-the-rise.

Acknowledgments

I am deeply grateful to so many people for helping me over the years I have been researching and writing this book. To my spiritual running buddies, thank you for whispering in my ear, teaching me about your spiritual practices, being patient with my (many) questions, and (in some cases) coming along for the ride. Words cannot express how truly grateful I am. This list is by no means exhaustive—largely because I wanted those of you not mentioned to continue to remain employable or funded by your VCs. (You know who you are.)

To A. J. Jacobs, Alexis Rosenzweig, Amy Christiansen, Angela Le, Annika Inez, Bethany Golden, Bobby Roth, Chade-Meng Tan, Charisse Czaja, Dayle Breault, Deepali Bagati, Gabrielle Bernstein, Gina Fortunato, Gopi Kallayil, Heather Hartnett, Ildiko Szollosi, Jeffrey Zurofsky, Jenna Arnold, Jennifer Lucarello, Kalina King, Kamla Rathi, Kanwar Singh, Karen McCullah, Karim SiAhmed, Kelly Luscombe and the Ojai crew, Kris Carr, Latham Thomas, Laura Choi, Linda Krisberg, Lynn Shafran, Madeleine Sackler, Marina Michelutti, Mark Bakacs, Megha Desai, Michael Skolnik, Michael Ventura, Michelle Murphy, Monika Sharma, Mridu Gulati, Nicole Burdock, Nicole DeMember, Nilofer Merchant, Ophira Edut, Pam Gallin, Pamela Landman, Parker, Rachel Goldstein, Rachna Khosla, Rashmi Sen, Rebecca Bradshaw, Regena Thomashauer, Richard Nichols, Russell Simmons, Ruth Ann Harnisch, Sally Kohn, Satya Twena, Simi Chhabria, Sophia Bush, T. J. Rathi, Terry Iacuzzo, Tiffany Dufu, Tina Hedges, Tyler Gage, my RV mates from Hong Kong who prefer to remain anonymous (even though I have photographic evidence of everything), my three amigos (Luis, Jakob, and Mario), and my families at Summit, dot-2dot, Google, Spark Camp, CSW, La Calaca, and TheLi.st: I feel lucky to know you and have each of you in my life.

Thank you, Ruth, D. W., and Rita and the amazing writers at Omi for the gift of my residency, slightly suspicious Russian cold medicine, and icy-cold vodka. You made me feel like a real writer.

Thank you, Tesha Lemond, for helping us keep Zia safe, loved, and fed as I traveled the globe on this crazy adventure—and for never calling the authorities when I came back from a questionable outing.

Thank you, K. W., for being the most extraordinary researcher and coach I could ever have dreamed of. You continuously pulled better stories from me. I literally couldn't have done this without you.

Thank you, Laura Mazer, my editor, and the entire Seal Press team for making my creative sabbatical a dream come true and for making this book better.

Thank you, Mel Berger, my agent at William Morris Endeavor, for believing in this book from day one. You had me at hello, too. And I swear I will convince you to meditate one day.

And finally, thank you:

Mom and Dad, for encouraging me to write this book, even though I suspect you both still secretly wish I had gone to med school. (It's definitely too late.)

Avanti, for being the best sister and friend I could ask for. You are the greatest healer I have encountered on this journey. Oh, and thank you for not charging me when you clear my energy fields in your bathroom (you big weirdo).

Atul, for helping me find my wings. I am forever grateful and love you more than I feel comfortable expressing in the acknowledgments of this book. I am glad we are on this ride together.

And Zia, for being my inspiration and muse. (And remember, you can fly too. Just please wear a helmet. And sunblock.) I love you.